STUDY GUIDE TO ACCOMPANY

1990 ANNUAL EDITION

WEST'S FEDERAL TAXATION: INDIVIDUAL INCOME TAXES

William H. Hoffman, Jr.
University of Houston

Eugene Willis
University of Illinois-Urbana

James E. Smith
College of William and Mary

Prepared by
Gerald E. Whittenburg
School of Accountancy
San Diego State University

West Publishing Company
St. Paul   New York   Los Angeles   San Francisco

COPYRIGHT © 1989 by WEST PUBLISHING CO.
50 W. Kellogg Boulevard
P.O. Box 64526
St. Paul, MN 55164-1003

Printed in the United States of America
96 95 94 93 92 91 90 89   8 7 6 5 4 3 2 1 0
ISBN 0-314-55623-0

TABLE OF CONTENTS

PREFACE

This Study Guide has been designed to be used as a supplement to the *1990 Edition of West's Federal Taxation: Individual Income Taxes*. Its purpose is to help you master the material presented in the text. The Study Guide contains two features to help you understand individual income taxes.

> *Chapter Highlights*-- This section provides statements about key concepts presented in the text.

> *Tests for Self-Evaluation*--Over 900 questions and problems are presented along with answers so that you may see how well you understand the material in the text. The answers are keyed to the page numbers in the text.

I recommend the following approach as a method to use this Study Guide effectively:

1. Study the textbook chapter.

2. Review the Chapter Highlights section of the Study Guide. If something is not clear to you, review the chapter in the textbook.

3. Mark the Test for Self-Evaluation and resolve your missed answers by referring to the solutions and to the textbook.

4. Work the problems that are assigned to you in the textbook.

Students should be reminded that the Study Guide is not designed to replace the textbook but should be used in connection with it. I would like to thank Vicky Wall and H. Whittenburg for their help in preparing this Study Guide.

Gerald E. Whittenburg, April 1989

1

AN INTRODUCTION TO TAXATION AND UNDERSTANDING THE FEDERAL TAX LAW

CHAPTER HIGHLIGHTS

A review of the history of the U.S. Federal tax system is helpful for the student to gain an understanding of the principles which have shaped the development of the system. This chapter introduces the student to the structure of the U.S. Federal tax system, the major types of taxes, and the organizational aspects of administering the tax law.

I. HISTORY OF U.S. TAXATION

    A.   There have been several income taxes in the past. The first income tax was enacted in 1634 in the Massachusetts Bay Colony. The first U.S. income tax was passed in 1861 to help finance the Civil War. The early individual income taxes were held to be unconstitutional by the Supreme Court in *Pollock v. Farmer's Loan and Trust Co.* In response to this Supreme Court decision, a constitutional amendment was passed to authorize the individual income tax. The Sixteenth Amendment, which was ratified in 1913, gave Congress the power to impose and collect an income tax. Before the Sixteenth Amendment, the corporate income tax was held to be an excise tax, and therefore deemed to be constitutional by the Supreme Court.

    B.   Various Revenue Acts were passed between 1913 and 1939. In 1939 these Acts were codified into the Internal Revenue Code of 1939, which was later recodified in 1954 and then renamed the 1986 Code. The *Internal Revenue Code of 1986* is the current U.S. tax law.

C.   Over the years the income tax has become the major source of revenue for the Federal government. During World War II, the tax went from a select tax to a mass tax.

The individual and corporate income tax constitutes 49 percent of all Federal budget receipts. Social Security taxes are 33 percent of Federal receipts.

D.   Adam Smith listed certain criteria with which to evaluate a particular tax or tax structure. These "canons of taxation" are equality, convenience, certainty, and economy.

II.   THE TAX STRUCTURE

A.   Tax Rates.

A progressive tax is one in which the tax rates increase as the tax base increases. The Federal income, gift, and estate taxes and most state income taxes are progressive taxes.

A proportional tax is one in which the rate of tax remains constant regardless of the size of the tax base.

III.   MAJOR TYPES OF TAXES

A.   Property taxes or ad valorem taxes are taxes that are based on value. The tax is usually imposed on realty or personalty. Realty taxes are a major source of revenue for local government, while personalty taxes have low compliance by taxpayers, except such items as inventory, automobiles, boats, etc.

B.   Transaction taxes impose a tax on transfers of property and are normally computed as a straight percentage of the value of the property involved.

Excise taxes are taxes on products such as gasoline, telephone usage, air travel, alcohol and tobacco. Both the Federal and state government usually impose some form of excise tax.

Sales taxes differ from excise taxes in that they are applied to many different transactions, while excise taxes are based on one product. A use tax is designed to prevent the resident of one state from buying products in another state and thereby avoiding the sales tax. Many states allow local sales taxes by cities, counties, etc., in addition to the general sales tax.

Death taxes are taxes imposed either on the right to pass property at death (estate tax) or the right to receive property from a decedent (inheritance tax).

The Federal estate tax is designed to prevent large concentrations of wealth from being kept within the same family. The unified transfer credit eliminates or reduces the estate tax liability for small estates. For deaths during 1988, estate tax on a taxable estate up to $600,000 is eliminated by a credit of $192,800.

Most states levy some form of death tax. In general, the rates are lower for close family members, and get larger the more distant the heir.

The Federal gift tax was enacted into law to complement the estate tax because without it, it would be possible to avoid the estate tax by making lifetime gifts and eliminating the gross estate. Taxable gifts are those gifts that exceed $10,000 per year per donee.

C.   In the United States income taxes are levied by the Federal government and most state governments and are the most popular form of tax. Income taxes are imposed on individuals, corporations, and certain estates and trusts. The Tax formula for individuals is:

> Income (broadly conceived)
> - <u>Exclusions</u>
> = Gross income
> - <u>Certain business deductions</u>
> = Adjusted gross income
> - Greater of itemized deductions or
>   standard deduction
> - <u>Exemptions</u>
> = **Taxable income**
>
> Tax on taxable income
> - <u>Credits and withholding</u>
> = **Tax due or refund**

A standard personal deduction is available to taxpayers. The standard deduction amount may be used in place of itemizing deductions for individual taxpayers.

The Federal income tax applies to corporations. The taxable income of a corporation is the difference between gross income and deductions.

Nearly all the states impose a state income tax on individuals and corporations. Most states pattern their income tax after the Federal income tax and use an adjusted form of Federal income as a base on which to apply the tax. Most states have some form of withholding procedures. The state taxing authorities work closely with the IRS and share information about audits and other changes in tax returns.

E.   Employment taxes such as FICA (Federal Insurance Contributions Act) are collected by the Federal government.

FICA taxes fund the social security system and are levied on both the employee and the employer. For 1989 the tax is 7.51% of the first $48,000 of wages for employees and 7.51% of the first $48,000 for employers. If an employee pays too much FICA because he or she worked two or more jobs, a credit for the excess amount may be claimed.

The FUTA tax is levied only on the employer with the purpose of providing the states with funds to administer the unemployment program. The FUTA tax is 6.2% on the first $7,000 of covered wages for 1989. A credit is allowed (up to 5.4%) for any FUTA paid to a state government so that the amount paid to the IRS could be as little as 0.8 percent.

IV.   TAX ADMINISTRATION

A.   The Internal Revenue Service (IRS), which is part of the Treasury Department, has responsibility for administering the Federal tax law. The IRS uses statistical sampling techniques to select tax returns for audit.

B.   IRS audits are classified as "office audits" or "field audits." Office audits are restricted in scope and are conducted in the IRS office. A field audit is comprehensive and is conducted on the premises of the taxpayer or the taxpayer's representative.

C.   The general statute of limitations for an IRS assessment is three years from the date the return is due, not the date it is filed. There is no statute of limitations if no return or a fraudulent return is filed.

D.   The interest rate used by the federal government is adjusted quarterly. The IRS charges one percent more than it pays to taxpayers. For the first quarter of 1989, the rate of interest is 11 percent for assessments and 10 percent for refunds. Besides interest, various penalties are applied for non-compliance. For "failure to file" a return a penalty of 5 percent per month is charged up to a 25 percent maximum. The penalty for "failure to pay" is one-half percent per month up to a maximum of 25 percent. If both penalties apply to the same return, one is used to offset the other.

V.   REVENUE NEEDS & ECONOMIC CONSIDERATIONS

A.   Raising revenue is a major function of taxation. However, there are several other functions of the U.S. tax law. One economic function of the tax law is to control the economy. Attempts at stimulation or temperance of the national economy have led to many recent amendments to the Internal Revenue Code.

The tax law contains many provisions to encourage investment and capital formation.

Lowering the tax rates provides taxpayers with more income to spend, and so is another method used to stimulate the economy. An increase in tax rates would have the opposite effect.

B.   Another economic consideration of the tax law is to encourage certain activities. The rapid amortization of pollution control facilities and Foreign Sales Corporations (FSC) are an example of these types of provisions in the tax law. IRAs and other pension plans are also an example of using the tax law to help the economic problem of capital formation.

C.   The encouragement of certain industries is another economic consideration of the tax law. Agriculture, for example, is an industry that has special tax benefits.

D.   Small businesses are generally considered to be good for the economy as a whole. Therefore, provisions of the tax law are designed to help small businesses. The S Corporation election is an example of the methods Congress uses to assist small businesses through tax law provisions.

VI.   SOCIAL CONSIDERATIONS

A.   The U.S. tax law contains many social objectives. Examples of such social objectives are:

Nontaxability of accident and health plans

Nontaxability of premiums for group-term insurance

Qualified pension and profit sharing plans

Deductions for contributions to charitable organizations

Credit for child care

Disallowance of expense deductions that are against public policy (fines, penalties, etc.)

VII.   EQUITY CONSIDERATIONS

A.   The Federal tax law attempts to alleviate the effect of multiple taxation in several areas. Examples include the deduction for state and local income tax and the foreign tax credit.

B.   The wherewithal to pay concept recognizes the inequity of taxing a transaction where the taxpayer lacks the means with which to pay the tax. The Federal tax rules for like-kind exchanges and involuntary conversions allow the taxpayer to defer recognition of gain when his or her economic situation has not changed significantly.

C.   Mitigating the effect of the concept of an annual accounting period is an equity consideration that deals with the inequities which arise from the arbitrary use of the annual accounting period to divide the taxpayer's life into taxable segments. The annual accounting period concept could lead to different treatment of two individuals who are, from a long range standpoint, in the same economic position. Measures to alleviate this inequity include the carryover of net operating losses, excess capital losses and excess charitable contributions, and the installment method of recognizing gain.

D.   One of the major problems in recent years has been bracket creep which was caused by inflation. Taxpayers were pushed into higher tax brackets without a real increase in income. This problem is addressed by indexing. Each year, beginning in 1989, the tax brackets and the standard deduction are indexed upward by the amount of inflation with the adjustment for inflation beginning in the 1990 tax year.

VIII.   POLITICAL CONSIDERATIONS

A.   Special interest legislation includes tax provisions sponsored as a result of the instigation of influential constituents. Such legislation is inevitable in our political system, and can sometimes be justified on economic, social or utilitarian grounds.

B.   Political expediency is responsible for the passage of tax provisions which have popular appeal, such as measures that insure wealthy taxpayers pay their "fair" share of tax, the lowering of individual income tax rates and increasing the exemption amount.

C.   State and local influences explain the nontaxability of interest received on state and local obligations, and the extension under Federal tax law of community property tax advantages to residents of common law jurisdictions.

IX.   INFLUENCE OF THE IRS

A.   As protector of the revenue, the IRS has a great deal of influence on shaping the tax law. In this role the IRS tries to close what it sees as loopholes in the tax law.

B.   Many provisions of the tax law are for administrative feasibility, and exist because they simplify the work of the IRS in collecting the revenue or administering the tax law. Withholding procedures place taxpayers on a pay-as-you-go basis and so aid the IRS in the collection of revenue. Interest and penalties imposed for noncompliance with tax laws are also of considerable help to the IRS.

X.   INFLUENCE OF THE COURTS

The Federal courts have influenced the tax law. Some court decisions have been of such consequence that Congress has incorporated them into the Internal Revenue Code. The rule that allows tax-free stock dividends is an example of a court decision being codified.

TEST FOR SELF-EVALUATION

True or False

Indicate which of the following statements are true or false by circling the correct answers.

T F 1. The first U.S. Federal income tax was enacted to provide revenues for the Civil War.

T **F** 2. The Supreme Court held that the 1894 income tax law was constitutional since it was a direct tax.

T **F** 3. The Sixteenth Amendment was necessary to enact the corporate income tax of 1909.

T F 4. The first Internal Revenue Code was the Code of 1939.

T F 5. The current tax law is the Internal Revenue Code of 1986.

T **F** 6. The corporate income tax provides the largest percentage of Federal tax revenues.

T F 7. During World War II, the income tax was converted from being a select tax to being a mass tax.

T F 8. The responsibility for administering the Federal tax law rests with the Treasury Department.

T **F** 9. The Internal Revenue Service openly discloses its audit selection techniques.

T F 10. The purpose of the gift tax is to prevent widespread avoidance of the estate tax.

T F 11. For 1989 the ceiling amount of income for which the FICA tax will be applied to is $48,000.

T **F** 12. The United States income tax rates are proportional.

T F 13. Tax collections from individual taxpayers account for about 38 percent of the Federal government's budget receipts.

T **F** 14. Ad valorem taxes are taxes that are based on income derived from property.

T **F** 15. Property taxes on personalty have a high rate of compliance, while taxes on realty have a low rate of compliance.

T⃝ F 16. Excise taxes are levied on specific products, while sales taxes are collected transactions involving a wide range of products.

T⃝ F 17. Excise taxes are sometimes used to influence social behavior.

T (F) 18. The Federal government is the only government allowed to impose excise taxes on products.

T (F) 19. The primary purpose of the estate tax is to generate revenue with which to operate the Federal government.

T⃝ F 20. After 1986, the estate tax credit and the gift tax credit is $192,800.

T (F) 21. State inheritance taxes usually tax all heirs at the same rate.

T (F) 22. The annual exclusion for Federal gift tax purposes is $47,000 per year per donee.

T (F) 23. The Federal income tax is imposed on individuals, corporations, partnerships, and certain fiduciaries.

T (F) 24. All states impose some form of income tax on individuals who reside in that state.

(T) F 25. Some cities impose an income tax along with the Federal and state income taxes.

T⃝ F 26. In recent years, tariffs have served the nation more as an instrument for carrying out protectionist policies than as a means for generating revenue.

T⃝ F 27. The interest rate used by the Internal Revenue Service is adjusted every quarter.

T⃝ F 28. The U.S. Federal income tax rate structure for individuals is becoming less progressive.

T⃝ F 29. Provisions of the U.S. income tax law are designed to help small businesses.

T⃝ F 30. An example of a social consideration in the tax law is the nontaxability of health plan benefits.

T (F) 31. The wherewithal to pay concept states that a taxpayer should pay the tax on all gains, even when his economic position has not changed.

T⃝ F 32. Many provisions of the tax law can be explained by looking at the influence of pressure groups on Congress.

(T) F 33. One role assumed by the Internal Revenue Service is that of "protector of the revenue."

T (F) 34. Some of the tax law is justified because it complicates the Internal Revenue Service's task of collecting revenue.

T (F) 35. The courts have established the rule that the relief provisions of the Code are to be broadly interpreted.

(T) F 36. Some court decisions have been of such consequence that Congress has written them into the tax laws.

(T) F 37. The tax law attempts to encourage technological progress.

(T) F 38. Economic considerations in the tax law help regulate the economy.

(T) F 39. One equity consideration of the tax law is the alleviation of multiple taxation.

(T) F 40. Carryback and carryover procedures help mitigate the effect of limiting a loss or deduction to the accounting period in which it was realized.

(T) F 41. The standard deduction, exemptions, and the tax brackets will be indexed for inflation in the future.

(T) F 42. In future years, budget deficit problems will probably influence many of the new tax provisions passed by Congress.

Fill-in-the-blanks

Complete the following statements with the appropriate word(s).

1. Adam Smith's "canons of taxation" are __equality__ , __convenience__ , __certainty__ , and __economy__ .

2. There are two kinds of tax rates. Tax rates may be __progressive__ or __flat or proportional__ .

3. Taxes imposed on luxury items such as alcoholic beverages, tobacco products, and highway fuels are called __excise__ taxes.

4. The Federal tax levied on the value of property transferred at death is the __estate__ tax.

5. The Internal Revenue Service is part of the Department of __Treasury__ .

6. Audits by the Internal Revenue Service are classified as ___*field*___ audits or ___*office*___ audits.

7. The general rule for the statute of limitation is ___3___ years, but it is ___6___ years if there is an omission of more than 25 percent of the gross income reported on a return.

8. The penalty for failure to file a tax return is ___5___ percent per month, up to a maximum of ___25___ percent.

Multiple Choice

Choose the best answer for each of the following questions.

___b___ 1. Which of the following is an employment tax?
   a. The gift tax
   b. FICA
   c. Custom duties
   d. Excise taxes
   e. None of the above

___c___ 2. Which of the following items will not be subject to indexing under the tax law?
   a. The standard deduction
   b. Personal and dependency exemptions
   c. The child care credit
   d. The individual tax brackets
   e. All of the above are indexed

___c___ 3. For 1989 the tax rate for Social Security on employees is:
   a. 7.00%
   b. 7.15%
   c. 7.51%
   d. 7.05%
   e. Some other amount

___d___ 4. The installment method of reporting gains is justified on the basis of:
   a. Mitigation of the annual accounting period
   b. Wherewithal to pay
   c. Social consideration
   d. Both a and b
   e. None of the above

___d___ 5. Jack Todd's gross income for 1989 is $60,000 and he has business deductions of $6,000. His itemized deductions are $7,000 and he has one personal exemption worth $2,000. For 1989 Jack's taxable income is:
   a. $54,000

b. $52,920
c. $47,000
d. $45,000
e. Some other amount

 6.   For 1989, Jeanne Emerson earned wages of $51,000. The total amount of FICA tax due on both Jeanne and her employer is:
a. $3,131.70
b. $7,209.60
c. $3,604.80
d. $6,263.40
e. Some other amount

7.   During 1989, Steve Jones earned $4,000 and Lynne Sass earned $12,000 from Bay Inc. The total FUTA tax payable before any state credits is:
a. $420
b. $240
c. $682
d. $660
e. Some other amount

8.   Byron Toole files his tax return 45 days late. Along with the return he remits a check for $6,000 which is the balance of the tax owed. Disregarding interest, what is Byron's penalty for failure to file?
a. -0-
b. $60
c. $540
d. $600
e. Some other amount

9.   The value added tax is:
a. Used by many countries in Western Europe.
b. A form of income tax on corporations.
c. Like a national sales tax on production.
d. Both a. and c. are correct.
e. All the above are correct.

10.   John Williams holds raw land as an investment. The land has a fair market value of $140,000 and cost John $84,000. The land is exchanged for other land worth $140,000, which is held as an investment. From this exchange John should report a taxable gain of:
a.   -0-
b. $56,000
c. $140,000
d. $84,000
e. Some other amount

_____ 11.   For the first three months of 1989, the interest rate charged by the IRS on money due to the government was:
a. 9%
b. 10%
c. 11%
d. 12%
e. 13%

_____ 12.   Michelle Roth overstated her deductions on last year's income tax return. During audit the IRS determined the overstatement was due to negligence by Michelle. As a result of the audit she owes additional income taxes of $20,000. The interest due to the underpayment amounts to $1,000. What is Michelle's total negligence penalty?
a. $1,500
b. $1,000
c. $500
d. $10,000
e. Some other amount.

_____ 13.   Vicky Wall filed her 19X3 individual tax return on January 15, 19X4. There was no understatement of income on the return, and the return was properly signed and filed. The statute of limitations for Vicky's 19X3 return expires on:
a. January 15, 19X7
b. April 15, 19X7
c. January 15, 19X0
d. April 15, 19X0

_____ 14.   Mike Shields had two jobs during 1989. He earned $20,000 from his first employer and $30,000 from his second employer. When Mike files his tax return he can claim a credit for excess FICA of how much?
a. -0-
b. $150.20
c. $375.50
d. $3,755.00
e. Some other amount

_____ 15.   Which of the following is not an economic consideration of the tax law?
a. Encouragement of small business
b. Encouragement of certain industries
c. The wherewithal to pay concept
d. Encouragement of certain activities
e. None of the above

_____ 16.   T owns an office building that he uses in his business. The building has a basis of $40,000 when it is destroyed by fire. T collects the insurance proceeds of $100,000 and within a short period reinvests all the proceeds in a new office building. How much gain should T recognize for tax pur-

poses?
a. -0-
b. $40,000
c. $60,000
d. $100,000
e. None of the above

_____ 17.   The net operating loss provision of the tax law is an example of:
a. An economic consideration
b. A social consideration
c. A political consideration
d. An equity consideration
e. None of the above

_____ 18.   Which of the following is not a social consideration in the tax law?
a. Qualified pension and profit sharing plan
b. Expensing land clearing cost
c. Child care credit
d. A speeding ticket paid by a truck driver is nondeductible
e. All of the above are social considerations

_____ 19.   Which of the following is the best example of a tax law provision designed to aid in controlling the economy?
a. Depreciation deduction
b. Child care credit
c. Personal exemption
d. Election to expense
e. None of the above

_____ 20.   Smith Corporation pays $2,000 per month rent on a building to Mary Smith, its sole shareholder. The fair market value of the rent determined at "arm's length" would be $900 per month. Smith Corporation will be allowed a monthly rental deduction of:
a. -0-
b. $900
c. $1,000
d. $2,000
e. None of the above

SOLUTIONS TO CHAPTER 1

True or False

1. True   (p. 1-2)

2. False   The income tax was unconstitutional because it was not apportioned. (p. 1-3)

3. False   The 1909 corporate income tax was held to be constitutional. (p. 1-3)

4. True   (p. 1-3)

5. True   (p. 1-3)

6. False   The individual income tax provides the largest percent. (p. 1-4)

7. True   (p. 1-3)

8. True   (p. 1-18)

9. False   The IRS does not disclose its audit selection techniques. (p. 1-19)

10. True   (p. 1-12)

11. True   (p. 1-16)

12. False   The U.S. income tax rates are progressive. (p. 1-5)

13. True   (p. 1-4)

14. False   Ad valorem taxes are based on the value of the property. (p. 1-6)

15. False   Realty has a high compliance rate. (p. 1-6)

16. True   (p. 1-9)

17. True   (p. 1-9)

18. False   State and local governments can also impose excise taxes. (p. 1-9)

19. False   The purpose of the estate tax is to prevent concentrations of wealth. (p. 1-11)

20. True   (p. 1-11)

21. False   Inheritance taxes tax distant heirs at a higher rate. (p. 1-11)

22. False   The exclusion is $10,000 per year. (p. 1-12)

23. False   The income tax is not imposed on partnerships. (p. 1-13)

24. False   Several states do not have a state income tax. (p. 1-14)

25. True   (p. 1-15)

26. True   (p. 1-17)

27. True   (p. 1-21)

28. True   (p. 1-5)

29. True   (p. 1-25)

30. True   (p. 1-25)

31. False   Wherewithal to pay states that gains are taxed when realized. (p. 1-27)

32. True   (p. 1-29)

33. True   (p. 1-30)

34. False   Some of the law is justified because it simplifies the work of the IRS. (p. 1-31)

35. False   The relief provisions are narrowly interpreted. (p. 1-32)

36. True   (p. 1-32)

37. True   (p. 1-24)

38. True   (p. 1-23)

39. True   (p. 1-26)

40. True   (p. 1-28)

41. True   (p. 1-29)

42. True   (p. 1-23)

Fill-in-the-Blanks

1. equality, convenience, certainty, economy (p. 1-4)

2. proportional, progressive (p. 1-5)

3. excise (p. 1-8)

4. estate (p. 1-10)

5. the Treasury (p. 1-18)

6. office, field (p. 1-20)

7. three, six (p. 1-21)

8. five, 25 (p. 1-21)

Multiple Choice

1. B (p. 1-15)

2. C (p. 1-29)

3. C (p. 1-16)

4. D (p. 1-28)

5. D $60,000 - $6,000 - $7,000 - $2,000 = $45,000. (p. 1-14)

6. B ($48,000 + $48,000) x 7.51% = $7,209.60 (p. 1-16)

7. C [$4,000 + $7,000 (maximum)] x 6.2% = $682.00 (p. 1-17)

8. D 5% per month or fraction thereof, or 10% x $6,000 = $600. (p. 1-21)

9. D (p. 1-18)

10. A (p. 1-27)

11. C (p. 1-21)

12. A (5% x $20,000) + (50% x $1,000) = $1,500   (p. 1-22)

13. B (p. 1-21)

14. B ($30,000 x 7.51%) + ($20,000 x 7.51%) - $3,604.80 (max) = $150.20 (p. 1-16)

15. C This is an equity consideration. (p. 1-27)

16 A This is an involuntary conversion. (p. 1-27)

17. D (p. 1-28)

18. B (p. 1-25)

19. A (p. 1-24)

20. B (p. 1-32)

2

WORKING WITH THE TAX LAW

CHAPTER HIGHLIGHTS

Familiarity with the statutory, administrative, and judicial sources of the tax law is essential in learning to work with tax legislation. This chapter considers the sources of tax law, the application of research techniques to tax problems, and the effective use of tax planning procedures.

I.   STATUTORY SOURCES OF THE TAX LAW

    A.   The Internal Revenue Code of 1939 was the first codification of all Federal tax provisions into a logical sequence. The 1939 Code was recodified into the 1954 Code, which was renamed the Internal Revenue Code of 1986. New tax laws are integrated into the 1986 Code.

    B.   For a tax bill to become law, it must be passed by both houses of Congress and signed by the President. Tax legislation is first considered in the House by the Ways and Means Committee and in the Senate by the Finance Committee. When the House and Senate cannot agree on the tax bill, the differences are worked out by the Joint Conference Committee.

    C.   The Code is arranged by Subtitles, Chapters, Subchapters, Parts, and Sections. However, to identify any part of the Code, it is only necessary to know the Section because these numbers are not repeated. The normal progression for a citation is Section, Subsection, Paragraph, and Subparagraph.

II.   ADMINISTRATIVE SOURCES OF THE TAX LAW

A.   There are numerous administrative sources of Federal tax law. These can be grouped as Treasury Department Regulations, Revenue Rulings and Procedures, and other pronouncements. All are issued by the U.S. Treasury Department or one of its instrumentalities such as the Internal Revenue Service or a District Director.

B.   Treasury Department Regulations are the Internal Revenue Service's official interpretation of the Code. They are arranged in Code section sequence with a prefix to designate the class of regulation.

C.   Revenue Rulings and Procedures are official pronouncements of the national office of the IRS. They do not, however, carry the same legal force as Regulations. Revenue Rulings usually are concerned with a restrictive problem or area, while Revenue Procedures are concerned with internal management practices of the IRS. Both Revenue Rulings and Procedures are published weekly by the U.S. government in the *Internal Revenue Bulletin*. Every six months the weekly bulletins are published in a bound volume entitled *Cumulative Bulletin*.

D.   The IRS also makes the following administrative communications:

Treasury Decisions (TDs) are published to promulgate new Regulations, or to announce the government's position on selected court decisions.

Individual Letter Rulings are issued on a taxpayer's request and describe how the IRS will treat a proposed transaction. These are available for public inspection after identifying details are removed.

Determination Letters are rulings that generally deal with completed transactions, and are issued from District Directors, as opposed to the National Office of the IRS.

Technical Advice Memoranda are private rulings initiated by the IRS during its audit activities.

Other items such as Announcements, Notices, and Prohibited Transaction Exemptions are published in the *Internal Revenue Bulletin*.

III.   JUDICIAL SOURCES OF THE TAX LAW

A.   After a taxpayer has exhausted some or all of the remedies available with the IRS, a dispute can be taken to the Federal courts. The dispute is first heard by a trial court (the court of original jurisdiction) with any appeal taken to the appropriate appellate court.

B.   The trial courts include the following:

The District Court is organized into geographical regions, and will hear cases involving any Federal matter. Taxpayers cannot choose a particular District Court but must use the one having jurisdiction over the case. Each District Court has only one judge and it is the only court which may have a jury trial.

The U.S. Claims Court has sixteen judges and meets in Washington D.C. The purpose of this court is to hear any case involving a monetary claim against the Federal government.

The Tax Court is a national court with nineteen judges. However, only one judge hears a case unless it is unusual. The Tax Court will follow decisions of the Court of Appeals in the jurisdiction the case is being heard. The Tax Court is the only court in which the taxpayer need not pay the deficiency before taking the dispute to court. Before 1943, the Tax Court was called the Board of Tax Appeals (BTA).

The small claims division of the Tax Court will hear matters involving up to $10,000 in tax. The decisions of the small claims division are final and cannot be appealed.

C.   The appellate courts include the following:

There are eleven numbered Courts of Appeals plus one for the District of Columbia, and one for the Federal District. Each Court of Appeals has jurisdiction in specific geographical regions of the country, except the Federal District, which hears cases only from the U.S. Claims Court.

The Supreme Court, a nine judge panel, has final say in all tax matters. Appeal to the Supreme Court is by Writ of Certiorari, and acceptance is not automatic.

D.   Court decisions are reported in a variety of different publications. Decisions of the District Court, U.S. Claims Court, Court of Appeals, and Supreme Court that deal with tax matters are reported in both the CCH, *U.S. Tax Cases (USTC)* and the P-H, *American Federal tax Reports (AFTR)* series. All District Court decisions are published by West Publishing Company in their *Federal Supplement (F.Supp.)* series. All decisions of the U.S. Claims Court after October 1982 are published in the *Claims Court Reporter (Cl.Ct.)*, by West Publishing. All decisions of the Court of Appeals are published by West in a reporter designated as the *Federal Second Series (F.2d)*. Supreme Court decisions are published by West in their *Supreme Court Reporter (S.Ct.)*, by the U.S. Government Printing Office in the *United States Supreme*

Court Reports (U.S.), and by the Lawyer's Co-Operative Publishing Company in its *United States Reports, Lawyer's Edition (L.Ed.)*.

The Tax Court issues two kinds of decisions, Regular and Memorandum. Generally, Regular decisions deal with a new or unusual point of law, while Memorandum decisions deal with an established point of law. The Regular decisions of the Tax Court are published in a series designated *Tax Court of the United States Reports (T.C.)*. Memorandum decisions are published by CCH in *Tax Court Memorandum Decisions (TCM)* and by Prentice Hall in *P-H T.C. Memorandum Decisions*.

A court decision citation usually consists of two parts: (1) the name of the case and the abbreviated title of the report volume and (2) the number or page of the report that contains the text of the decision. After each citation, a parenthetical reference identifies the court rendering the decision and the year the decision was reached.

E.   If the IRS loses at the trial court level, and if an appeal is not made, it does not indicate that the IRS agrees with the result or that it will not litigate similar situations in the future.

IV.   TAX RESEARCH

A.   The first step in tax research is to identify and refine the problem. All facts having a bearing on the problem must be gathered since any omission could have a substantial impact on the conclusion reached.

B.   The second step in tax research involves locating the appropriate tax law sources. Most tax research begins with the index volume of a tax service. A tax service is a comprehensive set of books on Internal Revenue law. The major tax services are arranged by Code section or topic. When using any tax service one should always check for current developments. Besides the tax services there are numerous tax periodicals, which are indexed in CCH's *Federal Tax Articles*.

C.   The third step in tax research, once a source of tax information has been located, is to assess the source in relation to the problem at hand. Some of the characteristics of sources that need to be assessed include conflicting Code provisions and the relative importance of Treasury Regulations, Revenue Rulings, and court decisions.

The language of the Code can be extremely difficult to comprehend, with extremely long sentences and many cross references between interrelated provisions. Also, occasional conflicts between old and new Code provisions arise. For these and other reasons, great care should be exercised when interpreting the Code.

The Treasury Regulations are not the law, but have the force and effect of law if they are reasonable interpretations of the Code. The burden of proof rests with the taxpayer to show that a Regulation is wrong. Certain "legislative regulations" are virtually impossible to overturn.

Revenue Rulings carry less weight than the Regulations, but are important reflections of the IRS's position on certain tax matters.

The validity of a court decision depends on the level of the court, the residence of the taxpayer and the current status of the decision.

D. The fourth step of the tax research process is arriving at a solution based on the information gathered. Often a clear cut answer is impossible to obtain, and a guarded judgment is the best solution that can be given.

E. Once a conclusion has been reached, it is necessary to communicate the findings to the client. This is normally done by preparing a memo that explains the findings and how the conclusions were reached. The memo should contain the following:

A clear statement of the issue(s).

A short review of the factual pattern.

A review of the tax law.

Any assumptions.

The solution recommended and the logic supporting the conclusion.

References consulted while doing the research.

V. TAX PLANNING

A. In tax planning, it is necessary to take into account many nontax considerations. What may produce the best tax result may not be an acceptable alternative to the taxpayer. As a general rule, tax planning involves producing the smallest tax within the nontax and legal constraints. Tax consideration should not impair the exercise of sound business judgment by the taxpayer.

B. There is a difference between tax avoidance and tax evasion. Tax avoidance is merely minimization through legal means, while evasion is illegal tax planning.

C. Computer tax research is part of the day-to-day tax practice for many tax professionals. The computer on-line data bases provide the tax practitioner instant access to the entire legal data base. The three major tax research data bases are Lexis, Westlaw, and Phinet. These data bases are searched by using a system of key words. The document(s) that meet the search criteria are then displayed on the computer screen for the tax researcher.

TEST FOR SELF-EVALUATION

True or False

Indicate which of the following statements are true or false by circling the correct answers.

T F 1. Both Revenue Rulings and Revenue Procedures are published weekly by the U.S. Government in the *Internal Revenue Bulletin.*

T F 2. There is only one U.S. Claims Court and it meets in Washington, D.C.

T F 3. The U.S. Claims Court has seven judges and the Tax Court has nineteen.

T F 4. Regulation Section 1.61 refers to Internal Revenue Code Section 61.

T F 5. Appeal to the Supreme Court is by Writ of Certiorari.

T F 6. Revenue Ruling 87-61 relates to Section 61 of the Internal Revenue Code.

T F 7. In general, a U.S. Tax Court Regular decision deals with a new or unusual point of law.

T F 8. The Internal Revenue Service usually acquiesces or nonacquiesces to all regular Tax Court decisions.

T F 9. To go to the Tax Court, a taxpayer must pay the tax and sue for a refund.

T F 10. A jury trial may be obtained in the Tax Court.

T F 11. *Bradford v. Comm.,* 56-1 USTC Para. 9552 (CA-6, 1956) is an example of a citation from Commerce Clearing House's *United States Tax Cases.*

T F 12. Prentice-Hall publishes Revenue Rulings in its *American Federal Tax Reports* (AFTR).

T F 13. The United States Tax Court is one of the federal trial courts that is a court of original jurisdiction.

T F 14. When confronted with a particularly troublesome problem, the taxpayer may always obtain an individual letter ruling.

T F 15. *Morris Alexander v. Comm.,* 61 T.C. 278 is an example of a citation from Commerce Clearing House's *Tax Court of the United States Reports.*

T F 16. Temporary Regulations are also issued as proposed Regulations and automatically expire within three years after the date of issuance.

T F 17.   In a challenge by the IRS, the burden of proof is on the taxpayer to show
            that a Regulation is wrong.

T F 18.   Tax avoidance is illegal tax planning while tax evasion is legal tax plan-
            ning.

T F 19.   A case is appealed from the U.S. Claims Court to the Court of Appeals and
            then to the Supreme Court.

T F 20.   *John Smith*, T.C. Memo 1980-32 is the 32nd Tax Court Memorandum decision
            of 1980.

T F 21.   The Tax Court follows the decisions of the Court of Appeals in the jurisdic-
            tion a case is being heard.

T F 22.   The District Courts hear cases involving both tax and nontax litigation.

T F 23.   The appellate courts are the Supreme Court, Courts of Appeals, and the U.S.
            Claims Court

T F 24.   The *Cumulative Bulletins* normally are published for six-month periods.

T F 25.   The prefix 1 designates an income tax Regulation when referring to a
            Treasury Department Regulation.

T F 26.   Tax legislation originates in the House of Representatives Ways and Means
            Committee.

T F 27.   Individual Letter Rulings and TAMs are not available for public inspection.

Fill-in-the-Blanks

Complete the following statements with the appropriate word(s) or amount(s).

1.   Federal tax legislation generally originates in the House of Representa-
     tives where it is first considered by the House _____ and
     _____ Committee.

2.   When the Senate version of a tax bill differs from that passed by the
     House, the _____ Conference Committee resolves the differences.

3.   To locate a provision in the Code, all that is necessary is the
     _____ number of that provision.

4.   The Treasury Department Regulations are arranged in Code _____
     sequence.

5. Every six months the *Internal Revenue Bulletins* are published in a bound volume designated as the _____ _____.

6. Individual Letter Rulings are issued by the _____ Office of the Internal Revenue Service, while determination letters are issued by the _____ Director.

7. The Tax Court and Claims Court are both _____ courts.

8. The Tax Court issues two kinds of decisions, _____ and _____ decisions.

Multiple Choice

Choose the best answer for each of the following questions.

_____ 1. Appeal from the Tax Court is to the:
a. Court of Appeals
b. District Court
c. U.S. Claims Court
d. Supreme Court
e. None of the above

_____ 2. If taxpayers choose not to pay a tax deficiency, then they must petition which court?
a. District Court
b. U.S. Claims Court
c. Tax Court
d. Court of Appeals
e. None of the above

_____ 3. Which of the following court(s) would have jurisdiction if a taxpayer paid a tax deficiency and sued for a refund?
a. Tax Court
b. District Court and U.S. Claims Court
c. Tax Court and District Court
d. U.S. Claims Court
e. None of the above

_____ 4. A decision of which of the following courts could not be found in CCH's *U.S. Tax Cases?*
a. District Court
b. Court of Appeals
c. Supreme Court
d. U.S. Claims Court
e. None of the above

_____ 5.   Which of the following does not publish a tax service?
a. Commerce Clearing House
b. Prentice-Hall
c. Research Institute of America
d. U.S. Government
e. None of the above

_____ 6.   The *Federal Tax Articles* index is a three-volume service published by:
a. U.S. Government
b. Prentice-Hall
c. Commerce Clearing House
d. Matthew Bender, Inc.
e. None of the above

_____ 7.   Tax evasion is:
a. Legally minimizing taxes
b. Illegally minimizing taxes
c. The same as tax avoidance
d. None of the above

_____ 8.   In *Walter H. Johnson*, 34 TCM 1056, 34 stands for:
a. The year of decision
b. The page number
c. The volume number
d. The paragraph number
e. None of the above

_____ 9.   Decisions by which court are published by West Publishing Company in its Federal Supplement (F.Supp.) Series?
a. District Court
b. Tax Court
c. U.S. Claims Court
d. Court of Appeals
e. None of the above

_____ 10. The largest grouping of material in the Internal Revenue Code is the:
a. Subtitle
b. Chapter
c. Part
d. Subchapter
e. None of the above

_____ 11. The maximum amount of tax that is within the jurisdiction of the Small Claims Division of the United States Tax Court is:
a. $1,500
b. $2,500
c. $5,000

    d. $10,000

    e. None of the above

_____ 12. Which of the following Federal courts is not a "national" court?

    a. Supreme Court

    b. District Court

    c. U.S. Claims Court

    d. United States Tax Court

    e. None of the above

_____ 13. The United States Tax Court:

    a. Has nineteen judges

    b. Will hear any Federal case

    c. Is an appeals court

    d. Has jurisdiction over the District Courts

    e. None of the above

_____ 14. The *Standard Federal Tax Reporter* is published by:

    a. Prentice-Hall

    b. Commerce Clearing House

    c. Research Institute of America

    d. Bureau of National Affairs

    e. None of the above

_____ 15. According to the text, the primary purpose of effective tax planning is:

    a. Eradicating the tax entirely

    b. Deferring the receipt of income

    c. Converting ordinary income into capital gain

    d. Eliminating tax in the current year

    e. None of the above

_____ 16. Which of the following best describes Westlaw, Lexis, or Phinet?

    a. A new computer tax service

    b. A computerized legal data base that can be used (among other things) for tax research

    c. An electronic spreadsheet for tax planning

    d. A computer program that can be used for estate planning for wealthy taxpayers

    e. A tax return preparation computer program

_____ 17. At the completion of the tax research process the results are generally set forth in which of the following ways?

    a. A phone call to the client

    b. A note to the IRS

    c. Preparing a tax research memo

    d. Adding the results to the LEXIS data base

    e. Nothing is done formally

_____ 18. Which of the following is not a tax periodical?
a. *Journal of Taxation*
b. *Taxation for Accountants*
c. *TAXES-the Tax Magazine*
d. *The American Tax Journal*
e. *Estate Planning*

_____ 19. The IRS considers only the primary sources of tax law to be "substantial authority." Which of the following is a primary source of tax law?
a. Tax treaties
b. Legal journals
c. Technical Advice Memoranda (TAM)
d. Tax textbooks
e. General Counsel Memoranda (GCM)

_____ 20. In Letter Ruling 8515087, the 087 refers to the:
a. Year of the Letter Ruling
b. Issue of the Bulletin in which the Letter Ruling appears
c. Day of the year the Letter Ruling was issued
d. The number of the Letter Ruling issued during the week

_____ 21. Which of the following is a "secondary" source of tax law?
a. A Tax Court case
b. A Revenue Ruling
c. A tax treaty between the U.S. and Mexico
d. An article on partnership tax in the *Tax Advisor*
e. All of the above are secondary sources

SOLUTIONS TO CHAPTER 3

True or False

1. True   (p. 2-9)

2. True   (p. 2-13)

3. False   The U.S. Claims Court has sixteen judges. (p. 2-13)

4. True   (p. 2-7)

5. True   (p. 2-16)

6. False   It is the 61st Revenue Ruling of 1979. (p. 2-9)

7. True   (p. 2-17)

8. False   IRS acquiesces or nonacquiesces to decisions it loses. (p. 2-18)

9. False   The taxpayer does not have to pay. (p. 2-13)

10. False   A jury trial is available only in the District Courts. (p. 2-13)

11. True   (p. 2-19)

12. False   Court decisions are published in the AFTR. (p. 2-12)

13. True   (p. 2-9)

14. False   There are many issues on which the IRS will not rule. (p. 2-9)

15. False   *Tax Court of the U.S. Reports* are published by the government. (p. 2-17)

16. True   (p. 2-26)

17. True   (p. 2-8)

18. False   Tax planning is legal while tax evasion is illegal. (p. 2-31)

19. True   (p. 2-15)

20. True   (p. 2-18)

21. True   (p. 2-16)

22. True   (p. 2-13)

23. False   The U.S. Claims Court is a court of original jurisdiction. (p. 2-14)

24. True   (p. 2-9

25. True   (p. 2-7)

26. True   (p. 2-3)

27. False   They are published by CCH, Prentice-Hall, and other publishers. (p. 2-10)

Fill-in-the-Blanks

1. Ways, Means (p. 2-3)

2. Joint (p. 2-3)

3. Section (p. 2-5)

4. Section (p. 2-7)

5. Cumulative Bulletin (p. 2-9)

6. National, District (p. 2-11)

7. national (pp. 2-15)

8. Regular, Memorandum (p. 2-17)

Multiple Choice

1. A (p. 2-15)

2. C (p. 2-13)

3. B (p. 2-13)

4. E (p. 2-19)

5. D (p. 2-23)

6. C (p. 2-24)

7. B (p. 2-31)

8. C (p. 2-18)

9. A (p. 2-19)

10. A (p. 2-5)

11. D (p. 2-12)

12. B (p. 2-15)

13. A (p. 2-13)

14. B (p. 2-33)

15. E (p. 2-30)

16. B (p. 2-33)

17. C (p. 2-29)

18. D (p. 2-24)

19. A (p. 2-28)

20. D (p. 2-10)

21. D (p. 2-28)

3

TAX DETERMINATION; PERSONAL AND DEPENDENCY EXEMPTIONS; AN OVERVIEW OF PROPERTY TRANSACTIONS

CHAPTER HIGHLIGHTS

This chapter continues to develop the components of the individual income tax formula. To determine Federal tax liability, an amount known as taxable income must be computed. Taxable income includes all realized income less deductions specifically provided in the tax law. Special deductions, the standard deduction and personal exemptions, are available for all taxpayers. An overview of property transactions is helpful at this point, though the subject will be covered in greater detail in later chapters.

I. THE TAX FORMULA

    A. Taxable income is calculated based on the following formula:

Income (broadly conceived)	$xxxxx
Less: Exclusions	(xxxxx)
Gross Income	xxxxx
Less: Deductions for A.G.I.	(xxxxx)
Adjusted Gross Income	$xxxxx
Less: the greater of	
Itemized Deductions, or	
the Standard Deduction	(xxxxx)
Exemptions	(xxxxx)
Taxable Income	$xxxxx

B.   The components of the tax formula can be broken down as follows:

Income includes all taxable and nontaxable income of the taxpayer.

Exclusions are items of income which Congress has chosen to exclude from the tax base for various social, economic, equity, and other reasons.

Gross income is defined in the Code as "all income from whatever source derived", but does not include unrealized gains.

Deductions for adjusted gross income include ordinary and necessary expenses incurred in a trade or business, certain reimbursed employee business expenses, alimony paid, and IRA contributions among others.

Adjusted gross income (AGI) is an important subtotal which serves as a basis for calculating limitations on certain itemized deductions.

Itemized deductions are expenses, personal in nature, for which Congress has specifically allowed a deduction. Taxpayers are allowed to use a standard deduction in lieu of itemizing deductions. See text for amounts.

Blind and aged taxpayers are given additional amounts of standard deduction. See text for amounts.

Certain taxpayers are required to make special computations for the standard deduction. These taxpayers are:

> a married taxpayer filing a separate return when either spouse itemizes deductions
>
> a nonresident alien
>
> individuals with short tax years

The calculation of taxable income for dependent minor children with unearned income over $500 is subject to special adjustments. Generally, dependent minor children cannot claim themselves as dependents on their own tax returns. Also, a dependent's standard deduction is limited to the greater of $500 or the individual's earned income for the year. However, if the individual's standard deduction exceeds the normal standard deduction, then the standard deduction is limited to the normal amount shown in the text.

Personal and dependency exemptions give some measure of equity in our tax system by providing relief for taxpayers with families. For 1989 the amount is $2,000.

II.   PERSONAL AND DEPENDENCY EXEMPTIONS

A.   The law provides for a personal exemption for the taxpayer and an additional exemption for the spouse if a joint return is filed. The determination of marital status is made at the end of the taxable year. If spouses enter into a legal separation agreement before the end of the taxable year, they are considered to be unmarried at the end of the taxable year.

B.   For an individual to qualify for the dependency exemption, five tests must be met. These tests are:

support

relationship or member of the household

gross income

joint return

citizenship or residency

See the flowchart for the relationship between the five tests.

For the support test to be met, over one-half of the dependent's support must be furnished by the taxpayer. The term "support" generally includes expenditures for food, shelter, clothing, medical care, and education.

The relationship test requires that the dependent be a relative specified in the Code. An individual can qualify as a dependent if he or she has a principal place of residence in the taxpayer's household for the entire year.

The dependent's gross income must be less than $2,000 (the 1989 exemption amount) unless the dependent is the taxpayer's child under 19, or a child that is a full-time student under the age of 24.

If the dependent is married, the supporting taxpayer is not permitted a dependency exemption if the person being supported files a joint return with his or her spouse.

A dependent must be a U.S. citizen or a resident of the U.S. or a country which is contiguous to the U.S.

DEPENDENCY EXEMPTION TESTS FLOWCHART

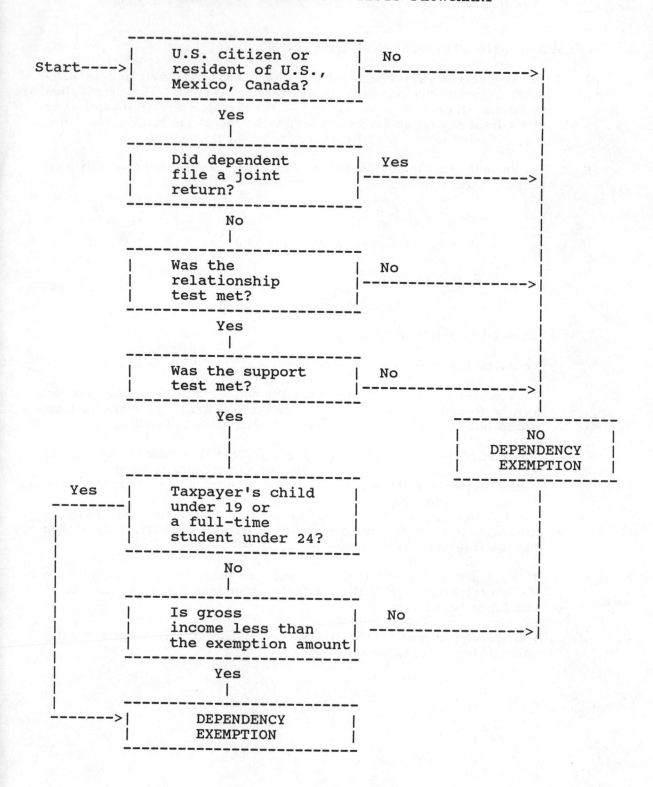

Under a multiple support agreement, one member of a group of taxpayers who furnishes over one-half of the support of a dependent can claim a dependency exemption even when no one person provides more than 50 percent of the support. Any person who contributed more than 10 percent of the support is entitled to claim the exemption if each person in the group who contributed more than 10 percent files a written consent.

For divorced parents, the Code has established rules to help settle disputes as to who is eligible to claim the children as dependents. For divorce decrees after 1984, the parent with custody is allowed to claim the exemption except where the parents agree in writing that the non-custodial parent can claim the exemption.

III.   TAX DETERMINATION

A.   In calculating their tax liability taxpayers use a tax table or a tax rate schedule.

B.   Taxpayers who cannot use the tax tables include estates and trusts, individuals claiming exclusion for foreign earned income, individuals filing a short period return, and individuals with taxable income larger than the amounts in the tables.

C.   For tax years after 1987 there is a 5 percent phase-out surtax on high income taxpayers. The surtax is paid until the taxpayer has recaptured the lower bracket tax saving and any exemption amounts claimed.

D.   For tax years after 1986 the "unearned income" of minor children is taxed at their parent's marginal rate. The provision applies to any child if the child:

> has not reached age 14 by the close of the tax year, and
>
> has at least one living parent, and
>
> has net unearned income for the tax year.

Net unearned income is unearned income less $500 and less the greater of $500 of standard deduction or the amount of allowable deductions directly connected with the production of unearned income.

For a child under 14 the parents may elect to report the child's income on the parent's tax return if the following conditions are met:

> income is from dividends and interest only
>
> income is over $500 and less than $5,000

no estimate tax has been paid by the child

there is no backup withholding on the child

IV.   FILING CONSIDERATIONS

A.   Filing Requirements.

An individual taxpayer must file a tax return if certain minimum amounts of gross income have been earned. (See text for the dollar amounts).

A self-employed individual with net earnings of $400 or more must file a tax return regardless of the dollar amount of gross income.

Individual taxpayers file either a Form 1040 (long form), Form 1040A (short form), or 1040EZ (certain single taxpayers).

B.   There are four different statuses under which a taxpayer can file. These are single, married filing jointly, married filing separately, and head of household. The amount of tax liability will vary with the filing status.

Single (Schedule X). Taxpayers who are unmarried on December 31, are single unless they qualify as head of household.

Married (Schedule Y). Taxpayers who are married on December 31, are married and must use married filing jointly or married filing separately tax rates.

Head of Household (Schedule Z). Taxpayers may file as head of household if the following conditions are met:

They are unmarried on December 31,

They provide over one-half the cost of a household, and

They have a relative as defined in the Code living in the household (certain unmarried relatives such as a child need not qualify as a dependent).

V.   GAINS AND LOSSES FROM PROPERTY TRANSACTIONS -- IN GENERAL

A.   The sale or other disposition of property may result in gain or loss. Realized gain or loss is the amount realized less the adjusted basis of the property. In general, the adjusted basis is the cost of the property plus capital additions, less depreciation (if any).

B.   All realized gains are recognized for tax purposes unless some provision of the tax law provides otherwise. Realized losses may or may not be recognized as a deduction for tax purposes. Losses on personal use property are generally not recognized.

VI.   GAINS & LOSSES FROM PROPERTY TRANSACTIONS -- CAPITAL GAINS

A.   Gains and losses from the sale or exchange of capital assets receive special treatment under the tax law.

B.   The Code defines a capital asset as property owned by the taxpayer other than items such as inventory, accounts receivable, depreciable property, or real estate used in a business.

The principal capital assets held by individuals for personal (non business) use include automobiles, a personal residence, and assets held for investment (such as stocks, bonds, and land).

C.   For tax years after 1986, net capital gain is taxed as ordinary income (with special rate limits in 1987).

D.   Capital losses are first offset against capital gains. For individuals net capital losses are deductible against other income up to a maximum of $3,000 per year. The excess loss carries forward for an unlimited period. Corporations may not use capital losses as deductions against ordinary income.

TEST FOR SELF-EVALUATION

True or False

Indicate which of the following statements are true or false by circling the correct answers.

T   F   1.   For divorces decrees after 1984, the mother is always eligible to claim the dependency exemption for any child of divorced parents.

T   F   2.   The standard deduction for 1989 is $3,100 for single taxpayers, $5,200 for married individuals filing jointly, and $2,600 for married individuals filing separately.

T   F   3.   Itemized deductions are deductible even if they do not exceed the standard deduction.

T   F   4.   If married individuals file separate returns and one spouse itemizes, both must itemize.

T   F   5.   For 1989 the personal and dependency exemption is $2,000.

T   F   6.   Taxpayers are allowed extra standard deduction amounts for old age and blindness.

T   F   7.   If taxpayers are married at the end of the taxable year, they are considered married for the entire year.

T   F   8.   The old age and blindness standard deduction can apply to a dependent of the taxpayer.

T   F   9.   For the support test to be met, a taxpayer must furnish over one- half of the support of the dependent.

T   F   10.   Social Security benefits can always be disregarded in determining the support of a dependent.

T   F   11.   A foster child qualifies as the taxpayer's child if he has his principal place of abode in the taxpayer's household.

T   F   12.   An individual whose gross income is over $2,000 cannot be a dependent of another taxpayer.

T   F   13.   If an individual is married and files a joint return with her spouse, she generally cannot qualify as a dependent of another taxpayer.

T   F   14.   A person who lives in Mexico or Canada could qualify as a dependent of a taxpayer.

T   F   15.   To qualify for a multiple support agreement, a group of taxpayers must supply over 50 percent of the support of an individual.

T   F   16.   In order for a taxpayer's dependent parents to qualify him or her for head of household filing status, the parents must live in the taxpayer's home.

T   F   17.   All realized gains are recognized for tax purposes unless some specific provision of the tax law provides otherwise.

T   F   18.   For individual taxpayers, net long-term capital losses carry forward for five years and carry back for three years.

T   F   19.   For 1989 long-term capital gains are taxed as ordinary income to individual taxpayers.

T   F   20.   Assets acquired after 1987 have to be held over one year in order to be long-term capital gains.

T   F   21.   Parents may elect to include their 10-year-old child's interest income of $7,300 on their tax return to prevent the child from having to file a tax return.

T   F   22.   The 33% tax bracket includes a 5% surtax to phase out the tax benefit for high income taxpayers caused by the use of the 15% bracket.

Fill-in-the-Blanks

Complete the following statements with the appropriate word(s) or amount(s).

1.   A parent who provides over one-half of the support of a _____ who is under 19 or who is a full-time student may claim a dependency exemption.

2.   A dependent must be a U.S. citizen or a resident of the United States, _____, or _____.

3.   The tax rate schedules are mainly used by _____ income taxpayers while the tax tables are used by low and middle income taxpayers.

4.   Taxpayers with income over the ceiling amount will be required to use the tax _____ schedule method in calculating their tax liability.

5.   The determination of marital status is generally made at the _____ of the tax year, except where a spouse dies during the year.

6.   Form 1040A, 1040EZ, or 1040 is due on or before the 15th day of the _____ month following the close of the tax year.

7.   The joint return rate schedule was originally enacted to establish equity for married taxpayers in common law states, because married taxpayers in _____ property states could split their income.

8.   Unmarried individuals who maintain a household for dependents are entitled to use the head of household tax rate schedule _____.

9.   Net capital losses may not be used to reduce ordinary income of a _____.

Multiple Choice

Choose the best answer for each of the following questions.

_____   1.   For 1989 the standard deduction amount for a single taxpayer would be:
a. -0-
b. $2,600
c. $3,100
d. $5,200
e. None of the above

_____   2.   During 1989, T, a single taxpayer with no dependents, has adjusted gross income of $20,000. She has itemized deductions of $6,500. What is T's taxable income?
a. $20,000
b. $14,900
c. $11,500
d. $15,850
e. None of the above

_____   3.   Jimmy is 10 years old and has $1,700 in interest earnings on a saving account at a local bank. If Jimmy is claimed as a dependent on his parent's tax return, what is Jimmy's "net unearned income?"
a. -0-
b. $1,700
c. $1,200
d. $700
e. None of the above

_____   4.   For 1989, the maximum net long-term capital gain tax rate (without the surtax) for individual taxpayers is:
a. 40%
b. 33%
c. 28%
d. 38.5%
e. None of the above

_____ 5.   A head of household taxpayer uses which of the following tax rate schedules?
a. Schedule X
b. Schedule Y
c. Schedule Z
d. Schedule G
e. None of the above

_____ 6.   A taxpayer's child under 19 or a full-time student under 24 does not have to
meet which of the following dependency tests?
a. Support test
b. Relationship test
c. Joint return test
d. Gross income test
e. Citizenship test

_____ 7.   Walter Kuhn is a divorced individual. He has a dependent son, age 6, who
is in the custody of his ex-wife. In addition, Walter supports his dependent
mother who lives in her own home. Walter's filing status would be:
a. Head of household
b. Married-joint
c. Married-separate
d. Single

_____ 8.   Which of the following is subtracted from the original basis to obtain the
adjusted basis of an asset?
a. Capital improvements
b. The gain realized
c. The gain recognized
d. Depreciation
e. None of the above

_____ 9.   During the current year, T sells his car for $8,000 (adjusted basis of $7,000)
and Exxon stock for $20,000 (adjusted basis of $10,000). What is T's recognized gain?
a. $11,000
b. $10,000
c. $8,000
d. $1,000
e. None of the above

_____ 10.   Dee Walsh is 66 years old and files as a single taxpayer. For 1989 her
standard deduction amount is:
a. $3,100
b. $3,700
c. $3,850
d. $4,300

_____ 11. Which of the following is a capital asset?
   a. Inventory
   b. Accounts Receivable
   c. Stock held by an individual taxpayer
   d. Real estate used in a business
   e. None of the above

_____ 12. The maximum deduction for capital losses against an individual taxpayer's income in 1989 is:
   a. $6,000
   b. $5,000
   c. $4,000
   d. $3,000
   e. None of the above

_____ 13. Which of the following in not a deduction for adjusted gross income?
   a. IRA deductible amounts
   b. Trade or business expenses
   c. Alimony
   d. Moving expenses
   e. None of the above

_____ 14. For individual taxpayers, unused capital losses can be carried forward:
   a. 3 years
   b. 4 years
   c. 5 years
   d. 7 years
   e. None of the above

_____ 15. During 1989 T had a long-term capital gain of $8,000 and a short-term capital loss of $2,000. What is the net amount (after any deduction) included in income for T?
   a. $3,600
   b. $2,400
   c. $6,000
   d. -0-
   e. None of the above

_____ 16. Mike Karp owns machinery, with an adjusted basis of $50,000, for use in his car-washing business. In addition, Karp owns his personal residence and furniture, which together cost him $100,000. The capital assets amount to:
   a. $-0-
   b. $50,000
   c. $100,000
   d. $150,000
   e. Some other amount   (CPA Adapted)

_____ 17. The highest individual tax rate in the United States for 1989 is:

    a. 15 percent
    b. 28 percent
    c. 33 percent
    d. 34 percent

_____ 18. For single taxpayers the 1989 phase-out range for the 15 percent bracket starts at:
    a. $44,900
    b. $64,200
    c. $83,130
    d. $74,850

Problems

1. In each of the independent cases below, indicate the total number of exemptions for the taxpayer, T. Assume any test not mentioned has been met.

_____ a. T is age 70, his wife is age 64, and they file a joint return.

_____ b. T is age 73, blind, and has adjusted gross income of $10,000. His wife is 66 and they file a joint return.

_____ c. T is age 66 and his wife is age 34. During the year Mrs. T gave birth to a son.

_____ d. T is unmarried and supports her 10-year-old sister who does not live with her. The sister had income of $2,865 from interest on a savings account.

_____ e. T and W have a foster child who lived with them the entire year. They provide over one-half the support of the foster child.

_____ f. T and his wife furnish all the support of F, T's father. F is 80 years old and blind. T and W file a joint return claiming F as a dependent.

2. Cathy West is a secretary, and for 1989 her salary was $18,630. Cathy is single, lives in an apartment and cannot itemize her deductions. During the year her employer withheld $3,510 from her salary. River Bank paid Cathy $750 interest on her savings account. Calculate Cathy's tax due or refund for 1989.

    Adjusted Gross Income   _____

    Standard Deduction   _____

    Exemption   _____

Taxable Income   _____

Tax Liability   _____

Withholding   _____

Tax Due or Refund   _____

Code Section Recognition

Indicate, by number, the appropriate Code section where the following items are found.

_____ 1. The standard deduction.

_____ 2. Tax rates for individual taxpayers.

_____ 3. Personal exemptions.

_____ 4. The definition of a dependent.

_____ 5. Definition of a capital asset.

_____ 6. Definition of a net capital gain.

SOLUTIONS TO CHAPTER 4

True or False

1. False Exemptions are generally based on which parent has custody. (p. 3-13)

2. True   (p. 3-6)

3. False Itemized deductions must exceed the standard deduction. (p. 3-7)

4. True   (p. 3-8)

5. True   (p. 3-7)

6. True   (p. 3-7)

7. True   (p. 3-10)

8. False The old age and blindness amounts are personal. (p. 3-7)

9. True   (p. 3-11)

10. False   Nontaxable items (except scholarships) must be used to test support. (p. 3-11)

11. True   (p. 3-15)

12. False   Certain children do not have to meet the gross income test. (p. 3-15)

13. True   (p. 3-15)

14. True   (p. 3-15)

15. True   (p. 3-12)

16. False   Dependent parent(s) do not have to live in the taxpayer's home. (p. 3-29)

17. True   (p. 3-30)

18. False   Net capital losses carry forward indefinitely for individuals. (p. 3-32)

19. True   (p. 3-31)

20. True   (p. 3-31)

21. False   (p. 3-22)

22. True   (p. 3-16)

Fill-in-the-Blanks

1. child (p. 3-15)

2. Mexico, Canada (p. 3-15)

3. upper (p. 3-15)

4. rate (p. 3-15)

5. end (p. 3-10)

6. fourth (p. 3-27)

7. community (p. 3-28)

8. Z (Appendix)

9. corporation (p. 3-33)

Multiple Choice

1. C (p. 3-6)

2. C $20,000 - 6,500 - 2,000 = $11,500. (p. 3-8)

3. D $1,700 - 1,000 = $700 (p. 3-23)

4. C (p. 3-31)

5. C (Appendix)

6. D (p. 3-14)

7. A (p. 3-29)

8. D (p. 3-31)

9. A (p. 3-31)

10. C $3,100 + $750 = $3,850 (p. 3-7)

11. C (p. 3-31)

12. D (p. 3-32)

13. D (p. 3-3)

14. E There is no time limit on the carryforward. (p. 3-32)

15. C $8,000 - 2,000 = $6,000 (p. 3-32)

16. C (p. 3-31)

17. C (p. 3-16)

18. A (p. 3-17)

Problems

1.   a. 2; 2 regular, (p. 4-10)

       b. 2; 2 regular, (p. 3-10)

c. 3; 2 regular, 1 dependency (p. 3-10)

d. 1; 1 regular, sister fails the gross income test (p. 3-14)

e. 3; 2 regular, 1 dependency (p. 3-14)

f. 3; 2 regular, 1 dependency, (p. 3-12)

2.
Adjusted Gross Income:	$19,380 ($18,630 + $750)
Standard deduction:	3,100
Exemption:	2,000
Taxable Income:	14,280
Tax Liability:	2,142 (15% of taxable income)
Withholding:	3,510
Refund:	$1,368

Code Section Recognition

1. Section 63.

2. Section 1.

3. Section 151.

4. Section 152.

5. Section 1221.

6. Section 1222.

4

GROSS INCOME: CONCEPTS AND INCLUSIONS

CHAPTER HIGHLIGHTS

The calculation of gross income is the first computation needed in the formula for taxable income. This chapter defines gross income and those items specifically included. The effect of the cash and accrual methods of accounting on the calculation of gross income is also discussed.

I.   GROSS INCOME

    A.   Section 61(a) of the tax law defines gross income as "income from whatever source derived." However, this definition is rather broad so the courts have established the principle that for income to be recognized for tax purposes, it must be realized. Therefore, increases in value would not be taxed as income until the property is disposed of.

    B.   Although financial accounting and tax accounting measurement concepts are frequently parallel, they have different purposes. The primary goal of financial accounting is to provide useful information to management, shareholders, creditors, and other interested parties, while the goal of tax accounting is the equitable collection of revenue.

    C.   Gross income is not limited to cash received. Income can be realized as money, property, or services received by the taxpayer.

D. Under the "recovery of capital doctrine" the proceeds from the sale or disposition of property are reduced by the basis to determine taxable gain. This is to ensure that income is not taxed until the capital initially invested is recovered. Many damages received in the settlement of a law suit are also excluded from income.

II. YEAR OF INCLUSION

A. As a general rule, taxpayers are required to use a calendar year to report income. However, taxpayers who keep adequate books and records (and meet certain other tests) may use a fiscal year.

B. The two generally accepted accounting methods for taxable income are the cash method and the accrual method.

The cash receipts method of accounting is used by most individuals and many small businesses. Under the cash method, property or services are included in the taxpayer's gross income in the "year of actual or constructive receipt."

The accrual method of accounting is used by many corporations. Under this method, income is recognized "in the year it is earned," regardless of when it is collected. Income is considered earned when (1) all events have occurred which fix the right to receive such income, and (2) the amount of the income can be determined with reasonable accuracy.

Chapter 18 contains the limitations applicable to accounting periods and methods.

C. Exceptions applicable to the cash method include the following:

The "doctrine of constructive receipt" limits an individual's ability to shift income arbitrarily to a later taxable year. If a taxpayer is entitled to receive income and the income is made available to him, it must be included in gross income.

Income set apart or made available is not constructively received if it is subject to substantial restrictions. For example, the increase in cash surrender value on ordinary life insurance is not taxed as the policy increases in value.

No income is realized when money is borrowed. Receipt of funds under an obligation to repay is not a taxable event.

When a lender makes a loan at an original issue discount, the accrued interest must be reported each year, regardless of the taxpayer's accounting method. Interest on long-term bonds issued at a discount must also be accrued. However, the tax law allows an exception to defer interest on U.S. Savings Bonds (Series E or EE). A taxpayer may chose to either defer the interest using the cash method or make an election to use the accrual method. By making the accrual election, the taxpayer prevents the bunching of income in a future year.

D.   Exceptions to the accrual method include the following:

"Prepaid income" is generally taxed in the year of receipt. Many court cases have been brought against the IRS by taxpayers arguing that the proper matching of revenue and expenses requires that income is recognized only when it is earned (e.g. the accrual method). The IRS has modified its position in several areas.

Generally, a taxpayer can elect to defer "advance payments for goods" if the taxpayer's method of accounting for the sale is the same for tax and financial reporting purposes. However if the seller collects more than the cost of the property, and delivery occurs more than one year after collection, prepayments must be included in gross income.

A taxpayer can defer "advance payments for services" to be performed by the end of the tax year following the year of receipt. Such "services" do not include interest, amounts received under guarantee or warranty, or prepaid rent.

III.   INCOME SOURCES

A.   Income from personal services must be included in the gross income of the person who "performs the services." A mere assignment of income will not shift the tax liability.

B.   Income from property (e.g. interest, dividends, rent) must be included in the gross income of the "owner of the property."

When property is sold with accrued interest, a portion of the selling price is treated as interest and taxed to the seller in the year of sale.

Dividends, unlike interest, do not accrue on a daily basis. Dividends are normally taxed to the taxpayer who is entitled to receive them.

C.   A partner in a partnership or a shareholder in a S Corporation must "include his or her share of income" from these entities on his or her individual tax return. Beneficiaries of estates and trusts are generally taxed on income earned by the estate or trust that is actually distributed or required to be distributed to them. Any excess income is taxed to the estate or trust.

D.   In nine states -- Louisiana, Texas, New Mexico, Arizona, California, Washington, Idaho, Nevada, and Wisconsin -- marital rights to the ownership of property are controlled by community property laws. Income from personal services (e.g. salaries and wages) and community property is treated as being earned equally by both spouses. Income from property is taxable to the person who owns the property except, in Texas, Louisiana, and Idaho. In those states the income from property is generally community income.

E.   Under Section 66, spouses living apart in community property states will be taxed only on their separate earnings from personal services if the following conditions occur:

The individuals live apart for the entire year.

They do not file a joint return with each other.

No portion of the income is transferred between the individuals.

IV.   ITEMS SPECIFICALLY INCLUDED IN GROSS INCOME

A.   For divorces after 1984 alimony is defined as cash payments only if the following three conditions are met:

the decree does not specify the cash payments are not alimony.

the payor and payee are not members of the same household.

there is no liability for payments after the death of the payee.

If the divorce decree is after 1986, different alimony recapture rules are used. Under the post-1986 rules, special recapture rules apply if the payments exceed $15,000 in the first or second year. In the third year, the payor must include the excess alimony payments for the first and second years in gross income and the payee is allowed a deduction for the excess alimony payments. The recaptured amount is computed as follows:

$$R = D + E$$

$$D = B - (C + \$15,000)$$

$$E = A - [\{(B - D + C) / 2\} + \$15,000]$$

Where,

R = amount of recapture in year 3.
D = recapture from year 2.
E = recapture from year 1.
A, B, C are the alimony payments in year 1, 2, and 3.

For 1985 and 1986 special rules apply if divorce cash payments in any one year exceed $10,000. To qualify as alimony, these payments must extend over at least six years. If during the first six years the payments decline by more than $10,000 between years, the amount of the decrease less $10,000, must be recaptured (included in the payor's income and deducted by the payee).

For post-1984 decrees, if cash payments would be reduced by a "contingency related to a child," then the payments are child support. Thus they are not deductible to the payor or income to the payee.

Under post-1984 rules, transfers of appreciated property to a former spouse under a divorce decree are not taxable events.

B.   Pre-1985 Divorce Alimony Rules. Alimony payments are taxable to the recipient and deductible to the payor if such payments are:

   made under a legal obligation such as a decree of divorce or separate maintenance.

   are for a period of more than 10 years or contingent.

   the payments are in discharge of a legal obligation arising from the marital or family relationship.

The Regulations define marital or family obligation as an obligation for support. Since the obligation for support must arise under state law, the alimony question varies with the state in which the taxpayer is domiciled.

C.   If a taxpayer makes a "below-market interest rate" loan to a related party, there can be imputed interest. The imputed interest is income to the lender and deductible to the borrower. The rate of imputed interest is the rate the Federal government pays on new borrowings. This rate is adjusted monthly and published by the IRS. These rules apply to the following types of loans:

   Gift loans

   Compensation-related loans

   Corporation-shareholder loans

   Tax avoidance loans

The below-market rules do not normally apply if the total loans between the related parties are $10,000 or less. On loans of $100,000 or less, the imputed interest cannot be greater than the net investment income earned by the borrower in that year, unless there is evidence of tax avoidance.

D.   Amounts received as annuity payments are included in gross income subject to the following rules:

For collections on or after the annuity starting date, the recipient may exclude a portion of the payment that represents a recovery of his or her investment. The formula is as follows:

$$\text{Percent Excluded} = \frac{\text{Investment in the contract}}{\text{Total expected return}}$$

The exclusion ratio applies until the annuitant has recovered his or her investment in the contract. Once the investment is recovered, the entire amount of subsequent payments is taxable. If the annuitant dies before recovering his or her investment, the unrecovered cost is deductible in the year the payments cease.

E.   Under Section 74, the fair market value of "prizes and awards" (other than qualified scholarships) is included in gross income. However, if the award is for recognition of religious, charitable, scientific, educational, artistic, literary, or civic achievement, and if the recipient transfers the prize to a qualified governmental unit or nonprofit organization then the award may be excluded from gross income. Certain employee achievement awards can be excluded from gross income. The maximum amount of such an employee award is $400 ($1,600 for qualified plan awards).

F.   There is an exclusion for premiums on "group-term" life insurance for the first $50,000 worth of insurance. Part of the premiums for insurance more than $50,000 are included in gross income based on a table supplied by the Internal Revenue Service. If the group-term insurance plan discriminates in favor of certain key employees, the Section 79 exclusion does not apply.

G.   All unemployment compensation benefits are included in gross income under the tax law.

H.   Part of Social Security benefits may be included in income. The amount included is the lesser of:

50% of Social Security Benefits, or
50% of [Modified AGI + 50% (Soc. Security benefits) - base amount]

Modified AGI is the taxpayer's AGI from all sources except Social Security, plus the two-earner marital deduction and any tax exempt interest income. The base amount is:

$32,000 for married filing jointly taxpayers
$0 for married filing separately taxpayers
$25,000 for all other taxpayers

TEST FOR SELF-EVALUATION

True or False

Indicate which of the following statements are true or false by circling the correct answers.

T   F   1.   The general definition of gross income is found in Section 161(a).

T   F   2.   The term "income" is used in the Code but is not separately defined.

T   F   3.   Economic income is the sum of the taxpayer's change in net worth and the actual consumption of goods and services during the tax period.

T   F   4.   An accountant's concept of income is based on the recognition principle.

T   F   5.   For any individual taxpayer, financial income and taxable income are always the same amount.

T   F   6.   For post-1984 divorce decrees, payments must be in cash to qualify as deductible alimony.

T   F   7.   Amounts received for damages to property or to goodwill of a business are income only to the extent the amount received exceeds the adjusted basis of the assets.

T   F   8.   Corporate taxpayers must always use the cash method of accounting.

T   F   9.   A cash basis taxpayer has some degree of control over the timing of the recognition of income and expenses.

T   F   10. The benefits of the group-term life insurance exclusion are not available to proprietors and partners.

T   F   11. U.S. "Series EE" savings bonds must always be treated using the cash method of accounting.

T   F   12. Prepaid income is always income in the year payment is received.

T   F   13. Income from personal services can be shifted to other taxpayers such as family members.

T   F   14. In all community property states (Texas, California, etc.), income derived from separate property is always separate income.

T   F   15. On the sale of stock, dividends are generally taxed to the person who is entitled to receive the dividends.

T F 16.   Income from property must be included in the gross income of the owner of the property.

T F 17.   If a taxpayer is entitled to receive income, which is made available to him, he cannot "turn his back" on it and refuse the income.

T F 18.   Most individual taxpayers use the cash method of accounting.

T F 19.   The recovery of capital doctrine means that the amount received from a sale of property is reduced by the adjusted basis in arriving at the taxable gain.

T F 20.   For pre-1985 divorce decrees, alimony and separate maintenance payments are not included in gross income.

T F 21.   For pre-1985 divorce decrees, payments paid for over 10 years will generally be treated as alimony.

T F 22.   For divorce decrees dated in 1985 and 1986, if the alimony payments decrease by more than $5,000 between years, then the excess over $5,000 will be recaptured.

T F 23.   The premiums on the first $50,000 worth of non-discriminatory group-term life insurance can be excluded from gross income.

T F 24.   If the interest charged on a loan is less than the Federal rate, the imputed interest is the difference between the amount that would have been charged at the Federal rate and the amount actually charged.

T F 25.   If a group-term life insurance plan discriminates in favor of key employees, the key employees must include the lesser of the actual premiums paid by the employer or the amount calculated from the Uniform Premiums table.

Fill-in-the-Blanks

Complete the following statements with the appropriate word(s).

1.   Income from property belongs to the _____ of that property under the assignment of income doctrine.

2.   Every partner in a partnership must report his or her _____ share of partnership income.

3.   Income from personal services is treated as being earned equally by both spouses in a _____ property state.

4.   The Supreme Court in *Eisner v. Macomber* added the _____

requirement to the judicial definition of income.

5.   The accrual accounting _____ is a basic component of our tax system.

6.   The primary goal of _____ accounting is to provide useful information to interested parties, while the goal of _____ accounting is to provide the equitable collection of revenue.

7.   The _____ accounting period is a basic component of the U.S. tax system.

8.   The Regulations require that the _____ method be used for determining purchases and sales when a taxpayer maintains an inventory.

9.   Dividends are generally taxed to the person who owns the stock as of the corporation's _____ date.

10.   Property may be held as _____ property in a community property state if it is acquired before marriage or by bequest or inheritance following marriage.

Multiple Choice

Choose the best answer for each of the following questions.

_____ 1.   A bank deposits $500 in interest in a savings account on December 31, 1989. The depositor withdraws $2,000 on January 3, 1990. How much income must be recognized for 1989?
              a. $2,000
              b. $500
              c. $1,500
              d. None of the above

_____ 2.   On December 1, 1989, T receives $3,000 for three months rent (December, January, and February) of an office building. T is an accrual basis taxpayer. How much income must be recognized for 1989?
              a. -0-
              b. $1,000
              c. $2,000
              d. $3,000
              e. None of the above

_____ 3.   Revenue Procedure 71-21 applies to which of the following?
              a. Prepaid rent
              b. Services
              c. Prepaid interest

d. Amounts under warranty contract
e. None of the above

_____ 4. T and his wife live in Texas. During the year T earned a salary of $20,000, and his wife earned a salary of $10,000. If they file separate income tax returns, T would report how much income?
a. -0-
b. $10,000
c. $15,000
d. $20,000
e. None of the above

_____ 5. Which of the following is not a community property state?
a. Texas
b. New York
c. California
d. New Mexico
e. Arizona

_____ 6. Dave Jones, a calendar year taxpayer, owns 30% of Z Corporation, an S Corporation. For the year ended December 31, 1989, Z Corporation had taxable income of $100,000. During the year the corporation paid dividends of $20,000. Dave's dividend income from other corporations was $25,000. What is Dave's taxable income from dividends for 1989?
a. $25,000
b. $45,000
c. $55,000
d. $125,000
e. None of the above

_____ 7. For 1989, Jill Adams, a single taxpayer received $10,000 in Social Security benefits. Her adjusted gross income was $40,000 and she had no tax-free interest income. How much of the Social Security benefits should Jill include in her income?
a. -0-
b. $5,000
c. $10,000
d. $7,500
e. Some other amount.

_____ 8. Judy Davis has savings bonds (Series EE) which increase by $600 in redemption value during 1989. In addition, Judy has $1,000 in interest on her savings account at Big Town Savings & Loan. If Judy has not made any elections and she is a cash basis taxpayer, she should report taxable interest income of:
a. -0-
b. $600
c. $1,000

    d. $1,600
    e. None of the above

_____ 9.   A lawyer drafts a will for a dentist in exchange for dental work. The dentist would normally have charged $400 for this work. Since the attorney normally charges $300 for drafting a will, he paid the dentist $100 in cash. Based on the transaction, how much should the dentist include in his gross income?
    a. -0-
    b. $100
    c. $300
    d. $400
    e. None of the above

_____ 10.   Lisa Smith owned stock, which originally cost $100,000, in X Corporation. She sold the stock for $75,000 plus 10% of X's income in the year of sale plus 10% of five additional years of income. The value of the future income cannot be determined in the year of sale. Collections in the first year are $84,000. What is Lisa's taxable gain?
    a. -0-
    b. $9,000
    c. $25,000
    d. $16,000
    e. None of the above

_____ 11.   In November 1989, John Lewis, entered into a contract to deliver goods to a customer in March 1990 for $12,000. John uses the accrual method of accounting for both financial and tax purposes. He collected $8,000 in 1989 and the balance in 1990. John did not have the goods in stock on December 31, 1989. The cost of the goods to him is $9,000. How much net income must John report in 1989?
    a. -0-
    b. $1,000
    c. $5,000
    d. $8,000
    e. None of the above

_____ 12.   Sky Corporation sells service contracts for 12 and 24 months. In September 1989, the company sold $8,000 of the 12-month contracts and $10,000 of the 24-month contracts. If the company services each customer each month (October, November, and December 1989), how much income should be reported for 1989 if Sky follows Rev. Proc. 71-21?
    a. $2,000
    b. $6,000
    c. $8,000
    d. $12,000
    e. None of the above

_____ 13. Vicki Cohen owned 25 percent in K&A Partnership. For the 1989 tax year the partnership had net income of $200,000. During the year Vicki withdrew $35,000 from her capital account. What is Vicki's reported share of net income from K&A?
   a. -0-
   b. $35,000
   c. $50,000
   d. $200,000
   e. None of the above

_____ 14. On July 15, the Board of Directors of R Corporation declared a $1 per share dividend, payable July 30 to shareholders of record on July 25. As of July 15 Norman Beatty owned 1,000 shares. On July 16 he sold 700 shares to Sam Wise for the fair market value, and he gave 300 shares to his son. How much dividend income must Norman report?
   a. -0-
   b. $300
   c. $700
   d. $1,000
   e. None of the above

_____ 15. Dave Berg, an employee of P.K. Inc., is covered by a group-term life insurance policy that has a face amount of $60,000. The company pays all the policy premiums, which amount to $500 per year. According to Regs. Sec. 1.79-3, the cost of a policy for a man Dave's age is 48 cents per $1,000 per month. How much income should Dave report on his tax return?
   a. -0-
   b. $57.60
   c. $500.00
   d. $345.60
   e. Some other amount

_____ 16. Robert Bowen is divorced in the current year. He makes cash payments to his ex-wife of $1,000 per month. When their son, who is in the wife's custody, turns 18-years-old the payments are reduced to $600 per month. How much can Robert deduct as alimony each month?
   a. -0-
   b. $400
   c. $600
   d. $1,000
   e. Some other amount

_____ 17. Assume the same situation as in question 16, except Jeff did not enter the radio contest, and the prize was awarded to him with no action on his part.
   a.   -0-
   b. $2,000
   c. $3,000
   d. $1,000

e. Some other amount

_____ 18. In the current year Dave Smith receives stock from his employer worth $25,000. The stock cannot be sold by Dave for seven years. Dave estimates that the stock will be worth $60,000 after the seven years. In the current year how much income must Dave recognize?
a. -0-
b. $25,000
c. $35,000
d. $60,000
e. Some other amount

_____ 19. T retired last year after investing $100,000 in an annuity, which pays $12,000 per year. T had a life expectancy of 10 years at the date the annuity was purchased. What is T's income for the current year?
a. -0-
b. $2,000
c. $10,000
d. $12,000
e. None of the above

_____ 20. Larry Boxer, a cash basis taxpayer, paid $42,000 for an 18-month certificate-of-deposit with a maturity value of $50,000. The effective interest rate on the certificate was 12 percent. If Larry bought the certificate on June 30 of the current year, how much interest income should he report?
a. -0-
b. $5,040
c. $2,520
d. $6,000
e. Some other amount

_____ 21. Under a current year's divorce decree, Oliver Whittington has to pay his ex-wife alimony. The cash payments are as follows:

Year 1	32,000
Year 2	25,000
Year 3	-0-

What is Oliver's alimony deduction for Year 1?
a. -0-
b. $32,000
c. $22,000
d. $12,000
e. Some other amount

_____ 22. Assume the same facts as question 21. What is the amount of alimony that Oliver will have to recapture in Year 3?
a. -0-

       b. $10,000
       c. $19,500
       d. $9,500
       e. Some other amount

_____ 23.   Under a current year's divorce decree, Van Ballew transfers appreciated property to his ex-wife. The property has a fair market value of $150,000 and an adjusted basis to Van of $60,000. From the transaction Van should report a taxable gain of:
       a.   -0-
       b. $60,000
       c. $90,000
       d. $150,000
       e. Some other amount

_____ 24.   If Van Ballew's wife in question #23 above were to sell the property 3 years later for $160,000, how much gain should she report?
       a.   -0-
       b. $90,000
       c. $100,000
       d. $10,000
       e. Some other amount.

_____ 25.   During the first six months of the current year the Federal imputed interest rate is 12 percent and for the second six months it is 14 percent. On January 1, a father gives his son an interest-free loan of $50,000. How much interest income must the father recognize and how much interest expense may the son deduct?
       a. -0-
       b. $6,500
       c. $6,000
       d. $7,000
       e. Some other amount

_____ 26.   Assume the same facts as in question 25. How much of a "gift" has the father made to his son?
       a. -0-
       b. $6,500
       c. $6,000
       d. $7,000
       e. Some other amount

Code Section Recognition

Indicate, by number, the appropriate Code Section where the following items are found.

_____ 1. The definition of gross income.

_____ 2. Provision allowing the IRS to determine accounting methods.

_____ 3. Treatment of community property income of spouses living apart.

_____ 4. Alimony and separate maintenance payments.

_____ 5. The taxation of income from annuities.

_____ 6. Prizes and awards.

_____ 7. Group-term life insurance.

_____ 8. Unemployment compensation payments.

_____ 9. Taxation of Social Security benefits.

SOLUTIONS TO CHAPTER 5

True or False

1. False The definition of gross income is found in Section 61. (p. 4-2)

2. True   (p. 4-2)

3. True   (p. 4-2)

4. False The accountant's concept is based on the realization principle. (p. 4-3)

5. False Financial income is different from taxable income. (p. 4-4)

6. True   (p. 4-22)

7. True   (p. 4-6)

8. False Corporations may use other methods. (p. 4-8)

9. True   (p. 4-8)

10. True   (p. 4-35)

11. False Taxpayers may elect the accrual method. (p. 4-13)

12. False Sometimes it may be accrued under Rev. Proc. 71-21. (p. 4-14)

13. False The assignment of income is not possible. (p. 4-16)

14. False In Texas, Louisiana, and Idaho it is community income. (p. 4-18)

15. True   (p. 4-16)

16. True   (p. 4-16)

17. True   (p. 4-10

18. True   (p. 4-7)

19. True   (p. 4-6)

20. False They are included in the gross income of the recipient. (p. 4-24)

21. True   (p. 4-24)

22. False The decrease must be over $10,000. (p. 4-24)

23. True   (p. 4-35)

24. True   (p. 4-27)

25. False It is the greater of. (p. 4-36)

Fill-in-the-Blanks

1. owner (p. 4-16)

2. distributive (p. 4-17)

3. community (p. 4-19)

4. realization (p. 4-4)

5. method (p. 4-9)

6. financial, tax (p. 4-5)

7. annual (p. 4-7)

8. accrual (p. 4-8)

9. record (p. 4-17)

10. separate (p. 4-18)

Multiple Choice

1. B (p. 4-8)

2. D The entire $3,000 is taxable when received. (p. 4-15)

3. B (p. 4-15)

4. C 50% ($20,000 + 10,000) = $15,000. (p. 4-19)

5. B (p. 4-18)

6. C 30% ($100,000) + 25,000 = $55,000. (p. 4-17)

7. B Lesser of:

> (1) 50% x $10,000 = $5,000, or
> (2) 50% x [$40,000 + 50%($10,000) - $25,000] = $10,000.
> (p. 4-36)

8. C (p. 4-12)

9. D $300 + 100 = $400. (p. 4-5)

10. A The $84,000 is a recovery of capital. (p. 4-6)

11. A The income is reported in 1990 (p. 4-14)

12. D 3/12 ($8,000) + 10,000 = $12,000. (p. 4-15)

13. C 25% ($200,000) = $50,000. (p. 4-27)

14. B Norman is taxed on the dividends related to 300 shares because the gift was after the declaration date. (p. 4-17)

15. B $.48 x [$60 - $50] x 12 months = $57.60. (p. 4-35)

16. C The contingent amount is disguised child support. (p. 4-24)

17. B (p. 4-34)

18. A (p. 4-11)

19. B
> $100,000/(12,000 x 10 years) x $12,000 = $10,000 excluded
> $12,000 - 10,000 = $2,000 included. (p. 4-34)

20. C (.12 x $42,000) x 1/2 year = $2,520 (p. 4-12)

21. B (p. 4-22)

22. C

 D = $25,000 - (0 + $15,000) = $10,000
 E = $32,000 - [($25,000 - $10,000 + 0)/2 +$15,000] = $9,500
 R = $10,000 + $9,500 = $19,500 (p. 4-23)

23. A (p. 4-22)

24. C $160,000 - $60,000 (p. 4-22)

25. B

Jan 1 to June 30 .12 x $50,000 x 1/2 year =	3,000
July 1 to Dec. 31 .14 x $50,000 x 1/2 year =	3,500
	6,500 (p.4-27)

26. B (p. 4-27)

Code Section Recognition

1. Section 61

2. Section 446

3. Section 66

4. Section 71

5. Section 72

6. Section 74

7. Section 79

8. Section 85

9. Section 86

5

GROSS INCOME: EXCLUSIONS

CHAPTER HIGHLIGHTS

This chapter focuses on those items which are specifically excluded from gross income by Congress or the IRS.

I. EXCLUSIONS FROM GROSS INCOME--STATUTORY AUTHORITY

    A.   As a general rule, everything received by a taxpayer is income unless a "specific statutory exclusion" can be found. Congress has chosen to exclude certain items from gross income for various social, economic, and equity purposes.

    B.   The courts also influence the determination of gross income. In one case, a District Court held that insurance reimbursement proceeds for the cost of temporary living quarters after a fire were income. However, Congress was not satisfied with this decision and enacted a provision to exclude such insurance proceeds from income.

II. GIFTS AND INHERITANCES

    A.   The value of property received by gift or inheritance is excluded from gross income under Section 102. A gift is a voluntary transfer of property by one taxpayer to another without any valuable consideration or compensation therefrom. The payment must be made out of affection, respect, admiration, charity, or like impulses.

B.   Gifts made in a business setting will usually be held not to be gifts and included in gross income. Payments which represent compensation for past, present, or future services are not gifts.

III.   LIFE INSURANCE PROCEEDS

A.   In general, the proceeds of life insurance are excluded from the income of the beneficiary of the policy. However, if the policy is transferred for valuable consideration or is an amount due from the decedent, the net proceeds of the policy will be included in income. The net proceeds will not be included if the policy is transferred to the following:

a partner of the insured

a partnership in which the insured is a partner

a corporation in which the insured is an officer or shareholder

a transferee whose basis in the policy is determined by reference to the transferor's basis

The first three exceptions facilitate the use of life insurance to fund buy-sell agreements.

B.   Interest that is earned on the reinvestment of life insurance contracts is subject to the income tax.

IV.   EMPLOYEE DEATH BENEFITS

A.   Payments made by an employer to a deceased employee's spouse, children, or other beneficiaries will generally be excluded from gross income. The maximum exclusion allowed to the employee's beneficiaries is a total of $5,000. The exclusion does not pertain to payments made out of legal obligation such as the decedent's accrued salary. The $5,000 exclusion must be split among the beneficiaries proportionally based on the total death benefits received.

B.   Amounts in excess of $5,000 may be excluded as a gift if they were made as an act of "affection or charity" by the employer. Generally, however the IRS considers employee death benefits to be compensation for prior services and not gifts.

V. SCHOLARSHIPS AND FELLOWSHIPS

    A. A scholarship is "an amount paid or allowed to, or for the benefit of, an individual, . . ., to aid such individual in the pursuit of study or research." The recipient must be a candidate for a degree at an educational institution.

    B. Scholarship grants for tuition and related expenses are excluded from income under Section 117 of the Code. Other scholarship amounts received (e.g. room and board) are included in the taxable income of the recipient.

VI. COMPENSATION FOR INJURIES AND SICKNESS

    A. A person who suffers harm caused by another is often paid damages. Generally, the reimbursement for loss of income is taxed in the same manner as the income being replaced by the damages. Payments for personal injury are specifically excluded from income of the person receiving the payment. When a payment contains amounts that are taxable and nontaxable the amounts received must first be allocated to the claims based on objective evidence. Any remaining amount will them be allocated among claims of a speculative nature (e.g. pain and suffering).

    B. Workers' compensation payments and benefits from accident and health insurance policies purchased by the taxpayer are specifically excluded from gross income under Section 104.

VII. EMPLOYER SPONSORED ACCIDENT AND HEALTH PLANS

    A. When persons suffer damages by another they are often entitled to damages. The receipt of damages are generally taxed the same as the income replaced.

    B. Premiums paid on "employer sponsored" accident and health plans are excluded from the income of the employee and are deductible by the employer. When the employee collects the insurance benefits, such benefits are considered taxable income with the following exceptions:

        Payments received for the medical care of the employee, spouse, and dependents are excluded except to the extent the payments are reimbursements for medical expenses which were deducted in the previous year.

        Payments for the permanent loss or the loss of the use of a member or function of the body or the permanent disfigurement of the employee, spouse, or dependent are also excluded.

    C. Amounts received under employer medical reimbursement plans are excluded unless the plan discriminates in favor of certain groups of employees

ed unless the plan discriminates in favor of certain groups of employees (e.g. management level). Benefits which are paid only to a particular group of employees must be included in income.

VIII.   MEALS AND LODGING

A.   An employee can exclude meals and lodging from his or her gross income if certain conditions are met. To qualify for the exclusion, meals must be furnished by the employer on the business premises of the employer and be for the convenience of the employer. In addition to these tests, lodging must be a condition of employment for an employee to be able to exclude it.

B.   An employee of an educational institution can exclude the value of campus housing provided by the employer. Generally, the employee does not recognize income if he or she makes annual rent payments equal to or greater than 5 percent of the value of the facility, with the excess included in gross income. A "minister of the gospel" can exclude the rental value of a home furnished as compensation. Military personnel are allowed exclusions under various circumstances.

IX.   OTHER EMPLOYEE FRINGE BENEFITS

A.   The following specific employee benefits are excluded from income of an employee by provisions in the tax law:

        The value of child care services paid by an employer, enabling the employee to work.

        The value of gymnasium and athletic facilities.

        An employee of a nonprofit educational institution can exclude undergraduate tuition granted to family members.

The maximum exclusion cannot exceed $5,000 per year ($2,500 if married filing separately) for the above items. For married taxpayers, the annual exclusion cannot exceed the earned income of the spouse with the lesser amount of earned income. For an unmarried taxpayer, the exclusion cannot exceed the taxpayer's earned income.

B.   The tax law establishes four broad classes of nontaxable employee benefits. These benefits are:

        No-additional cost services. An employee of an airline can fly for free if the seat would otherwise be empty.

        Qualified employee discounts. Employees do not have to report as income employer discounts up to 20 percent.

Working condition fringes. Employees can exclude those items from gross income that would be deductible if the employees had paid them. In addition, certain nondeductible items such as free parking do not have to be included as income.

De minimis fringes. Small amount of benefits such as using the company copy machine do not have to be reported as income.

C. Employer sponsored plans must not benefit only certain groups of employees. The requirements for the benefit plans are:

The plan must be in writing.

The employees' rights under the plan must be legally enforceable.

The plan must be established with the intention of being maintained indefinitely.

Employees must be provided with notice of benefits available under the plan.

The plan must be maintained for the exclusive benefit of employees, their spouse, and dependents.

The plan must not discriminate in favor of highly paid employees.

X. FOREIGN EARNED INCOME

A. A U.S. citizen is generally subject to U.S. tax on total worldwide income. However, qualified U.S. citizens working abroad can exclude up to $70,000 per year of earned income. In addition, an exclusion is allowed for a reasonable amount of housing cost in the foreign country in excess of a base amount. The base amount of "housing allowance " is the amount over 16 percent of the pay for a GS-14 (step 1) federal employee.

B. To qualify for the exclusion the taxpayer must either be a resident of the foreign country, or present in the country for 330 days during any 12 consecutive months.

C. The taxpayer may include the foreign income in gross income and elect to claim a credit for foreign taxes paid as an alternative to (A) above.

XI. MUNICIPAL BOND INTEREST

A. Taxpayers can exclude interest on the "obligations of state and local governments" from their gross income. However, there are exceptions for arbitrage bonds, industrial development bonds, and certain other bonds.

XII. DIVIDENDS

A. A dividend payment to a shareholder with respect to the ownership of stock is included in income. Distribution to the extent of earnings and profits are taxable and any distributions in excess of basis are taxed as capital gains.

B. The following items are not considered regular dividends for tax purposes:

> payments received on savings and loan deposits,
>
> patronage dividends from cooperatives,
>
> mutual life insurance dividends, and
>
> capital gains dividends from mutual funds.

XIII. TAX BENEFIT RULE

A. Under the tax benefit rule, if a taxpayer obtains a deduction for an item in one tax year and in a later year recovers a portion of the prior deduction, the "recovery produces taxable income" in the year it is received. Items subject to this rule include bad debts, prior taxes, and delinquency amounts.

B. The recovery of a deduction which did not yield a tax benefit in a prior year is not included in income under the tax benefit rule.

XIV. INCOME FROM THE DISCHARGE OF INDEBTEDNESS

A. The transfer of appreciated property in satisfaction of a debt is treated first as a sale of the property and then as payment of the debt. Any gain on the sale of the property must be recognized as income.

B. Under the Bankruptcy Act, the discharge of indebtedness is not recognized as income to the taxpayer whose debt is forgiven. The amount of debt forgiven is applied against the taxpayer's basis in the assets, effectively deferring the gain until the assets are sold.

TEST FOR SELF-EVALUATION

True or False

Indicate which of the following statements are true or false by circling the correct answers.

T F 1.   Public assistance payments (welfare) are generally nontaxable.

T F 2.   Gifts in a business setting are always excluded from gross income.

T F 3.   A $5,000 employee death benefit exclusion is allowed to the beneficiaries of the employee.

T F 4.   Life insurance proceeds are always excluded from gross income of the recipient.

T F 5.   A surviving spouse can exclude up to $1,000 per year of interest received on life insurance proceeds.

T F 6.   A transfer of appreciated property in satisfaction of a debt is a realizable event in taxation.

T F 7.   The maximum exclusion for employee child care fringe benefits is $5,000 per year.

T F 8.   Under the tax benefit rule if a taxpayer obtains a deduction in one year and later receives a portion of the prior deduction, the recovery produces taxable income.

T F 9.   There are limits on the use of tax-exempt bonds to finance private business activities.

T F 10.   A United States citizen is generally subject to U.S. tax on his total income regardless of the geographic origin of the income.

T F 11.   To be excludible, meals for an employee must be on the business premises and be for the convenience of the employer.

T F 12.   Workers' compensation benefits are included in the gross income of the taxpayer receiving the benefits.

T F 13.   The foreign earned income exclusion is $70,000, plus a limited exclusion for foreign housing costs.

T F 14.   To qualify for the foreign income exclusion, the taxpayer must be either a bona fide resident of the foreign country or present in the country for 250 days during any 12 consecutive months.

T F 15. Dividends on a mutual life insurance policy are taxable to the owner of the policy only if the policy has a cash surrender value of $5,000 or more.

T F 16. "Cafeteria" plans allow employees to choose nontaxable benefits rather than cash compensation and have the benefits remain nontaxable to the employee.

T F 17. Ministers can exclude the rental value of a home furnished as compensation or a rental allowance used to provide a home.

T F 18. Professor Gomez's son attended the private university where he teaches. The university waived the tuition of $6,000 for the son. Professor Gomez must include the $6,000 in his income because his son went to school for free.

T F 19. Scholarship income used for expenses other than tuition and books is treated as earned income for purposes of calculating the standard deduction.

T F 20. If the amount of a scholarship eligible for exclusion is not known at year end the transaction is held open until the education expenses are paid.

T F 21. Generally, punitive damages are not taxed to the recipient because they represent a penalty to the person causing the damages.

T F 22. Generally, if an employee has an option of taking cash instead of employer-provided housing then the amount is taxable.

T F 23. Under employer-sponsored benefit plans the employees' rights under the plan must be legally enforceable.

T F 24. Employer-paid parking for company officers qualifies as a working condition fringe benefit and would not be income to the officers.

Fill-in-the-Blanks

Complete the following statements with the appropriate word(s) or amount.

1.   Amounts received as qualified scholarships are _____ from gross income.

2.   To be excluded from income, meals must be on the _____ of the employer and be furnished for the _____ of the employer.

3.   U.S. taxpayers are allowed a _____ for foreign income taxes paid.

4.   The interest on _____ and _____ bonds is usually exempt from the Federal income tax.

5.   If a taxpayer obtains a deduction for an item in one year and later recovers a portion of that deduction, the recovery produces income under the tax _____ rule.

Multiple Choice

Indicate for Questions 1 to 7 the amount "included" in 1989 gross income for T (an individual) in each of the following independent situations. (Note: Unless otherwise stated, assume T is a cash basis calendar year taxpayer, and the year involved is 1989).

_____   1.   During 1989 T, a single taxpayer, received $1,100 in dividends on his Texaco Inc. stock and $600 on Harrod Stock (a U.K. Corporation).
a. -0-
b. $1,100
c. $1,700
d. $1,600
e. Some other amount

_____   2.   During 1989 T received gifts of $7,000 in cash and an automobile with a fair market value of $2,000 (cost $12,000).
a. -0-
b. $2,000
c. $7,000
d. $12,000
e. Some other amount

_____   3.   A Corporation sues Z Corporation and recovers $500,000 lost income damages and $300,000 in punitive damages for loss of income.
a. $-0-
b. $300,000
c. $500,000
d. $800,000
e. Some other amount.

_____   4.   During 1989 T recovered $10,000 of $18,000 that was written off for tax purposes in 1986.
a. -0-
b. $10,000
c. $15,000
d. $5,000
e. Some other amount

_____   5.   T received $50,000 (cash value of the policy is $24,000) as the beneficiary

of his father's life insurance policy.
a. -0-
b. $50,000
c. $24,000
d. $26,000
e. Some other amount

_____ 6.   T inherited several AT&T bonds. The bonds had a fair market value of
            $70,000 at the date of death. After receiving the bonds, he was also paid
            $2,000 in interest.
            a. -0-
            b. $72,000
            c. $70,000
            d. $2,000
            e. Some other amount

_____ 7.   As the result of an accident on the job T is disabled. Under workers'
            compensation insurance, he received $7,200 during 1989.
            a. -0-
            b. $2,000
            c. $7,200
            d. Some other amount

_____ 8.   Pat Brown (a single taxpayer) received the following income for 1989.

Salary	30,000
Dividends from G.M. stock	1,000
Interest on City of Houston bonds	2,000
Life insurance proceeds	10,000
Dividends on Mexican stock	1,600

            What is Pat's gross income for 1989?
            a. $42,600
            b. $31,000
            c. $32,600
            d. $30,000
            e. Some other amount

_____ 9.   Sam Houston died in the current year. His employer paid $8,000 to his
            widow and $4,000 each to his two children as a qualified death benefit. Of
            the $8,000 she received, how much may his widow exclude from her gross
            income?
            a. -0-
            b. $2,500
            c. $5,000
            d. $8,000
            e. Some other amount

_____ 10. T works for a hospital which provides employees free meals in a lunch room. During 1989 the value of the meals received by T are $2,300. If T had eaten all the meals available at the hospital, he would have eaten $4,800 worth of meals. The reason the hospital provides the meals is so that employees will be available for emergencies. How much will T have to include in his income from the free meals?

a. -0-

b. $2,300

c. $4,800

d. $2,500

e. Some other amount.

_____ 11. In the current year Armadillo Airlines covers an employee with a qualified dental plan at a cost of $200. In addition, its employees are allowed to fly for free on a standby basis, and this same employee takes free flights valued at $3,000. Also the employee is given free parking at the airport worth $400 per year. Of these amounts, how much must the employee include in his gross income for the current year?

a. -0-

b. $200

c. $3,200

d. $3,600

e. Some other amount

_____ 12. Chris Audette had adjusted gross income of $5,000 after deducting a bad debt of $2,000. Her itemized deductions and personal exemptions were $6,600. The next year, much to her surprise, Chris collected the bad debt. How much must she include in income for the year of recovery?

a. -0-

b. $200

c. $400

d. $1,000

e. Some other amount

_____ 13. Janis Rasmussen owed Friendly Bank and Trust an unsecured note of $50,000. She paid off the note with stock worth $50,000 (basis of $40,000). How much gain must Janis recognize on the transfer of the stock to the bank?

a. -0-

b. $10,000

c. $40,000

d. $50,000

e. Some other amount

_____ 14. Mike Fontaine is an employee of Mega Corporation. As an employee, Mike received the following fringe benefits.

Benefit	Value
Free use of company gym	$200
10% discount on $250 TV	25
Free company parking	400
Personal use of copy machine	8

If the plan does not discriminate, what amount of these fringe benefits must Mike report as income on his tax return?
a. -0-
b. $1,233
c. $600
d. $400
e. Some other amount

_____ 15. During the current year Alfred Allen sustained a serious injury while on the job. As a result of his injury, Allen received the following amounts during the same year:

Workers' compensation	$2,400
Reimbursement from employer's accident and health plan for medical expenses paid by Allen	1,800
Damages for personal injuries	8,000

How much of the above amounts should Allen include in his gross income for the current year?
a. $12,200
b. $8,000
c. $1,800
d. -0-

Questions 16 to 19 use the following information.

Laura Lewis has been legally separated from her husband, Herman, since 1987. Their three-year old son, Ronald, lived with Laura for the entire year of 1989. Under the written separation agreement between Laura and Herman, Herman is obligated to pay Laura $300 per month for alimony and $200 per month for child support, or a total of $6,000 annually. However Laura received a total of only $300 from Herman during 1989. Laura's other income in 1989 was from the following sources:

Salary	$20,000
Interest on insurance dividends left on deposit with a life insurance company	100
Interest on federal income tax refund	60

In addition, Laura's father, Albert, gave Laura a gift of 500 shares of Liba Corporation common stock in 1989. Albert's basis for the stock was $4,000. At the date of the gift, the fair market value of the Liba stock was $3,000.

_____ 16. What is Laura's filing status for 1989?
   a. Single
   b. Married filing separate return
   c. Unmarried head of household
   d. Married head of household

_____ 17. How much alimony is included in Laura's 1989 taxable income?
   a. -0-
   b. $300
   c. $3,600
   d. $6,000

_____ 18. How much interest is included in Laura's 1989 taxable income?
   a. -0-
   b. $60
   c. $100
   d. $160

_____ 19. How much is included in Laura's 1989 taxable income for the 500 shares of Liba stock?
   a. -0-
   b. $3,000
   c. $3,500
   d. $4,000   (CPA adapted)

Questions 20 to 22 use the following information.

John Budd, who was 58 at the time of his death on July 1, 1988, received $1,000 interest in 1989 on municipal bonds. John's wife, Emma, age 57, received a $300 television set in 1989 as a gift for opening a long-term savings account at a bank. On John's death, Emma received life insurance proceeds of $60,000 under a group policy paid for by John's employer. In addition, an employee death benefit of $7,500 was paid to Emma by John's employer. Emma did not remarry in 1989. Emma is the executrix of John's estate.

_____ 20. How much taxable interest was received by John and Emma in 1989?
   a. -0-
   b. $300
   c. $1,000
   d. $1,300

_____ 21. How much of the group-term life insurance proceeds should be excluded

from 1989 taxable income?
   a. -0-
   b. $5,000
   c. $50,000
   d. $60,000

_____ 22. How much of the employee death benefit should be excluded from 1989 taxable income?
   a. -0-
   b. $4,500
   c. $5,000
   d. $7,500   (CPA adapted)

Code Section Recognition

Indicate, by number, the appropriate Code Section where the following items are found.

_____ 1. Gifts and inheritances.

_____ 2. Life insurance proceeds.

_____ 3. Scholarships.

_____ 4. Damages for workers' compensation.

_____ 5. Exclusion for meals and lodging.

_____ 6. Interest on state and local obligations.

_____ 7. Tax benefit rule.

SOLUTIONS TO CHAPTER 6

True or False

1. True   (p. 5-3)

2. False Gifts in a business setting are included in gross income. (p. 5-4)

3. True   (p. 5-7)

4. False They are included if the policy was for valuable consideration. (p.5-5)

5. False (p. 5-6)

6. True   (p. 5-28)

7. True   (p. 5-17)

8. True   (p. 5-25)

9. True   (p. 5-27)

10. True   (p. 5-24)

11. True   (p. 5-14)

12. False Workers' compensation is excluded from gross income. (p. 5-12)

13. True   (p. 5-25)

14. False 330 days, not 250 days. (p. 5-25)

15. False The dividends are nontaxable without any limits. (p.5-27)

16. True   (p. 5-18)

17. True   (p. 5-16)

18. False The tuition is not income. (p. 5-17)

19. True   (p. 5-9)

20. True   (p. 5-9)

21. False They are taxable. (p. 5-11)

22. True   (p. 5-15)

23. True   (p. 5-22)

24. True   (p. 5-21)

Fill-in-the-Blanks

1. excluded (p. 5-8)

2. business premises, convenience (p. 5-14)

3. credit (p. 5-24)

4. state, local (p. 5-26)

5. benefit (p. 5-28)

Multiple Choice

1. C $1,100 + $600 = $1,700. (p. 5-27)

2. A (p. 5-4)

3. D $300,000 + $500,000 = $800,000 (p. 5-10)

4. B (p. 5-28)

5. A (p. 5-5)

6. D (p. 5-4)

7. A (p. 5-12)

8. C $30,000 + 1,000 +1,600 = $32,600. (pp. 5-5, 5-26, 5-27)

9. B ($8,000/16,000) x 5,000 = $2,500 excluded. (p. 5-7)

10. A (p. 5-14)

11. A (p. 5-19)

12. C $7,000 - 6,600 = $400 tax benefit from deduction. (p. 5-28)

13. B $50,000 - $40,000 (p. 5-29)

14. A (p. 5-20, 5-21)

15. D (p. 5-10, 5-12, 5-13)

16. C discussed in another chapter

17. B discussed in another chapter

18. D (p. 5-6)

19. A (p. 5-4)

20. B The T.V. set is interest. (p. 5-4)

21. D discussed in another chapter

22. C (p. 5-7)

Code Section Recognition

1. Section 102

2. Section 101

3. Section 117

4. Section 104

5. Section 119

6. Section 103

7. Section 111

6

DEDUCTIONS AND LOSSES: IN GENERAL

CHAPTER HIGHLIGHTS

All deductions are a matter of legislative grace. For an expenditure to be deductible, it must be specifically authorized by Congress. This chapter is an introduction to the general deductions allowed in determining adjusted gross income and taxable income. Specific provisions in the tax law which disallow certain deductions are discussed in detail.

I.   CLASSIFICATION OF DEDUCTIONS

    A.   Deductions for individual taxpayers fall into one of two classifications, "deductions for" adjusted gross income, or "deductions from" adjusted gross income.

        Section 62 specifies the expenses which are deductible for adjusted gross income. The common deductions for AGI include:

            trade or business deductions

            certain reimbursed employee business expenses

            losses on the sale of property other than personal use property

            rent and royalty expenses

alimony (Section 125)

contributions to self-employed retirement plans

deductions for retirement savings (Section 219)

certain lump-sum pension distributions

penalties on early withdrawals from saving accounts

qualified performing artist expenses

repayment of certain unemployment benefits

certain estate depreciation and depletion deductions

reforestation expenses deduction

The more common deductions from AGI include:

expenses for the production or collection of income

expenses for the management, conservation, or maintenance of property held for the production of income

expenses with the determination, collection, or refund of any tax.

charitable contributions

medical expenses in excess of 7.5 percent of adjusted gross income

certain state and local taxes (e.g. real estate, state and local income taxes).

personal casualty losses.

certain personal interest

certain miscellaneous deductions (subject to a 2% AGI limitation)

B.   Trade or business expenses are deductible for AGI. For any business expenditure to be deductible, it must be "ordinary and necessary." An ordinary expense is one that is normal, usual, or customary in the type of business being conducted by the taxpayer. A necessary expense is one that is appropriate and helpful in furthering the taxpayer's trade or business. Certain payments such as charitable contributions, illegal bribes and kickbacks, and fines and penalties are excluded as trade or business deductions.

C.   Reasonableness Requirement. Besides being ordinary and necessary, the Code requires some deductible expenses such as salaries, to be "reasonable." The courts have expanded this requirement to cover all business expenses.

II.   TIMING OF EXPENSE RECOGNITION

A.   Timing of Expense Recognition. In general, the taxpayer's method of accounting (cash or accrual) will determine the period in which a deduction can be taken. However, there are several exceptions to each method. The cash method of accounting cannot be used by:

corporations (other than S corporations)

partnerships, where one of the partners is a corporation

certain trusts

tax shelters

There are exceptions for small businesses, farms, and certain personal service corporations, regarding whether or not they can use the cash method.

B.   The expenses of cash basis taxpayers must be paid in cash before they can be deducted. The issuance of a note or other promise to pay does not qualify as a cash payment. Cash expenditures for assets which will not expire or be consumed by the end of the tax year following payment must be capitalized.

C.   Accrual basis taxpayers can deduct an expense by meeting the "economic performance test." This test is met only when the service, property, or use of property giving rise to the liability is actually performed for, provided to, or used by the taxpayer.

II.   DISALLOWANCE POSSIBILITIES

A.   Public Policy Limitation. The Code will deny a deduction for an expenditure that is against public policy. Expenses that are against public policy include bribes, kickbacks, fines, and penalties. In general, legal expenses are deductible if incurred in the taxpayer's trade or business.

The usual expenses relating to the operation of illegal business, other than those contrary to public policy, are deductible. However, under the tax law illegal drug traffickers are no longer allowed a deduction for the ordinary and necessary expenses incurred in their business. They are only allowed a deduction for cost of goods sold.

B.   Political Contributions and Lobbying Activities. Generally, no business deduction is allowed for political contributions. However, a taxpayer may deduct certain lobbying expenditures if he has a direct interest in the proposed legislation. Dues or expenses paid to an organization of individuals with a common direct interest in proposed legislation are also deductible. No expenses which were incurred to influence the public on political matters may be deducted.

C.   Investigation expenses for determining the feasibility of entering a new business or expanding an existing business are deductible if a taxpayer is already engaged in a similar business. If the taxpayer is not engaged in a similar business, and a new business is acquired, such expenses are capitalized and amortized over 60 months or more. In the event the new business is not acquired, investigation expenses are usually nondeductible.

D.   Hobby Losses. Under Section 183, if a taxpayer can show that an activity was entered into with the intent of making a profit, and not for personal pleasure, then any losses are fully deductible.

The hobby loss rules apply when the taxpayer cannot show that the activity was engaged in for profit. Hobby expenses are only deductible up to the amount of hobby income. The expenses are deductible in the following order:

> amounts deductible under other Code sections (e.g. interest)

> amounts deductible as if the activity is engaged in for profit, but only if those amounts do not affect the basis of property (e.g. maintenance).

> amounts deductible as if the activity is engaged in for profit which affect the basis of property (e.g. depreciation).

The tax law presumes that if a profit is made for "three of five consecutive years" (two of seven years for activities involving horses) then the activity is presumed to be engaged in for profit, and the hobby loss rules do not apply.

If the above presumption is not met, the activity may still qualify as a business if the taxpayer can show a profit-making intent. The Regulations stipulate nine relevant factors in distinguishing between profit seeking activities and hobbies. The relevant factors are:

> whether the activity is conducted in a business-like manner

> the expertise of the taxpayers

> time and effort expended

expectation that the assets will appreciate

the previous success of the taxpayer in similar activities

the history of income and loss from the activity

the relationship of profits to losses

the financial status of the taxpayer

elements of personal pleasure in the activity

E. Vacation homes have loss rules similar to the hobby loss provisions. If the home is used for personal purposes for more than the greater of 14 days or ten percent of the days actually rented, then the deductions for depreciation, maintenance, etc., will be limited to the revenue generated. If the vacation home is rented for less than 15 days, all rental income is excluded and all rental expenses, other than mortgage interest and property taxes, are disallowed. Expenses must be allocated between personal and rental days. Taxes and interest are allocated on the basis of 12 months and other expenses are allocated on the basis of total days used.

F. Expenditures Incurred for the Taxpayer's Benefit or Obligation. For an expenditure to be deductible, it must be incurred for the taxpayer's "benefit or be the taxpayer's obligation." Thus a taxpayer cannot claim a deduction for paying the expenses of another individual.

G. Disallowance of Personal Expenditures.

No deduction is allowed for personal, living, or family expenses unless specifically provided in the Code. Exceptions provided in the Code include:

charitable expenses

medical expenses

moving expenses

expenses for the determination, collection, or refund of tax

tax advice in divorce proceedings

H. Disallowance of Unrealized Losses. For a loss to be deductible, a loss must in fact be suffered by the taxpayer. "Losses in value" will not cause a tax deduction. Any loss deducted is limited to the taxpayer's adjusted basis in the asset.

I.   Disallowance of Deductions for Capital Expenditures. These costs are added to the basis of the property and may be written off over the life of the property if the property is depreciable or amortizable. Often it is difficult to distinguish repairs and maintenance from capital expenses. The Code defines a capital expenditure as "any amount paid out for new buildings or for permanent improvements or betterments made to increase the value of any property or estate." Other expenditures are considered repairs and maintenance.

Exceptions in the Code regarding the deductibility of capital expenditures include the election to expense certain mineral development costs, intangible drilling costs, farm expenditures, and research expenditures.

J.   Transactions Between Related Parties. The tax law places restrictions on transactions between certain related parties due to the potential for "sham" transactions and tax avoidance schemes. Losses, unpaid expenses and interest are "not deductible" if incurred between related parties. However, any unrecognized loss may be used to reduce any future gain on the property.

Related parties (as defined in Section 267) include:

siblings, spouses, ancestors, and lineal descendants of the taxpayer

a corporation owned more than 50 percent (directly or indirectly) by the taxpayer

two corporations owned more than 50 percent by the same taxpayer if either corporation is a personal holding company

a series of other complex relationships between trusts, corporations, estates, and individual taxpayers

Under the constructive ownership rules, stock owned by certain related parties is deemed to be owned by the taxpayer for the above 50 percent tests. See text for the rules.

K.   Substantiation Requirements. To be deductible, travel, entertainment, and business gifts must meet substantiation requirements under Section 274 of the Code. To meet this requirement, the taxpayer must substantiate the following:

the amount of the expense

the time and place for travel or entertainment (or date of gift)

the business purpose of the expense

the business relationship of the taxpayer to the person involved

Evidence, such as receipts or paid bills, is required for expenditures of amounts over $25. Other documentation can be diaries, account books, or other expense records which are updated at or near the time of the expenditure.

TEST FOR SELF-EVALUATION

True or False

Indicate which of the following statements are true or false by circling the correct answers.

T F 1. The courts have established the doctrine that an item is not deductible unless a specific Code Section allows the deduction.

T F 2. To be deductible under Section 162 or 212, an item must be ordinary and necessary.

T F 3. Alimony, medical expenses, and state and local taxes are deductions from adjusted gross income.

T F 4. The term "trade or business" is clearly defined by statute in the Code.

T F 5. Expenses incurred in the determination, collection, or refund of any tax are deductible under Section 212

T F 6. To be deductible, salaries must be reasonable.

T F 7. As a general rule, taxable income shall be computed under the method of accounting that the taxpayer regularly uses to compute income and keep his or her books.

T F 8. Prepaid interest may be deducted in the current period by a cash basis taxpayer.

T F 9. Legal expenses are never deductible as ordinary and necessary business expenses if incurred in a trade or business activity.

T F 10. In order for an accrual basis taxpayer to deduct an expense, it must pass the "economic performance test."

T F 11. Investigation expenses are always deductible by a taxpayer entering a new trade or business.

T F 12. If an activity shows a profit for three of five years (two of seven years for horses), then the Code presumes it is not a hobby.

T F 13. Section 280A limits the deductions related to a vacation home if the taxpayer uses it for personal purposes for more than the greater of 14 days or 10 percent of the days actually rented.

T F 14. A taxpayer can claim a deduction for interest he paid on his son's mortgage.

(The son is not a dependent).

T F 15. In general, Section 262 disallows deductions for personal, living, and family expenses.

T F 16. The tax law disallows a deduction for expenses incurred in producing tax-exempt income.

T F 17. The Code allows the use of reasonable estimates in deducting travel and entertainment expenses.

T F 18. Section 267 disallows losses and certain deductions between related parties.

T F 19. Goodwill is a depreciable asset for tax purposes.

T F 20. Personal legal fees are generally deductible by individual taxpayers.

T F 21. All expenses for vacation homes are deductible for tax purposes.

T F 22. To be deductible, an expense must be incurred for the taxpayer's benefit or arise from the taxpayer's obligation.

T F 23. Expenses of hobbies are deductible from AGI subject to the 2 percent of AGI limitation..

T F 24. The courts have held that taxes and interest on a vacation home should be allocated over 365 days a year, while the IRS allocates taxes and interest on the basis of total days of use.

T F 25. T rented her condo in Utah for 180 days. Therefore, if she used the condo for 20 days of personal use, it would be classified as a "vacation home."

Fill-in-the-Blanks

Complete the following statements with the appropriate word(s) or amount.

1. The items that are disallowed under the related party rules are _____, unpaid interest and unpaid expenses.

2. For travel and entertainment to be deductible, the following substantiation is required: amount, time and place, business _____, and business _____.

3. On December 1, 19X1, a taxpayer pays three months rent of $3,000 on a building used in her business. If she is a cash basis taxpayer, her rent deduction for 19X1 is _____.

4.   The nondeductibility of bribes, kickbacks, fines, and penalties is justified by being against _____ _____.

5.   If an activity is deemed to be a hobby, the trade or business expenses are deductible only to the extent of the _____ from the hobby.

6.   One basic concept in the tax law is that a deduction cannot be taken until a loss is _____.

7.   Section 212 allows a deduction for expenses due to the production or _____ of income.

8.   Expenses under the accrual method of accounting are deductible when _____ and under the cash method when _____.

9.   Lobbying expenditures are deductible provided the proposed legislation is of _____ interest to the taxpayer.

Multiple Choice

Choose the best answer for each of the following questions.

_____ 1.   Which of the following is not a deduction for adjusted gross income?
       a. Alimony
       b. State income tax
       c. Trade or business expenses
       d. IRA contributions
       e. None of the above

_____ 2.   Section 212 covers expenses for the production or collection of income and tax return preparation fees. Which of the following is not a Section 212 deduction?
       a. Repairs expense on a rental house
       b. A fee paid to a CPA for preparing a tax return
       c. Interest expense on a personal residence
       d. Safe deposit box rental used to store stock certificates
       e. None of the above

_____ 3.   Phil Wolfe is a physician. In his spare time he wants to become a famous stock car racer. In the current year Phil incurs the following costs:

Stock car purchases	40,000
Entry fees	5,000
Driving lessons	10,000
Travel expenses to races	15,000
	70,000

Of the races entered by Phil this year, his total earnings are $250. In all probability, the IRS will allow Phil a deduction for what amount (before any 2% limit)?
a. -0-
b. $250
c. $30,000
d. $70,000
e. None of the above

_____ 4. Under Section 183, if an activity is not engaged in for profit, deductions will be limited in that activity. Which of the following is likely to be deemed a hobby by the IRS?
a. A CPA in private practice
b. A ranch owned by an executive that has shown a profit for four of the last five years
c. An individual borrowing money to open a gift shop
d. A physician who operates a photography studio at a loss for five consecutive years
e. None of the above

_____ 5. Several years ago, Mary Smith purchased a house on a hillside in California for $150,000 to be used as her personal residence. During the current year there is a recession in the local area. As a result, her house is now worth only $80,000 (which can be substantiated by Mary). Mary's deductible tax loss for the current year is:
a. -0-
b. $70,000
c. $80,000
d. $150,000
e. Some other amount

_____ 6. During the current year, Lee Marvin pays $5,000 to an attorney to obtain a divorce. Of this amount, $2,000 is for tax advice about the divorce settlement. How much, if any, of the $5,000 is deductible?
a. -0-
b. $2,000
c. $3,000
d. $5,000
e. None of the above

_____ 7. David La Rue made illegal business kickbacks of $10,000 and paid fines of $8,000 during the current year. How much of the expense can be deducted on his tax return?
a. -0-
b. $8,000
c. $10,000
d. $18,000
e. None of the above

_____ 8.   If a taxpayer paid $5,000 interest on a note, the proceeds of which were used to purchase Texas state bonds, and the bonds produced interest of $4,000, how much of an interest deduction would she be allowed?
a. -0-
b. $1,000
c. $4,000
d. $5,000
e. None of the above

_____ 9.   T owns 33 percent of the stock in T Corporation, 33 percent is owned by T's mother, and 33 percent by T's father. On January 1, 19X1, T loans T Corporation $100,000 at 9 percent interest. T Corporation is an "accrual" basis taxpayer while T is a cash basis taxpayer. T Corporation pays the current interest on December 29, 19X1. How much is deductible to T Corporation for 19X1?
a. -0-
b. $4,500
c. $9,000
d. None of the above

_____ 10.   T pays $5,000 interest on his home mortgage, and pays $3,000 on his son's mortgage. The son does not qualify as T's dependent. How much of an interest deduction will T be allowed?
a. -0-
b. $3,000
c. $5,000
d. $8,000
e. None of the above

_____ 11.   T rents her vacation home for 30 days and lives in it for 10 days during the current year. Her gross income from rent payments was $4,000 and she incurred the following expenses:

Taxes and interest	3,000
Utilities and maintenance	800
Depreciation	4,000
Total	$7,800

Using the IRS approach, what amount of income or loss must T report from this rental?
a. -0-
b. $200 income
c. $3,800 loss
d. $1,850 loss
e. None of the above

_____ 12.   Robert Lee owns a chain of motels in California. He flies to Arizona to

investigate the possibility of buying an automobile dealership. All of the expenses for the trip are deductible in the current year if:
a. The automobile dealership is purchased
b. The auto dealership is not purchased
c. Would never be deductible
d. Robert already owns an auto dealership and does not purchase the Arizona dealership
e. None of the above

_____ 13. During the current year, Mary Burnette purchased a lot with an old house on it for $100,000. She immediately had the house demolished at a cost of $15,000. Four months later the lot is sold for $160,000. How much gain should be recognized by Mary?
a. -0-
b. $15,000
c. $45,000
d. $60,000
e. None of the above

_____ 14. Under Section 267(c), the disallowance between related parties provision, which of the following is not a related family member?
a. Spouse
b. Son or daughter
c. Grandchild
d. Grandparent
e. All of the above are related

_____ 15. Which of the following expenses are not deductible under Section 212?
a. Trade or business expenses
b. Expenses for the production of income
c. Expenses for the management, conservation, or maintenance of property held for the production of income
d. Expenses for the determination, collection, or refund of any tax
e. None of the above

_____ 16. Pancho Suggs is in the business of importing certain illegal substances from Mexico. In this business, Pancho incurs the following expenses:

Cost of goods sold	200,000
Payoffs to customs agents	100,000
Cost of installing false bottom in trunk of car	10,000
Distribution expenses	50,000
Packaging (baggies)	5,000
Kickbacks to narcotic agents	75,000
	440,000

Of the total, what amount would be deductible by Pancho?
a. -0-
b. $440,000
c. $340,000
d. $200,000
e. None of the above

Code Section Recognition

Indicate by number the appropriate Code Section where the following items are found.

_____ 1. Deduction for trade or business expenses.

_____ 2. Deduction for expenses in producing income.

_____ 3. Loss deductions.

_____ 4. Deductions for adjusted gross income (AGI).

_____ 5. Hobby losses.

_____ 6. Vacation home rentals.

_____ 7. Losses between related parties.

_____ 8. Capital expenditures.

_____ 9. Expenses relating to tax-exempt income.

_____ 10. Casualty losses.

SOLUTIONS TO CHAPTER 7

True or False

1. True   (p. 6-2)

2. True   (p. 6-5)

3. False   Alimony is a dfor. (p. 6-3)

4. False   The term is not defined in the Code. (p. 6-5)

5. True   (p. 6-4)

6. True   (p. 6-6)

7. True   (p. 6-8)

8. False   Only points on a personal residence may be deducted. (p. 6-9)

9. False   Legal expenses are deductible if connected with a trade or business. (p. 6-12)

10. True   (p. 6-10)

11. False   The expenses are not deductible. (p. 6-14)

12. True   (p. 6-16)

13. True   (p. 6-19)

14. False   The interest deduction is not the taxpayer's obligation. (p. 6-18)

15. True   (p. 6-22)

16. True   (p. 6-29)

17. False   Travel and entertainment must be substantiated. (p. 6-28)

18. True   (p. 6-26)

19. False   Goodwill is not depreciable. (p. 6-25)

20. False   Legal fees are not generally deductible except for tax advice. (p. 6-12)

21. False   Vacation home expenses are limited to income. (p. 6-18)

22. True   (p. 6-22)

23. True   (p. 6-17)

24. True   (p. 6-20)

25. True   (p. 6-19)

Fill-in-the-Blanks

1. losses (p. 6-26)

2. purpose, relationship (p. 6-24)

3. $3,000 (p. 6-8)

4. public policy (p. 6-11)

5. income (p. 6-15)

6. realized (p. 6-24)

7. collection (p. 6-4)

8. incurred, paid (p. 6-9)

9. direct (p. 6-14)

Multiple Choice

1. B (p. 6-3)

2. C (p. 6-4)

3. B (p. 6-17)

4. D (p. 6-15)

5. A Deductions are not allowed for losses in value. (p. 6-22)

6. B (p. 6-12)

7. A (p. 6-12)

8. A (p. 6-29)

9. C 9% ($100,000) = $9,000; the interest is paid. (p. 6-27)

10. C (p. 6-22)

11. D Note: this is not a vacation home because it is only used 10 days.

Gross income	$4,000
Less: rental expenses	
Taxes & interest (75%)	(2,250)
Utilities and maintenance (75%)	(600)
Depreciation (75%)	(3,000)
Loss	(1,850) (p. 6-20)

12. D (p. 6-14)

13. C $160,000 - 100,000 - 15,000 = 45,000. (p. 6-24)

14. E (p. 6-27)

15. A (p. 6-4)

16. D $200,000. Drug dealers are allowed cost of goods sold only. (p. 6-13)

Code Section Recognition

1. Section 162

2. Section 212

3. Section 165

4. Section 62

5. Section 183

6. Section 280A

7. Section 267

8. Section 263

9. Section 265

10. Section 165

7

PASSIVE ACTIVITY LOSSES

CHAPTER HIGHLIGHTS

The treatment at-risk amounts and passive losses is one of the areas of concern for many taxpayers. The purpose of these rules is to limit the use of tax shelters to reduce a taxpayer's tax liability. The rules necessary to operationalize the at-risk rules and the passive loss limitation are very complex, but must be understood in order to have a working knowledge of the U.S. income tax system.

I. THE TAX SHELTER PROBLEM

For many years tax shelters were a major problem to the Congress and the IRS. However, the ability of taxpayers to avoid or reduce tax through the use of tax shelters have been limited by the at-risk rules and the passive loss rules. These two provisions have made the tax shelter investments of the past nearly obsolete. If they make investments in many activities, especially real estate, taxpayers must have a general working knowledge of these provisions because of their impact on tax liability.

II. AT-RISK RULES

A. The tax laws provide an at-risk limitation on losses from business and income-producing activities. Any loss deduction is limited to the amount at-risk. The amount at risk is generally the sum of the following:

The adjusted basis of property and cash contributed to the activity,

The amount borrowed for the activity for which the taxpayer has personal liability

Any share of the net earnings, decreased by losses and withdrawals from the activity.

A taxpayer is not consider at-risk with respect to borrowed amounts if either one of the following is true:

The taxpayer is not personally liable for the repayment of the debt (nonrecourse loans).

The lender has an interest (other than as a creditor) in the activity (except to the extent provided by the Regulations).

Recapture of previously allowed losses occurs to the extent the at-risk amount is reduced below zero. This occurs when the amount at-risk is reduced by distributions to the taxpayer, changes in status of debt from recourse to nonrecourse, or by any arrangement that affects the taxpayer's risk of loss.

Generally a taxpayer's amount at risk is determined separately with respect to separate activities. However, activities are treated as one activity if the activities constitute a trade or business and either of the following is true:

The taxpayer actively participates in the management of the trade or business

In the case of a partnership or S corporation, 65 percent of the entities losses are allocable to persons who actively participate in the management of the trade or business.

III. PASSIVE LOSS RULES

A. Overview of Passive Loss Rules.

For tax years after 1986, income and losses are classified into three categories:

Active (salary. etc.)

Passive (income from a limited partnership interest)

Portfolio (interest, dividends, etc.)

Passive losses cannot be used to offset income from the other two categories. Tax credits from passive activities can be offset only against tax derived from passive income. The unused loss and credit may be carried over to offset future passive income or used when the taxpayer disposes of his investment in the passive activity.

B.   Taxpayers Subject to the Passive Loss Rules. The passive loss rules apply to individuals, estates, trusts, closely held C corporations, and personal service corporations. The reason that passive loss rules apply to personal service corporations is to prevent taxpayers from sheltering personal service income by acquiring passive activities at the corporate level. A personal service corporation is a corporation which meets the following conditions:

the principal activity is personal services, and

services are substantially performed by owner-employees.

C.   Disallowed Passive Losses.

The passive loss rules are effective for passive activities acquired after October 22, 1986. The passive loss limitation for activities acquired before October 23, 1986 are phased in over five years. The phase-in is as follows:

1987	65% allowed
1988	40% allowed
1989	20% allowed
1990	10% allowed
1991	0% allowed

D.   Passive Activity Defined.

A passive activity is defined as any one of the following:

Any trade or business in which the taxpayer does not "materially participate."

Any rental activity (certain exceptions apply to small individual real estate owners, see below),

Any limited partnership

E.   Material Participation.

If a taxpayer materially participates in nonrental activity, any loss from that activity will treated as an active loss that can offset other active income. The Code provides that material participation requires the taxpayer to be involved in the operation of the activity on a regular, continuous and substantial basis. The Temporary Regulations provide the following specific tests.

1. The individual participates in the activity for more than 500 hours during the year.

2. The individual's participation in the activity for the year constitutes substantially all the participation in the activity of all individuals (including non-owner employee) for the year.

3. The individual participates in the activity for more than 100 hours during the year, and the individual's particaption in the activity for the years is no less than the particaption of any other individual (including non-owner employees) for the year.

4. The activity is a significant participation activity for the taxable year, and the individuals aggregate participation in all significant participation activities during the year exceeds 500 hours. A significant participation activity is one which the individual's participation exceeds 100 hours during the year.

5. The individual materially participated in the activity for any five taxable years (whether or not consecutive) during the ten taxable years that immediately precede the taxable year.

6. The activity is a personal service activity and the individual materially participated in the activity for any three preceding taxable years (whether or not consecutive).

7. Based on the facts and circumstances, the individual participates in the activity on a regular, continuous, and substantial basis during the year.

F. Rental Activities.

According to the tax law, any rental activity is to be treated as a passive activity. A rental activity is defined as any activity where payments are principally for the use of tangible property. An activity is generally a rental activity if it meets the following conditions:

> tangible property held in connection with the activity is used by customers or held for use by customers, and

> the expected gross income form the activity represents payments principally for the use of such property.

There are six exceptions to the definition of rental activity. These are as follows:

1.   The average period of customer use for such property is seven days or less.

2.   The average period of customer use for such property is 30 days or less, and significant personal services are provided by the owner of the property.

3.   Extraordinary personal services are provided by the owner of the property without regard to the average period of customer use.

4.   The rental of such property is treated as incidental to a non-rental activity of the taxpayer.

5.   The taxpayer customarily makes the property available during defined business hours for nonexclusive use by various customers.

6.   The provision of the property for use in an activity conducted by a partnership, S corporation, or joint venture in which the taxpayer owns an interest.

There is a limited exception for rental real estate activity losses. Generally up to $25,000 of rental losses by an individual may be deducted against active and portfolio income. This annual $25,000 deduction is reduced by 50 percent of the taxpayer's AGI in excess of $100,000. Thus the entire deduction is phased out when AGI reaches $150,000. If a married taxpayer files separately, then the $25,000 deduction is reduced to zero. The phase out is calculated without regard to the IRA deduction, social security benefits, and net losses from passive activities. To qualify for the $25,000 deduction, the taxpayer must meet the following two requirements:

Actively participate in the rental activity.

Own 10 percent or more interest in the activity.

G.   Calculation of Passive Losses.

Passive activity loss should be computed by performing the following two procedures:

Compute the passive loss or income for each separate passive activity.

Offset net passive income from profitable activities against net passive losses from unprofitable activities.

H.   Identification of Passive Activity.

The IRS has not yet pronounced Regulations on what constitutes a passive activity. The only guidance to date is in IRS Notice 88-94 which gives taxpayers considerable leeway as to how various business segments are to be treated under the passive loss rules.

I.   Suspended Losses and Credits.

If a passive loss is disallowed because of insufficient passive income to offset it, it becomes suspended. A taxpayer's basis in the investment is reduced by deductions even if the deductions are not allowed in the current year. Suspended losses are carried over indefinitely and are applied against future years' passive income. If the passive activity is disposed of, the suspended losses can be offset against nonpassive and portfolio income. Therefore suspended losses for each passive activity must be determined separately on a prorata basis.

Credits arising from passive activities can only be used against regular tax attributable to passive income. Any excess passive credits are carried over indefinitely into future years. If a taxpayer has a passive loss for a tax year, then no passive credits can be used. If the taxpayer's tax is calculated using the alternative minimum tax (see Chapter 12), then no passive credits can be used. The passive credit is lost if there is no regular tax generated when the activity is disposed of.

J.   Disposition of Passive Interests.

When a taxpayer disposes of his or her entire interest in a passive activity, any disallowed suspended losses are deductible. In general, if the current and suspended losses of passive activities exceed the gain realized or if the sale results in a realized loss, the sum of the following is treated as a loss which is not from a passive activity:

        Any loss from the activity for the tax year (including suspended losses, plus

        Any loss realized on the disposition

in excess of

        Net income or gain for the tax year from all passive activities (without regard the activity disposed of).

TEST FOR SELF-EVALUATION

True or False

Indicate which of the following statements are true or false by circling the correct answers.

T F 1. The passive loss rules apply to real estate activities for tax years after 1986.

T F 2. All debt on property qualifies as an amount at risk.

T F 3. Passive losses cannot offset active and portfolio income for taxpayers after 1986.

T F 4. The $25,000 exception on rental losses applies only to corporations and partnerships.

T F 5. In general, the $25,000 rental exception is reduced by 50% of a taxpayer's modified AGI over $100,000.

T F 6. An investment as a limited partner is always a passive activity for purposes of the tax law.

T F 7. Credits from passive activities can be used to offset a regular tax liability or a tax liability arising from the alternative minimum tax.

T F 8. Passive credits are carried back three years and then forward for ten years, and if not used in that time period they are lost forever.

T F 9. The amount at-risk is decreased each year by the taxpayer's share of income and by the taxpayer's share of losses and withdrawals from the activity.

T F 10. Recapture of previously allowed losses occurs to the extent the at-risk amount is reduced below zero.

T F 11. Generally, a taxpayer's amount at-risk is separately determined with respect to separate activities.

T F 12. Passive loss rules apply to individuals, estates, trusts, closely held C corporations, and personal service corporations.

T F 13. Individual taxpayers are allowed to offset passive losses against portfolio income, but not against active income.

T F 14. In general, personal service corporations are subject to the passive loss rules.

T F 15.   If a taxpayer participates in an activity for more than 300 hour during the year, then they materially participate in that activity.

T F 16.   If a taxpayer's participation in an activity for the taxable year constitutes substantially all the participation in the activity of all individuals for the year, then the taxpayer material participates in the activity.

T F 17.   If a taxpayer materially participated in an activity for any five of the ten preceding tax years, then the taxpayer materially participates in the activity for the current year.

T F 18.   If the average period of customer use of rental property is seven days or less, then the activity is not a passive activity.

T F 19.   The owner of a public golf course that sells weekly and monthly passes would be subject to the passive loss rules.

T F 20.   When a passive activity is sold, the suspended loss can be used to offset any realized gain.

Fill-in-the-Blanks

Complete the following statements with the appropriate word(s) or amount.

1.   Tax credits attributable to passive activities can be carried forward _____.

2.   A transfer at death of a taxpayer's interest in activity results in the suspended losses to the extent they exceed the _____ in basis allowed.

3.   In a disposition of a taxpayer's interest in a passive activity by gift, the suspended losses are added to the _____ of the property.

4.   Any losses disallowed for any given taxable year may be carried _____.

5.   For passive losses after October 22, 1986 _____ percent of the loss is disallowed.

Multiple Choice

Choose the best answer for each of the following questions.

_____ 1.   Colm O'Broin invests $20,000 in a limited partnership which financed the rest of its operations by the use of nonrecourse loans. If Colm's share of the loss this year is $25,000, how much may he deduct on his tax return in

the current year?
a. $-0-
b. $5,000
c. $20,000
d. $25,000
e. Some other amount

_____ 2.   T's AGI this year is $120,000 without deducting IRA contributions or pas-
sive losses. What is the maximum amount that T can deduct if he has real
estate losses of $18,000 from a rental house?
a. $-0-
b. $15,000
c. $18,000
d. $3,000
e. Some other amount

_____ 3.   Leonie Huddie's adjusted basis in a passive activity was $20,000 at the
beginning of the year. Her loss from the activity during the year was
$4,000 and she had no other passive activity income for the year. Her
passive activity credits for the year were $1,000. At the end of the year her
adjusted basis in the passive activity would be:
a. $20,000
b. $19,000
c. $16,000
d. $15,000
e. Some other amount

_____ 4.   Carol Smith owes $40,000 of tax, disregarding net passive income, and
$55,000 of tax considering both net passive and other taxable income
(before any credits). The maximum amount of passive credit that can be
used by Carol for this year is:
a. $-0-
b. $15,000
c. $40,000
d. $55,000
e. Some other amount

_____ 5.   T invests $25,000 in a limited partnership in 1988 which has a loss of $5,000
for the year. During 1989, the partnership has net income of $10,000. What
is T's amount at-risk at the end of 1989?
a. -0-
b. $25,000
c. $30,000
d. $15,000
e. Some other amount

_____ 6.   The passive loss rules are applied at the owner level for which of the following entities?

    a. S corporations
    b. Partnerships
    c. C corporations
    d. A and B
    e. A and C

_____ 7. Megan Inc., a closely held corporation, has $600,000 of passive losses from rental activity, $500,000 of active business income, and $200,000 of portfolio income. How much of the passive loss may offset other income?
    a.   -0-
    b. $200,000
    c. $300,000
    d. $500,000
    e. Some other amount

_____ 8. Same as number 7, except Megan is an individual. How much of the passive loss may offset other income?
    a.   -0-
    b. $200,000
    c. $300,000
    d. $500,000
    e. $600,000

_____ 9. Which of the following items is not portfolio income?
    a. Interest on savings account
    b. Dividends on U.S. Corporations
    c. Interest on U.S. Savings Bonds
    d. Dividends on Foreign Corporations
    e. All the above are portfolio income

_____ 10. If an activity is a personal service activity, how many prior years must an individual participate in the activity to be considered martially participating in the activity in the current year?
    a. One
    b. Two
    c. Three
    d. Five
    e. Seven

Code Section Recognition

Indicate, by number, the appropriate Code Section where the following items are found.

_____ 1. Passive loss limitations.

_____ 2. The at-risk rules.

SOLUTIONS TO CHAPTER 7

True or False

1. True   (p. 7-2)

2. False   It cannot be nonrecourse debt. (p. 7-3)

3. True   (p. 7-2)

4. False   It applies to individuals (p. 7-26)

5. True   (p. 7-26)

6. True   (p. 7-9)

7. False   They can only be used against passive tax. (p. 7-23)

8. False   Passive loss credits carry forward only. (p. 7-24)

9. False   Income increases the amount at-risk. (p. 7-3)

10. True   (p. 7-4)

11. True   (p. 7-4)

12. True   (p. 7-6)

13. False   Passive losses cannot offset portfolio income. (p. 7-5)

14. True   (p. 7-6)

15. False   The test is 500 hours per year. (p. 7-11)

16. True   (p. 7-12)

17. True   (p. 7-13)

18. True   (p. 7-16)

19. False   Exception 5 to general rental rule.   (p. 7-18)

20. True   (p. 7-23)

Fill-in-the-Blanks

1. indefinitely   (p. 7-23)

2. step-up   (p. 7-29)

3. basis   (p. 7-30)

4. forward   (p. 7-23)

5. 100   (p. 7-7)

Multiple Choice

1. C   Limited to the amount at-risk.   (p. 7-3)

2. B $25,000 - (50% of AGI over $100,000) = $15,000.   (p. 7-26)

3. C   (p. 7-22)

4. B   (p. 7-23)

5. C $25,000 - $5,000 + $10,000 = $30,000   (p. 7-3)

6. D   (p. 7-6)

7. D   Corporations can offset active income   (p. 7-7)

8. A   Individuals cannot offset active income   (p. 7-7)

9. E   (p. 7-5)

10. C   (p. 7-14)

Code Section Recognition

1. Section 469

2. Section 465

8

DEDUCTIONS AND LOSSES: CERTAIN BUSINESS EXPENSES AND LOSSES

CHAPTER HIGHLIGHTS

This chapter discusses certain business expenses and losses which are deducted from gross income to arrive at the taxpayer's adjusted gross income. Casualty losses are also discussed, though depending on circumstances they can be either deductions for or from adjusted gross income.

I.   BAD DEBTS

    A.   When a taxpayer sells goods or services on credit and the accounts receivable subsequently become worthless, a bad debt deduction is allowed provided the income arising from the debt was previously recognized. Cash basis taxpayers are allowed no deduction since income is not reported until cash is collected.

    B.   Allowable methods. For tax years after 1986, all taxpayers, except for certain financial institutions, must use the specific charge-off method for deducting bad debts. The specific charge-off method allows a deduction when a specific debt becomes partially or totally worthless.

    C.   As a result of the repeal of the use of the reserve method, the balance in any bad debt reserve is includible in income ratably over a period of four years, starting in 1987.

D. Business Versus Nonbusiness Bad Debts. Bad debts fall into one of two classifications: business bad debts and nonbusiness bad debts. Debts that arise from a taxpayer's trade or business are business bad debts, while all other debts are nonbusiness bad debts. The primary difference in the tax treatment is that business bad debts are an ordinary deduction, while nonbusiness bad debts are treated as short-term capital losses.

E. Under the tax law qualified individuals can elect to deduct losses on deposits in qualified financial institutions as personal casualty losses in the year in which the loss can be reasonably estimated.

F. Loans Between Related Parties. Loans between related parties create problems in determining whether the loan was real, or a gift. If there is no debtor-creditor relationship established, the debt to a related party may be a gift. If the debt is not repaid, the bad debt deduction will be lost and a gift tax may be incurred.

II. WORTHLESS SECURITIES

A. Losses arising from worthless securities, such as stocks and bonds, are generally treated as capital losses.

B. Securities in Affiliated Corporations. If stock is from an affiliated company, in which the corporate holder owns 80 percent of the voting power of all classes of stock and at least 80 percent of each class of nonvoting stock of the affiliated company, then ordinary loss treatment is allowed.

C. Small Business Stock. Another exception to the capital loss rule on worthless securities is for qualified "small business or Section 1244 stock." Individual taxpayers are allowed ordinary loss treatment (limited to $50,000, or $100,000 for a joint return, per year) for losses on stock that qualifies as small business stock. Any losses over the above limits are capital losses.

III. LOSSES OF INDIVIDUALS

A. Casualty Losses. An individual taxpayer may elect to deduct losses under Section 165(c) in each of the following circumstances:

the loss was incurred in a trade or business,

the loss was incurred in a transaction entered into for profit, or

the loss was caused by casualty or theft.

A casualty loss is "the complete or partial destruction of property resulting from an identifiable event of a sudden, unexpected or unusual nature."

Thus, casualties would include such items as hurricanes, tornadoes, floods, storm, shipwrecks, fires, auto accidents, and mine cave-ins.

B.   Events that are not casualties are those due to "progressive deterioration," such as termite damage, rust, and erosion. They are not considered casualty losses since they are not "sudden and unexpected."

C.   Theft Losses. A theft loss includes larceny, embezzlement, and robbery. It does not include misplaced items. Theft losses are deductible in the year the loss is "discovered," not the year of theft. A partial deduction is allowed if a settlement is arrived at which is less than the property's fair market value.

D.   When to Deduct Casualty Losses. As a general rule, casualty losses are deducted in the year of the casualty. However, if the casualty is in the area designated as a disaster area by the President of the United States, then the taxpayer may elect to treat the loss as having occurred in the previous taxable year. When a "reasonable prospect of full recovery" exists, no deduction for a casualty loss may be taken.

E.   Measuring the Amount of the Loss.

In computing the amount of a casualty loss, it is necessary to divide the property into that held for personal use and that held for business use. Property held for "personal use" is subject to a $100 statutory reduction in the otherwise allowable deduction. This $100 reduction does not apply to business use property. The personal casualty losses are deductible only to the extent they exceed 10 percent of A.G.I.

The actual amount of the gross deduction is the lesser of (1) the adjusted basis of the property, or (2) the decrease in fair market value of the property. The only exception to this rule is the complete destruction of business property, in which case the adjusted basis is used to measure the loss.

To determine the dollar amount of a casualty loss, an appraisal before and after the casualty is needed. An estimation of the amount of the loss may also be made through the cost of repairs to the damaged property.

F.   Casualty Gains and Losses. If a taxpayer's casualty gains exceed casualty losses, the gains and losses will be treated as capital gains and losses. If the casualty losses exceed the casualty gains, then the gains and losses are ordinary items. The losses are after the $100 limitation and any net loss is deductible subject to the 10 percent of AGI limitation.

IV.   RESEARCH AND EXPERIMENTAL EXPENDITURES

A.   Section 174 of the Code defines the tax treatment of research and experimental expenditures. A taxpayer may elect to expense all such costs in the current year. If the election is made for the first year in which the expenses are incurred, the taxpayer does not need the consent of the IRS.

B. A taxpayer may also elect to defer and amortize research and experimental expenditures over a period of not less than 60 months. If the election to expense or defer is not made, the taxpayer must capitalize such expenses. If the property is depreciable they may then be written off.

C. Taxpayers are allowed a 20 percent research and experimental credit through the 1988 tax year (see Chapter 13).

V. NET OPERATING LOSSES

A. To remove inequities that may be caused by the requirement that annual tax returns be filed, taxpayers are allowed a deduction for net operating losses (NOL). A NOL deduction is allowed in a given period for a business related loss incurred in another period. In computing a NOL, several adjustments have to be made to reflect a true economic loss.

B. Carryback and Carryover Periods. Once the NOL is calculated, the amount can be carried back or forward. For loss years after 1975, the loss is carried "back three years and forward fifteen years." Also, the taxpayer may elect to carry the loss forward only.

C. Computation of the NOL.

Adjustments must be made to an individual's taxable loss so that it reflects only losses related to the operation of a trade or business, since the NOL is intended as a relief provision only for business income and loss.

The following items are the most common ones that must be added to the taxpayer's taxable income to arrive at the NOL deduction:

> deductions for personal and dependency exemptions
>
> NOL carryovers and carrybacks from other years,
>
> capital losses
>
> nonbusiness deductions are limited (see text for limitations)

A taxpayer who does not itemize deductions adds the excess of nonbusiness deductions over nonbusiness income by substituting the standard deduction for itemized deductions.

D. When an NOL is carried into a non-loss year, the taxable income and tax must be recomputed. Deductions based on the amount of adjusted gross income, such as medical expenses, must be recomputed based on the new A.G.I. after the NOL. Any tax credits limited by tax liability must also be recomputed based on the reduced amount of tax due. After computing the refund claim for a carryover year it is necessary to recompute the loss to determine how much of the loss is left to carry into other years.

TEST FOR SELF-EVALUATION

True or False

Indicate which of the following statements are true or false by circling the correct answers.

T   F   1.   To be written off as a bad debt, accounts receivable must have been previously included in income.

T   F   2.   Non-financial institutions must use the specific charge-off method for bad debts.

T   F   3.   Pre-1987 reserve for bad debts accounts must be included in income over 5 years starting in 1987.

T   F   4.   Qualified insolvent financial institution losses are deducted by individuals as short-term capital losses for tax years after 1982.

T   F   5.   Consumer surveys, advertising, and promotions qualify under Section 174 as research and experimental expenditures.

T   F   6.   Sometimes, loans between related parties may be classified as gifts.

T   F   7.   Worthless securities always generate an ordinary loss.

T   F   8.   Worthless securities are treated as having become worthless on the last day of the taxable year.

T   F   9.   Within certain dollar limits, a loss on "Section 1244 stock" is an ordinary loss, as opposed to a capital loss.

T   F   10.   Losses on the disposition of stock in an affiliated company are long-term capital losses.

T   F   11.   All casualty and theft losses are subject to a $100 statutory floor on the deductions.

T   F   12.   A loss caused by rust will be deductible as a casualty loss under Section 165.

T   F   13.   To be deductible, a casualty damage must be to the taxpayer's property.

T   F   14.   Disaster area casualty losses must be deducted in the year of the casualty.

T   F   15.   The gross amount of a casualty loss deduction is the larger of (1) the adjusted basis of the property, or (2) the decrease in fair market value.

T   F   16.   For 1989, the general rule for NOL carryovers is three years back and seven years forward.

T   F   17.   Exemptions are allowed as a deduction in arriving at an NOL for an individual taxpayer.

T   F   18.   A taxpayer may elect to expense research and experimental expenditures.

T   F   19.   For 1989, the maximum loss on Section 1244 stock is $50,000 for a joint return.

T   F   20.   "Small Business Stock" under Section 1244 can only be common stock.

T   F   21.   Exemptions are subtracted from taxable income in arriving at a net operating loss.

T   F   22.   No deduction for exemptions is allowed for a year into which an NOL is carried.

Fill-in-the-Blanks

Complete the following statements with the appropriate word(s) or amount(s).

1.   In taking a deduction for bad debts, a taxpayer may use the _____ _____ method.

2.   A business bad debt is an _____ loss, while a non-business bad debt is a short-term loss.

3.   A theft loss is taken in the year of _____, not in the year of occurrence.

4.   The three tax treatments for research and experimental expenditures are capitalize, _____, and defer.

5.   If the deferral method is chosen for research and experimental costs, they must be written off over a period not less than _____ months.

6.   As a general rule, net operating losses are carried back _____ years and carried forward _____ years.

7.   For individual taxpayers, adjustments are required to bring the tax loss to a true _____ loss.

8.   When a net operating loss is carried into a non-loss year, the _____ income and income tax must be recomputed.

Multiple Choice

Choose the best answer for each of the following questions.

_____   1.   Simple Simon, a calendar year taxpayer, owns stock in Big Corporation (a
              publicly-held company). The stock was acquired on November 1st of last
              year. The cost of the stock was $10,000. On March 1st of the current year
              the stock became worthless. Simple should report (before any limitations) a:
              a. $10,000 short-term capital loss
              b. $10,000 long-term capital loss
              c. $10,000 ordinary loss
              d. No gain or loss

_____   2.   Liz Roberts owns Section 1244 stock in X Corporation with a basis of
              $120,000. During the current year she sells the stock for $40,000. If Liz is
              single, she should report:
              a. $60,000 long-term capital loss
              b. $60,000 ordinary loss
              c. $50,000 long-term capital loss and $10,000 ordinary loss
              d. $50,000 ordinary loss and $30,000 long-term capital loss
              e. None of the above

_____   3.   For tax purposes, research and experimental expenses may be:
              a. Capitalized and amortized
              b. Capitalized and not amortized
              c. Expensed
              d. Deferred and written off over 60 months or more
              e. All the above

_____   4.   Robert Chamberlain loaned his friend, Fred, $6,000. Fred used the money
              to start a business. In the current year Fred went bankrupt and the debt
              became worthless. Robert should report:
              a. No deduction for the loss
              b. $6,000 long-term capital loss
              c. $3,000 short-term capital loss
              d. $6,000 short-term capital loss
              e. None of the above

_____   5.   Martha Altus owns a small retail store. Before 1987 she used the reserve
              method for bad debts. As of December 31, 1986, the balance in the reserve
              account was $6,400. For 1989, she would include in income how much of
              the balance in her allowance account?
              a. -0-
              b. $1,600
              c. $6,400
              d. $3,200
              e. Some other amount

_____ 6.   During the current year Tim Kelley's house was broken into. His stereo and
TV were taken. The stereo had a basis of $600 and a FMV of $250, while
the TV's basis was $400 and its FMV was $500. What is Tim's theft loss
deduction, before the ten percent adjusted gross income limitation?
a. -0-
b. $550
c. $650
d. $750
e. None of the above

_____ 7.   Which of the following would be deductible as a personal casualty loss?
a. Rust on the panels of an automobile
b. Decrease in value of a home because of a new sewer plant nearby.
c. Moth damage to some clothes.
d. A tree blows over in a storm and damages the roof of a house.
e. None of the above are a casualty

_____ 8.   Linda Mckaig had a casualty gain of $6,000 in the current year and a casu-
alty loss of $4,000 (after deducting the $100 limitation). Her adjusted gross
income for the year is $25,000. Both the casualties are from long-term
assets. Linda should report:
a. $2,000 ordinary income
b. $1,500 casualty loss and $6,000 ordinary income
c. $6,000 ordinary gain and $2,000 capital loss
d. $6,000 capital gain and $4,000 capital loss
e. No gain or loss should be reported

Problems

1. T, a married individual, had the following income and deductions for 1989:

Income:

Gross income from business	71,720	
Interest on savings account	600	72,320

Deductions:

NOL carryover from 1988	300	
Business expenses	75,000	
Net loss on rental property	1,000	
Personal exemptions (2)	4,000	
Itemized deductions	4,000	(84,300)
Taxable income		**(11,980)**

Calculate T's NOL for 1989.

2. During 1989 T had the following casualty losses:

Asset	Adjusted Basis	FMV Before	FMV After
A	$2,000	$3,000	-0-
B	$2,000	$1,800	-0-
C	$3,000	$2,000	-0-
D	$2,000	$3,000	$500

Assets A and B are personal assets while C and D were used in T's business at the time of the casualty. Determine the amount of the deductible casualty loss (disregarding the 10 percent of adjusted gross income limitation) for:

_____ Asset A

_____ Asset B

_____ Asset C

_____ Asset D

Code Section Recognition

Indicate by number the appropriate Code Section where the following items are found.

_____ 1. Bad debt deduction.

_____ 2. Worthless securities.

_____ 3. Casualty and theft losses.

_____ 4. Research and experimental expenditures.

_____ 5. Net operating losses.

_____ 6. Losses between related parties.

_____ 7. Losses on small business stock.

SOLUTIONS TO CHAPTER 8

True or False

1. True   (p. 8-2)

2. True   (p. 8-2)

3. False The period is 4 years. (p. 8-3)

4. False They are deducted as casualty losses. (p. 8-5)

5. False They do not qualify. (p. 8-17)

6. True   (p. 8-5)

7. False They usually generate a capital loss. (p. 8-7)

8. True   (p. 8-7)

9. True   (p. 8-7)

10. False The losses are ordinary losses. (p. 8-7)

11. False Business casualties are not subject to the $100 floor. (p. 8-11)

12. False Rust is not sudden and unexpected. (p. 8-8)

13. True   (p. 8-8)

14. False   They may be deducted in the prior year. (p. 8-10)

15. False   The deduction is the lesser of the basis or decrease in FMV. (p. 8-11)

16. False   The carryforward period is 15 years. (p. 8-19)

17. False   Exemptions are not allowed in arriving at an NOL. (p. 8-20)

18. True   (p. 8-17)

19. False   The maximum for a joint return is $100,000. (p. 8-7)

20. False   Preferred stock is included under Section 1244. (p. 8-7)

21. False   Exemptions are added to taxable income. (p. 8-20)

22. True   (p. 8-25)

Fill-in-the-Blanks

1. specific charge-off (p. 8-2)

2. ordinary (p. 8-4)

3. discovery (p. 8-9)

4. expense (p. 8-17)

5. sixty (p. 8-18)

6. three, fifteen (p. 8-19)

7. economic (p. 8-20)

8. taxable (p. 8-23)

Multiple Choice

1. B   (p. 8-7)

2. D   (p. 8-7)

3. E   (p. 8-17)

4. C (p. 8-4)

5. B $6,400/4 years = $1,600 per year. (p. 8-3)

6. B $250 (stereo) + 400 (TV) - 100 (limit) = $550. (p. 8-11)

7. D (p. 8-8)

8. D There is a net casualty gain, therefore all gains and losses are capital (p. 8-14)

Problems

1. Taxable Income for 1989   ($11,980)

Add:		
NOL from 1988		300
Personal Exemptions		4,000
Itemized Deductions	4,000	
Less: Interest Income	600	3,400	(7,700)
Net Operating Loss for 1989		**($4,280)** (p. 8-23)

2. $1,900 Asset A Decrease in FMV ($3,000 - 0), limited to $2,000 - $100 = $1,900

    $1,700 Asset B Decrease in FMV $1,800 - $100 = $1,700

    $3,000 Asset C Adjusted basis $3,000 (Note, complete destruction)

    $2,000 Asset D Decrease in FMV ($3,000 - $500), limited to $2,000 (p. 8-12)

Code Section Recognition

1. Section 166

2. Section 165

3. Section 165

4. Section 174

5. Section 172

6.   Section 267

7.   Section 1244

9

DEPRECIATION, COST RECOVERY, AMORTIZATION, AND DEPLETION

CHAPTER HIGHLIGHTS

The tax law provides for the capital recovery of the cost of assets through depreciation, cost recovery, amortization and depletion. This chapter looks at the methods of capital recovery allowed under the Code as deductions from AGI. In addition, the types of assets that qualify for capital recovery are discussed.

I. DEPRECIATION AND AMORTIZATION

    A.   Section 167 permits a deduction for depreciation in the form of a reasonable allowance for the exhaustion, wear and tear, and obsolescence of business property and property held for the production of income.

            The Regulations hold that tangible property is depreciable only to the extent that it is subject to wear and tear, to decay or decline from natural causes, to exhaustion and to obsolescence. Intangible property is not subject to depreciation unless the property has a definite useful life, such as patents and copyrights. Goodwill is not amortizable because it does not have a measurable useful life.

            The basis for depreciation is generally the adjusted cost basis. However, personal use property converted to business or income-producing use will have a depreciable basis equal to the lower of its adjusted basis or fair market value when converted.

B.   Other Depreciation Considerations. Property placed in service before January 1, 1981 is subject to different rules than property placed in service after that date.

Before 1981, the taxpayer had a choice of the following allowable depreciation methods:

The straight-line method (cost basis less salvage value divided by the estimated useful life).

The declining balance method using a rate not more than twice the straight-line rate. Various classes of property were limited to a rate less than 200 percent declining balance. Salvage value is not taken into account under the declining balance method. However, no further depreciation can be claimed once net book value and salvage value are equal.

Any other consistent method which did not result in greater total depreciation being claimed during the first two thirds of the useful life than would have been allowable under the double declining balance method. Permissible methods included the sum-of-the-years digits', machine-hours, and units-of-production methods.

In determining the depreciable basis, the taxpayer must take into account the salvage value. However, the salvage value of tangible personal property with an estimated useful life of three years or more, may be disregarded if it is less than 10 percent of the basis. This allowance does not apply to livestock.

The Tax Reform Act of 1969 placed limitations on the use of accelerated methods. The following table summarizes the limitations on depreciation of real property acquired before January 1, 1981 and after July 24, 1969:

	Nonresidential Realty	Residential Realty
New property	150% DB, SL	200% DB, SYD
		150% DB, SL
Used property	SL	125% DB if
		EUL is greater
		than 20 years; SL

The Asset Depreciation Range (ADR) system established guideline lives for the depreciation of pre-1981 property. The rules were complex and have been eliminated.

II.   ACCELERATED COST RECOVERY SYSTEM (ACRS)

A.   General Considerations.

The accelerated cost recovery system applies to most property acquired after 1980. The ACRS is designed to aid capital formation by providing a rapid write-off for capital goods. The recovery periods under ACRS are based on property classifications. These are two classifications and the appropriate one is determined by whether the property was placed in service before 1987 or after 1986. The annual deduction amount for personalty is found in the tables in the text. It is given as a percentage of the basis.

B.   Personalty: Recovery Period and Methods.

Eligible personalty (and certain realty) is recovered under the following recovery classes:

Pre-1987 Acquisitions

3 year: Autos, trucks, R&D equipment, and certain horses.

5 year: Property that is not in another class.

10 year: Public utility property with an ADR life of 18 to 25 years.

15 year: Public utility property with an ADR life over 25 years.

Post-1986 Acquisitions

3-year: ADR midpoints of 4 years or less, except autos and light trucks

5-year: ADR midpoints of more than 4 and less than 10 years, including autos, light trucks, R&D equipment, etc.

7-year: Property that is not in another class.

10-year: ADR midpoints of more than 16 but less than 20 years.

15-year: ADR midpoints of 20 or more but less than 25 years.

20-year: ADR midpoints of 25 or more years.

The pre-1987 ACRS rates are based on the 150 percent declining- balance method, using the half-year convention, and disregarding salvage value. The post-1986 ACRS rates are based on the 200 or 150 percent declining balance method, depending on the class.

One-half of the investment tax credit (which was repealed for property placed in service after 1985) taken on property placed in service after 1982 must be used to reduce the basis of the property. As an alternative to reducing the basis of the property, a reduced investment credit of 4 percent for three-year-property and 8 percent for other property may be taken.

C.   Realty: Recovery Periods and Methods.

Pre-1987 real estate under ACRS is written off over 15, 18, or 19 years depending on when it was acquired (see text for the various ACRS tables). Post-1986 real estate is written off over 15 (land improvements), 27.5 (residential), or 31.5 (nonresidential) years.

Instead of using the accelerated methods under ACRS, taxpayers may elect to use the straight-line method depreciation. The pre-1987 straight-line write-off is limited to the following periods:

      3 year property: 3, 5, or 12 years
      5 year property: 5, 12, or 25 years
      10 year property: 10, 25, or 35 years
      15 year property: 15, 35, or 45 years
      18 year property: 18, 35, or 45 years
      19 year property: 19, 35, or 45 years

Post-1986 straight-line election is based on the property's class life, using a half-year or mid-month convention, whichever is applicable.

See the text for various methods of calculating straight-line ACRS.

E.   Election to Expense.

Section 179 permits an election to expense certain depreciable assets used in a trade or business, up to a $10,000 annual limit. The amount expensed cannot exceed the amount derived from the taxpayer's trade or business. Furthermore, the amount expensed is reduced dollar-for-dollar when the property placed in service exceeds $200,000 for the year.

F.   Other Aspects of ACRS. To prevent transactions that attempt to change pre-1981 property into post-1980 recovery property without actually changing ownership, the ACRS provision contain "anti-churing" rules. The taxpayer must use pre-1981 depreciation rules if the property was owned or used during 1980 by the taxpayer or a related person.

G.   Business and Personal Use of Autos and Other Listed Property. A taxpayer must show that property used for both business and personal use is used predominately for business (greater than 50%) in order to use ACRS. If it is not used predominately for business, acquisition cost must be recovered using straight-line deprecation.

H.   Under the "luxury auto" rules, passenger automobiles are limited to a $2,560 deduction the first year, $4,100 for the second year, $2,450 for the third year, and $1,475 for each subsequent year. These limits are imposed before the percentage reduction for personal use of the automobile. Also, the annual limits apply to any election to expense under Section 179.

I.   Alternative Depreciation System (ADS). For post-1986 property ADS must be used for the following:

> depreciation for the alternative minimum tax
>
> property used outside the U.S.
>
> property leased by a tax-exempt entity
>
> property financed by tax-exempt bonds
>
> certain imported property
>
> depreciation allowances for earnings and profits

See text for the ADS calculation.

III.   DEPLETION

A.   Payment for natural resources is recovered through depletion. Intangible drilling and development costs, however can be handled in one of two ways if the drilling is successful. If the well is dry these costs are lost. On a successful well, such costs can either be (1) expensed in the year incurred, or (2) capitalized and written off through depletion. These costs include the cost of making property ready for drilling, erecting derricks, and drilling the well.

B.   Depletion Methods.

The owner of an interest in a wasting asset is entitled to a depletion deduction. The tax law allows for two types of depletion, cost and percentage.

Cost depletion is based on the adjusted basis of the asset. The basis is divided by the estimated recoverable units of the asset to arrive at a cost per unit. This cost is multiplied by the units sold to arrive at the deduction allowed.

Percentage depletion is based on a percentage specified in the Code which is applied to the gross income from the property to arrive at the amount of depletion allowed. Such depletion may not exceed 50 percent of the taxable income from the property before the depletion allowance.

If intangible drilling costs are capitalized, the basis for cost depletion is increased. If such costs are expensed, the 50 percent limit for the percentage depletion deduction will be decreased.

IV.   REPORTING PROCEDURES

A.   Sole proprietors engaged in a trade or business should file a Schedule C with their Form 1040. Part I of Schedule C is used for reporting items of income. Part II is used for reporting deductions such as bad debts, depletion, and depreciation.

B.   If depreciation is claimed, it should be supported by a Form 4562.

TEST FOR SELF-EVALUATION

True or False

Indicate which of the following statements are true or false by circling the correct answers.

T F 1.   If depreciation is not claimed for a particular year, the basis for the asset remains unchanged.

T F 2.   An asset purchased in 1979 and depreciated using the straight-line method can be changed to the ACRS method provided the taxpayer uses the remaining cost recovery life.

T F 3.   The basis of personal use property converted to business use is the lower of its adjusted basis or fair market value on the date of conversion.

T F 4.   The alternative depreciation systems must be used on all automobiles.

T F 5.   Cost depletion is determined by dividing the fair market value of the asset by the estimated recoverable units expected.

T F 6.   A taxpayer may disregard salvage value in applying the ACRS percentages.

T F 7.   ACRS contains provisions to prevent the conversion of non-ACRS property into ACRS property.

T F 8.   Assets that do not decline in value on a predictable basis are not depreciable under ACRS.

T F 9.   Under ACRS, realty may be depreciated using the component method.

T F 10. Depreciation, depletion, and amortization are different words to describe the process of deducting the cost of an asset.

T F 11. Under ACRS an automobile used in a business is seven-year recovery property.

T F 12. In the current year, residential rental real estate under ACRS is generally written off over 27.5 years.

T F 13. For 1989, the maximum amount that can be expensed under Section 179 is $10,000.

T F 14. If more than 40 percent of the non-realty assets acquired during a year are acquired in the last quarter, then the taxpayer must use the mid-quarter ACRS tables to calculate the ACRS deduction.

T   F   15.   The annual limits for automobile deductions do not apply to any election to expense under Section 179.

T   F   16.   ACRS and other depreciation, amortization, and depletion are reported on Form 4562.

Fill-in-the-Blanks

Complete the following statements with the appropriate word(s) or amount(s).

1.   Post-1986 nonresidential real estate is written off over _____ years.

2.   For the taxpayer to be entitled to a depletion deduction, he or she must have an _____ interest in the property.

3.   Percentage depletion may not exceed _____ percent of the taxable income from the property before the allowance for depletion.

4.   An automobile is _____ year property under ACRS.

5.   The pre-1987 tables under ACRS for writing off realty are based on a _____ percent declining balance depreciation method.

6.   Under the pre-1987 ACRS straight-line election, five year property may be written off over _____, _____, or _____ years.

7.   For 1989, the maximum amount that can be expensed under Section 179 is $_____ .

8.   The methods of depletion under the tax law are called _____ depletion and _____ depletion.

9.   To use ACRS on listed property such as an automobile, the business use of the property must be more than _____ percent.

Multiple Choice

Choose the best answer for each of the following questions.

_____   1.   Section 167 permits a depreciation deduction for which of the following reasons?
a. Exhaustion
b. Wear and tear
c. Obsolescence
d. All the above

_____ 2.   Which of the following is not depreciable?
a. A delivery truck
b. Goodwill
c. An office building
d. Office equipment
e. None of the above

_____ 3.   For non-ACRS property, salvage value is not used in calculating depreciation on which of the following methods?
a. Declining-balance
b. Straight-line
c. Sum-of-the-years-digits
d. Units-of-production
e. None of the above

_____ 4.   For new residential rental property acquired after July 24, 1969, and before 1981, the maximum depreciation rate that can be used is:
a. Sum-of-the-years-digits
b. 200% declining-balance
c. 150% declining-balance
d. 125% declining-balance
e. None of the above

_____ 5.   The Big Tex Oil Company purchases an oil lease for $1,000,000. After exploration, oil is discovered and it is estimated that 100,000 barrels of oil are in the lease. If during 1989 Big Tex produces 15,000 barrels of oil from the lease and sells 12,000 barrels, what is the amount of cost depletion allowed Big Tex?
a. -0-
b. $120,000
c. $150,000
d. $1,000,000
e. Some other amount

_____ 6.   The Pit Sulfur Company has gross income of $200,000 from certain property subject to depletion. The expenses related to that property are $140,000, and a statutory depletion rate of 22 percent is applicable. What is the amount of depletion using percentage depletion?
a. -0-
b. $44,000
c. $30,000
d. $13,200
e. Some other amount

_____ 7.   On July 1, 1989 farmer John acquires a new tractor at a cost of $30,000. If John is married and files a joint return for 1989, what amount can John expense under Section 179 and what amount is subject to regular ACRS depreciation?

a. $0, $30,000
b. $10,000, $30,000
c. $5,000, $25,000
d. $10,000, $20,000
e. Some other amounts

_____ 8. Sun Corporation acquires $200,000 worth of three-year property and $210,000 worth of five-year property in 1989. If the election to expense is not made, what is Sun's ACRS deduction using the half-year method?
a. $108,667
b. $101,500
c. $81,500
d. $97,205

_____ 9. For 1989, what is the maximum amount of qualified expense property that can be placed in service during the year without causing a reduction in the $10,000 expense deduction?
a. $100,000
b. $125,000
c. $150,000
d. $200,000
e. Some other amount

_____ 10. For pre-1987 five-year class property, which of the following cannot be used as a life for a straight-line election?
a. 5 years
b. 8 years
c. 12 years
d. 25 years
e. None of the above

_____ 11. On September 1, 1989, Mike Shields places in service an automobile with a cost of $40,000. The car is used 90 percent for business and 10 percent for personal use. What is Mike's ACRS deduction?
a. $2,560
b. $2,304
c. $4,100
d. $3,690
e. Some other amount

_____ 12. Same as Question 11 above. What is Mike's ACRS deduction in 1990?
a. $2,560
b. $3,304
c. $4,100
d. $3,690
e. Some other amount

_____ 13. Maggie McCall acquires an apartment building on June 3, 1989 for $600,000.

What is Maggie's cost recovery for earnings and profits during the first year under the alternative depreciation system (ADS)?
a. $8,124
b. $10,769
c. $7,993
d. $15,000
e. Some other amount

_____ 14. The percentage depletion rate on coal is:
a. 22%
b. 15%
c. 14%
d. 10%
e. 5%

Problems

1. Each of the following assets was acquired in 1989. Determine the appropriate ACRS recovery class for each.

_____ a. A used delivery truck

_____ b. A used office building

_____ c. A new drill press

_____ d. A new duplex held for rental

_____ e. A used apartment building

_____ f. A new computer

_____ g. Public utility property with a life of 30 years

2. On August 8, 1989, Steve Brownell acquired an apartment building (27.5-year property) as an investment. Steve does not use straight-line ACRS on this building. The apartment cost $500,000 and has an estimated salvage value of $100,000. Using the table in the text, give the ACRS deduction for the first four years for this apartment.

Year 1 _____

Year 2 _____

Year 3 _____

Year 4 _____

Code Section Recognition

Indicate by number the appropriate Code Section where the following items are found.

_____ 1. Depreciation deduction.

_____ 2. Accelerated Cost Recovery System.

_____ 3. The election to expense.

_____ 4. Depletion deduction.

_____ 5. Percentage depletion.

SOLUTIONS TO CHAPTER 9

True or False

1. False   The basis decreases by the amount allowable. (p. 9-3)

2. False   Taxpayers cannot convert non-ACRS property into ACRS property. (p. 9-20)

3. True   (p. 9-4)

4. False   Regular ACRS is used on autos. (p. 9-21)

5. False   Adjusted basis is used, not fair market value. (p. 9-28)

6. True   (p. 9-10)

7. True   (p. 9-20)

8. True   (p. 9-9)

9. False   The component method cannot be used. (p. 9-15)

10. True   (p. 9-2)

11. False   Automobiles are five-year property. (p. 9-12)

12. True   (p. 9-16)

13. True   (p. 9-19)

14. True   (p. 9-14)

15. False   The limit does apply to Section 179. (p. 9-23)

16. True   (p. 9-31)

Fill-in-the-Blanks

1. 31.5 (p. 9-16)

2. economic (p. 9-28)

3. fifty (p. 9-29)

4. five (p. 9-12)

5. 175 (p. 9-15)

6. five, twelve, twenty-five (p. 9-17)

7. $10,000 (p. 9-19)

8. cost, percentage (p. 9-28)

9. fifty (p. 9-22)

Multiple Choice

1. D (p. 9-3)

2. B (p. 9-4)

3. A (p. 9-5)

4. B (p. 9-7)

5. B ($1,000,000/100,000 barrels) x 12,000 = $120,000. (p. 9-28)

6. C ($200,000 - 140,000) x 50% = $30,000 maximum. (p. 9-29)

7. D (p. 9-19)

8. A ($200,000 x 33.33%) + ($210,000 x 20%) = 108,667   (p. 9-15)

9. D (p. 9-19)

10. B (p. 9-17)

11. B $2,560 x 90% = $2,304   (p. 9-24)

12. D $4,100 x 90% = $3,690   (p. 9-24)

13. A $600,000 x 1.354% = $8,124   (p. 9-27)

14. D   (p. 9-30)

Problems

1.   a. 5-year

      b. 31.5-year

      c. 7-year

      d. 27.5-year

      e. 27.5-year

      f. 7-year

      g. 20-year   (p.9-11 to 9-13

2.   Year 1 $500,000 X 1.364% = $6,820

       Year 2 $500,000 X 3.636% = $18,180

       Year 3 $500,000 X 3.636% = $18,180

       Year 4 $500,000 X 3.636% = $18,180   (p. 9-44)

Code Section Recognition

1. Section 167

2. Section 168

3. Section 179

4. Section 611

5. Section 613

10

DEDUCTIONS: EMPLOYEE EXPENSES

CHAPTER HIGHLIGHTS

Some employee expenses are treated as expenses incurred in a trade or business, and thus are deductions for adjusted gross income. Other employee expenses, the itemized deductions, are deductible from adjusted gross income. This chapter deals primarily with deductions falling within the first category, whereas the itemized deductions are discussed in the next chapter.

I. CLASSIFICATION OF EMPLOYMENT RELATED EXPENSES

    A. Self-employed Versus Employee Status.

        One major problem in taxation is to determine if an employer- employee relationship exists or if an individual is self-employed. An employer-employee relationship exists when the employer has the right to specify the result and the ways and means by which the result will be obtained.

        A self-employed person is required to file a Schedule C, and all allowable expenses incurred will be deductions for adjusted gross income.

    B. Deductions for A.G.I.

        Certain employee expenses are deductible for adjusted gross income, while the rest are deductible from adjusted gross income. The dfors are reimbursed employee-related expenses.

C.   Itemized Deductions.

After classifying deductions as dfor or dfrom, it is necessary to group the
itemized deductions into two groups. The first group are deductible in full
for taxpayers who itemized, while the second group of deductions are added
together and reduced by 2% of AGI.

Miscellaneous itemized deductions not subject to the 2% of AGI limitation
are:

> --Work-related handicapped expenses
> --Certain estate taxes
> --Certain claim of right adjustments
> --Amortizable bond premiums
> --Gambling losses to the extent of winnings
> --Certain short sale deductions
> --Certain terminated annuity payments
> --Certain cooperative housing costs

The second group of itemized deductions (subject to a 2% limitation) are:

> --All unreimbursed employee expenses (after a 20% limit, if any)
> --Professional dues and subscriptions
> --Union dues and work uniforms
> --Employment-related education expenses
> --Malpractice insurance premiums
> --Job hunting expenses
> --Office in the home and outside sales expenses
> --Legal, accounting, and tax return fees
> --Hobby expenses
> --Investment expenses
> --Custodial fees for income-producing property or IRAs
> --Collection fees for interest and dividends
> --Appraisal fees for casualty losses or charitable deductions

D.   Percentage Reduction for Meals and Entertainment.

Deductions for meals and entertainment (including facilities) are limited to
80% of the otherwise allowable deductions. This rule applies to taxes and
tips relating to meals and entertainment. Cover charges, parking, and room
rental fees are also subject to the 80% rule.

Transportation expenses are not affected by this provision. If meals and
entertainment are part of luxury water travel and are not separately stated,
then the 80% rule does not apply.

The 80% rule does not apply in the following cases:

--Compensation of employees
--Income of independent contractors
--Meals and entertainment in a subsidized eating facility
--Where the de minimis rule applies
--Where employees are fully reimbursed for business and entertainment (the 20% reduction applies to the person making the reimbursement).
--Certain employer-paid recreation expenses
--Samples and promotional activities available to the public
--Expenses for charitable and fundraising events
--Expenses sold in a bona fide transaction
--Qualified meeting, convention, seminar, and annual meeting programs that include a meal.

E.   Reimbursed Expenses.

An employee must render an adequate accounting to his or her employer if there is an exact or excess reimbursement to the employee. When an adequate accounting has been made, the employee may omit the reimbursement from income and ignore the expenses up to the amount of the expenses. After 1988, employees who do not make an adequate accounting are required to include reimbursements in income and itemized their deductions subject to the 2% floor if the employer allows the employee to keep reimbursements that are not spent.

II. TRANSPORTATION EXPENSES

A.   A taxpayer is permitted a deduction from AGI subject to the 2% floor for unreimbursed, employment-related transportation expenses. Such expenses include those incurred by an outside salesperson and the cost of commuting to a second job from a first job. However, from home to work and back is not deductible.

B.   In computing automobile expenses a taxpayer has two choices, actual cost or an automatic mileage method. Under the automatic mileage method the taxpayer can deduct 24 cents per mile for the first 15,000 miles and 11 cents per mile for mileage over 15,000 miles annually. If an automobile is fully depreciated the mileage deduction is limited to 11 cents per mile. Parking fees and tolls can be deducted in addition to the amount calculated under the automatic mileage method.

See the text for restrictions which apply to changing from one method to another, the use of a fully depreciated vehicle, and the use of more than one vehicle for business purposes.

Any reimbursement the employee receives for transportation expenses must be used to reduce the deduction and may even produce income if the reimbursement exceeds the expenses.

III.   TRAVEL EXPENSES

A.   An employee will be allowed a second tier deduction for unreimbursed travel expenses. Travel expenses include meals and lodging while away from home in the pursuit of a trade or business, along with reasonable laundry and incidental expenses. Entertainment expenses are not included as travel and are discussed elsewhere.

B.   To meet the away from home test, an employee usually must stay overnight. An overnight stay is a period substantially longer than an ordinary day's work and requires rest, sleep or relief from the work period. To go into travel status a taxpayer must be away from his tax home. Generally, if a taxpayer has a work assignment of less than one year it is regarded as temporary, if the work assignment is more than two years it is regarded as indefinite. For periods between one and two years, the facts and circumstances determine each specific case.

C.   If a trip combines both business and pleasure and is within the United States, transportation is deductible only if the trip is primarily for business. If the trip is primarily a vacation, expenses relating to business other than transportation are still deductible.

D.   Disallowed and Limited Travel.

Expenses related to attending a convention, seminar, or similar meeting are disallowed unless the expenses are related to a trade or business of the taxpayers. Therefore, most investment or tax seminars will not qualify under this rule.

Luxury water travel is limited to twice the highest amount generally allowable for a day of travel for federal employees serving the United States.

No deduction is allowed for travel that, by itself, is deemed to be educational by the taxpayer. This rule does not apply with respect to a deduction for travel necessary to engage in an activity that gives rise to a business deduction related to travel.

Expenses incurred to attend conventions outside North America are disallowed unless the taxpayer can show that it is reasonable that the convention be held in a foreign location.

IV.   MOVING EXPENSES

A.   Moving expenses are deductible by employees from (not subject to the 2% limit) adjusted gross income. Reimbursements from the employer must be included in gross income under Section 82. The two basic tests that must be met for moving expenses to be deductible are a distance test and a time requirement.

B.   The distance test requires that the taxpayer's new job location be at least 35 miles farther from the taxpayer's old residence than the old residence was from the former place of employment. If the move was made for personal reasons, or the new job did not require a change in residence, no deduction is allowed.

C.   A time requirement is also necessary for an employee to qualify for the moving expense deduction. An employee must stay at the new location for 39 weeks in the twelve month period following the move and self-employed individuals must stay at the new location for 78 weeks, during the next two years.

D.   Moving expenses are deductible in the year of payment. However, if the employee is to be reimbursed for the expenses in the following year, an election can be made to deduct the expenses in that year.

E.   There are limits on various classes of moving expense deductions. The five classes are:

1) Expenses of moving household and personal belongings

2) Expenses of traveling to the new residence

3) Expenses of house-hunting trips

4) Temporary living expenses

5) Residential buying, selling, or leasing expenses

There is no dollar limit on classes 1 and 2. Classes 3 and 4 combined are limited to $1,500. For classes 3, 4, and 5 the total is limited to $3,000.

V.   EDUCATIONAL EXPENSES

A.   An employee may deduct expenses (subject to the 2% limit) for education as ordinary and necessary business expenses provided such items were incurred either (1) to maintain or improve existing skills required in the present job, or (2) to meet the express requirements of the employer or the requirements imposed by law to retain the employment status. However, expenses are not deductible if they are required to meet the minimum educational standards for the taxpayer's job or if they qualify the taxpayer for a new trade or business.

Many states require that teachers take additional courses to retain their position. Such expenses would qualify as deductible since they are incurred in meeting requirements imposed by law or the employer for retention of employment.

The deductibility of educational expenses said to "maintain or improve existing skills" is a heavily litigated subject. The deduction is disallowed in cases where the deduction qualifies the taxpayer for a new trade of business. For example, the expenses of a business executive or accountant incurred in obtaining a law degree are specifically not deductible under this provision.

VI. ENTERTAINMENT EXPENSES

A. Entertainment expenses can be categorized as those directly related to business and those associated with business. Directly related to expenses are those related to an actual business meeting or discussion. "Associated with" expenses are those that promote the general goodwill of the business. However, the entertainment must serve a specific business purpose.

B. Business meals are 80% deductible if the following conditions are met:

>   The meal is directly related to or associated with the active conduct of a trade or business,
>
>   The expense is not lavish or extravagant, and
>
>   The taxpayer (or an employee) is present at the meal.

C. A deduction for the cost of a ticket for entertainment activity is limited to the face value of the ticket. Deductions for skyboxes at sports arenas are generally disallowed except to the extent of the cost of a regular ticket.

D. Entertainment expenses must be substantiated by contemporaneous records under Section 274(d) to be deductible. The substantiation must include the amount, time and place, business purpose, and business relationship.

E. Business gifts are limited to $25 per donee per year. Excluded from the $25 limit are certain gifts costing $4 or less, gifts used for advertising, and gifts or awards for employees for length of service, etc. that cost under $400.

VII. OTHER EMPLOYEE EXPENSES

A. There is no deduction for an office in the home unless it is used exclusively and on a regular basis as the taxpayer's principal place of business or as a place of business which is used by patients, clients, or customers. The deductions for office in the home cannot exceed gross income from the business activity, reduced by all other deductible expenses attributable to the business but not allocable to the use of the home itself (unless the item would otherwise be deductible).

B. Expatriates who meet certain tests are allowed an annual exclusion on earned income from foreign countries as discussed in Chapter 5. In cases where the foreign country has high income taxes, the expatriate would be better off electing the foreign tax credit instead of the exclusion. An additional exclusion is allowed on the basis of housing costs incurred.

TEST FOR SELF-EVALUATION

True or False

Indicate which of the following statements are true or false by circling the correct answers.

T F 1.   Expenses of self-employed taxpayers are deductible for adjusted gross income as trade or business expenses.

T F 2.   An employer-employee relationship exists if the employer has the right to specify the result and the ways and means by which the result is to be attained.

T F 3.   A self-employed individual is required to file Schedule C of Form 1040.

T F 4.   Unreimbursed employee travel expenses are a deduction from adjusted gross income.

T F 5.   All miscellaneous deductions are subject to the 2 percent of AGI limitation.

T F 6.   To the extent employee expenses are reimbursed, they are deductions for adjusted gross income.

T F 7.   If an employer reimburses an employee for more than his or her expenses, the excess is not income to the employee.

T F 8.   Travel and transportation expenses are defined as the same expenses for tax purposes.

T F 9.   Commuting expenses from home to one's place of employment are nondeductible.

T F 10. An employee will be allowed a deduction for the cost of commuting from a primary job to a second job.

T F 11. Taxpayers must always use the automatic mileage method to determine an automobile expense deduction.

T F 12. If a taxpayer has two or more vehicles in use at the same time, he or she may use the automatic mileage method.

T F 13. A taxpayer cannot change to the automatic mileage method if the election to expense or accelerated depreciation has previously been taken.

T F 14. If an automobile has been fully depreciated under the straight-line method, the taxpayer may use a mileage rate of 21 cents per mile.

T   F   15.   Unreimbursed travel expenses are a deduction from adjusted gross income.

T   F   16.   Union dues are deductible (subject to the 2% limitation) for tax purposes.

T   F   17.   To be deductible a home office must be used exclusively and on a regular basis as the taxpayer's principal place of business or as a place which is used by patients, clients, or customers.

T   F   18.   All business gift deductions are limited to $25 per donee.

T   F   19.   Law school expenses are always deductible.

T   F   20.   The cost of a Bar exam or CPA exam review course is generally deductible.

T   F   21.   The moving expense deduction allowable for an auto is 9 cents per mile for 1989.

T   F   22.   Expenses of moving household and personal belongings are not subject to a dollar limitation.

T   F   23.   Business meals are only 80 percent deductible.

T   F   24.   Luxury water travel is limited to three times the Federal employee daily travel rate.

T   F   25.   Travel as a form of education is not allowed as a deduction for individual taxpayers.

Fill-in-the-Blanks

Complete the following statements with the appropriate word(s) or amount(s).

1.   To qualify for a travel deduction, a taxpayer must be away from home for a _____ period.

2.   The taxpayer's new job location must be at least _____ miles farther from the taxpayer's old residence than the old residence was from the former place of employment to qualify for a moving expense deduction.

3.   The minimum time requirement to qualify for a moving expense deduction is _____ weeks for an employee and _____ weeks for a self-employed individual.

4.   The total expense for house-hunting trips and temporary living quarters cannot exceed _____ dollars.

5.   An education expense will not be deductible if it qualifies the taxpayer for a
      _____ trade or business.

6.   Foreign convention expenses are limited if the convention is held outside
      _____ _____.

7.   Educational expenses are deductible if they are to maintain or improve
      _____ skills or to meet the requirements of an _____.

8.   Entertainment expense deductions are categorized as those _____ related
      to business and those _____ with business.

9.   For an office in the home to be deductible, it must be used exclusively and on a
      regular basis as the taxpayer's _____ place of business, or a place which
      is used by _____, _____ or _____.

10.   Special clothing, to be deductible, must be specifically required as a condition of
      _____ and not be adaptable to _____ wear.

Multiple Choice

Choose the best answer for each of the following questions.

_____ 1.   Which of the following educational expenses would be deductible?
              a. Travel expenses for general knowledge.
              b. CPA review course expenses.
              c. Law school educational expenses.
              d. Expenses of a senior in college who has already accepted a job.
              e. None of the above are deductible

_____ 2.   The substantiation requirements for business entertainment under Section
              274 do not include:
              a. The amount
              b. Credit card receipts
              c. The business purpose
              d. The business relationship
              e. None of the above

_____ 3.   An employee drove her automobile 20,000 miles on business. The car is not
              fully depreciated. Using the automatic mileage method, her deduction is:
              a. $4,800 for AGI
              b. $4,800 from AGI
              c. $4,150 from AGI
              d. $4,150 for AGI
              e. Some other amount

_____ 4.   Which of the following is not subject to the 2 percent limitation on miscel-

laneous deductions?
a. Unreimbursed employee expenses
b. Outside sales expenses
c. Union dues
d. Investment expenses
e. Amortizable bond premiums

_____ 5. Cathy McGrath is a high school teacher. She has set aside one room in her house as a home office where she grades papers, prepares for class, etc. No revenue is produced from this activity. Depreciation and maintenance are $400 on the home office. How much of the expenses are deductible by Cathy?
a. -0-
b. $400
c. $500
d. $900
e. Some other amount

_____ 6. T is self-employed and while traveling spends $120 on meals and $200 on transportation and lodging. What of the above can T deduct?
a. $296
b. $320
c. $256
d. $280
e. Some other amount

_____ 7. T spent $600 on dues to professional organizations and $250 for subscriptions to professional journals. T's AGI is $30,000. If T is not an outside salesperson or self-employed, how much may she deduct?
a. -0-
b. $850
c. $600
d. $250
e. Some other amount

_____ 8. Which of the following would be an employer-employee relationship?
a. A plumber who comes to your home to do work
b. A CPA who prepares a tax return
c. A physician who pays a nurse to help him in his office
d. A gardener who takes care of individual lawns for a monthly fee
e. None of the above

_____ 9. A self-employed CPA moves from California to Texas to establish a new practice. To qualify for a moving expense deduction, which of the following must be true?
a. He must work for another CPA in Texas for one year
b. He must have been in practice for three years in California
c. He must obtain a license to practice from the state of Texas

d. He must stay in the new location for 78 weeks

e. None of the above

_____ 10.   Fran Huffman is a CPA who has a small tax practice in her home in addition to working her regular job. The gross income from this practice is $5,500 for the year. Based on square footage, the portion of mortgage interest and real estate tax allocable to the business amounts to $3,000. The allocable portion of maintenance, utilities, and depreciation is $3,500. How much of the maintenance, utilities, and depreciation are deductible by Fran?

a. -0-

b. $3,500

c. $2,500

d. $500

e. Some other amount

_____ 11.   Mike Reynolds, a staff accountant for a CPA firm, incurred the following expenses:

Travel	$200
Transportation	$500
Dues and Subscriptions	$300

Mike gave his employer an adequate accounting and received a reimbursement of $1,000 to cover these expenses. What amount is deductible from adjusted gross income?

a. -0-

b. $60

c. $300

d. $700

e. Some other amount

_____ 12.   In 1989, Rachel Mollering, an employee of Big CPA firm, spent $3,000 in business expenses not subject to the 80% limitation. She was reimbursed $4,000 for these expenses. An adequate accounting was not made to her employer. If Rachel's AGI was $50,000 for the year she would include $4,000 income and deduct what amount as an itemized deduction?

a. -0-

b. $2,000

c. $4,000

d. $3,000

e. Some other amount

Problems

1. In 1989 Dorothy Hicks was transferred from San Francisco to San Diego. She paid
    $4,000 to have her personal and household goods moved. In addition, she had
    temporary living expenses of $900 and qualified house- hunting expenses of $800.
    During the move, Dorothy drove the 500 miles to San Diego, incurring travel
    expenses of $200. In selling her residence, Dorothy incurred $6,500 in expenses.
    Dorothy received no reimbursement for her moving expense. Calculate Dorothy's
    moving expense deduction using the following worksheet.

    Transportation expenses $_____

    Travel, meals and lodging $_____

    House-hunting expenses $_____

    Temporary living expenses $_____

    Total $_____

    Amount of househunting and
    temporary living allowed $_____

    Qualified house sale expenses $_____

    Total $_____

    Amount of househunting, temporary living,
    and house sale expense allowed $_____

    Moving deduction $_____

2. Ray Whittington, a college professor, incurred the following business-related
    expenses for which he was not reimbursed.

Mileage	16,500 miles
Travel (meals $200)	$750
Air Transportation	$600

Calculate Ray's employee expense deduction for 1989.

Mileage $_____

Travel $_____

Transportation $_____

Total $_____

3.   Chee Chow, a college professor, accepted a position with the IRS in Washington
      D.C. The assignment was designated as temporary and was for a 12-month period.
      Chee left his wife and children in Houston and rented an apartment in Washington
      during his employment. Chee's AGI for the year is $50,000. He incurred the
      following expenses, none of which were reimbursed by the IRS.

      Air fare for weekend trips to visit his family-- $4,000

      Rent on Washington Apartment-- $10,000

      Meals, in Washington-- $5,000

      Entertainment of IRS employees-- $5,500

      Which, if any, of these expenses are deductible by Chee? Are they deductions for
      or from AGI?

Code Section Recognition

Indicate, by number, the appropriate Code Section where the following items
are found.

_____ 1. Deductions for adjusted gross income.

_____ 2. Transportation expenses.

_____ 3. Travel expenses.

_____ 4. Moving expense deduction.

_____ 5. Entertainment expenses deductions and limitations.

_____ 6. Office in the home.

SOLUTIONS TO CHAPTER 10

True or False

1. True   (p. 10-2)

2. True   (p. 10-2)

3. True   (p. 10-3)

4. True   (p. 10-4)

5. False Only certain deductions are subject to the 2% limitation. (p. 10-34)

6. True   (p. 10-2)

7. False The excess is income. (p. 10-9)

8. False They are different categories of deductions. (p. 10-15)

9. True   (p. 10-12)

10. True   (p. 10-12)

11. False They may use actual operating cost. (p. 10-13)

12. False Employees with two vehicles must use actual operating cost. (p. 10-14)

13. True   (p. 10-14)

14. False The taxpayer is limited to 11 cents per mile. (p. 10-14)

15. True   (p. 10-15)

16. True   (p. 10-34)

17. True   (p. 10-32)

18. False Employees may be given up to $400 if the gift is for retirement, etc. (p. 10-32)

19. False The taxpayer is being qualified for a new trade or business. (p. 10-25)

20. False The taxpayer has not met the minimum standards. (p. 10-25)

21. True   (p. 10-23)

22. True   (p. 10-22)

23. True   (p. 10-6)

24. False It is two times the rate. (p. 10-17)

25. True   (p. 10-18)

Fill-in-the-Blanks

1. temporary (p. 10-15)

2. 35 (p. 10-21)

3. 39, 78 (p. 10-21)

4. $1,500 (p. 10-23)

5. new (p. 10-25)

6. North America (p. 10-19)

7. existing, employer (p. 10-25)

8. directly, associated (p. 10-27)

9. principal, patients, clients, customers (p. 10-32)

10. employment, regular (p. 10-34)

Multiple Choice

1. E (p. 10-25)

2. B (p. 10-31)

3. C 24 cents (15,000) + 11 cents (5,000) = $4,150 from AGI. (p. 10-14)

4. E (p. 10-4)

5. A (p. 10-32)

6. A 80% of $120 plus $200 = $296 (p. 10-6, 10-15)

7. D $600 + 250 -(2% of $30,000) = $250. (p. 10-34)

8. C (p. 10-2)

9. D (p. 10-21)

10. C $5,500 - $3,000 = $2,500   (p. 10-32)

11. A It is all reimbursed (p. 10-9)

12. B $3,000 - (2% of $50,000) = $2,000   (p. 10-10)

Problems

1.

Transportation expenses		$4,000
Travel, $200 + .09(500)		245
House-hunting expenses	$800	
Temporary living expenses	$900	
Total	$1,700	
Amount of househunting and temporary living allowed	$1,500	
Qualified house sale expenses	$6,500	
Total	$8,000	
Amount of househunting, temporary living, and house sale expense allowed		$3,000
Moving deduction		$7,245

2.

Mileage (15,000 x .24) + (1,500 x .11)	$3,765
Travel ((80% of $200) + $550)	$710
Transportation	$600
Total	$5,075

3. The entertainment expenses are not deductible. The other expenses are deductible from AGI. Chee's total deduction would be as follows:

Air fare	$4,000
Rent	10,000
Meals (80%)	4,000

Total	$18,000
2% of AGI	(1,000)
Deduction	$17,000

Code Section Recognition

1. Section 62

2. Section 162

3. Section 162

4. Section 217

5. Section 274

6. Section 280A

11

DEDUCTIONS AND LOSSES: CERTAIN ITEMIZED DEDUCTIONS

CHAPTER HIGHLIGHTS

Personal expenses are generally disallowed as deductions. However, Congress has specified certain personal expenses to be allowed as itemized deductions. This chapter summarizes the provisions which allow deductions for medical expenses, state and local taxes, interest expenses, and charitable contributions.

I.   MEDICAL EXPENSES

A.   General Requirements.

Taxpayers are allowed a deduction for medical expenses for the care of the taxpayer, spouse, and dependents. Medical expenses are deductible only to the extent that they exceed 7.5 percent of adjusted gross income. The term medical care means expenditures incurred for the "diagnosis, cure, mitigation, treatment, or prevention of disease," or for "affecting any structure or function of the body."

Expenses to improve the taxpayer's general health such as programs to stop smoking or to lose weight are not deductible. The expenses must be for curing a specific ailment.

If a patient is placed in a nursing home for personal or family reasons, expenses are deductible only to the extent of actual medical or nursing attention received. If the patient is placed in the home primarily for medical reasons, the expenses are fully deductible.

The expenses of keeping a dependent at a special school for the mentally or physically handicapped may be deductible as medical expenses.

B. Capital improvements for medical care are deductible to the extent that the cost exceeds the increase in value of the related property. However, the cost for capital expenditures that enable a handicapped individual to live independently and productively are fully deductible.

C. Expenditures for transportation to and from the point of treatment are deductible as medical expenses. If taxpayers use their personal automobiles, then the deduction is 9 cents per mile. Qualified lodging that is part of medical care is deductible up to $50 per night per person.

D. Medical insurance premiums are included in medical expenses subject to the 7.5 percent limitation. A self-employed person who is not covered under a medical plan may deduct as a business expense (Schedule C) up to 25 percent of medical insurance for his or her family. Any excess can be claimed as a medical expenses.

E. Medical expenses for dependents are deductible if they are legitimate medical expenses. The gross income test and joint return test need not be met for a dependent to qualify for the medical deduction.

F. Reimbursements. If a taxpayer receives an insurance reimbursement for the medical expenses deducted in a previous year, the reimbursement must be included as income in the year of receipt. The reimbursement is income only if the expense provided a tax benefit in the previous year.

If the taxpayer used the standard deduction amount in the year the medical expenses were incurred instead of itemizing deductions, any reimbursements received need not be included in gross income.

II. TAXES

A. Taxpayers are allowed a deduction for the payment of certain state and local taxes to reduce the effect of multiple taxation. The law defines a tax as an enforced contribution exacted under legislative authority. Under Section 164, the following taxes are deductible:

state, local, and foreign real property taxes

state, and local personal property taxes

state, local, and foreign income taxes

windfall profit tax

environmental tax

Federal income taxes, employee Social Security taxes, estate and inheritance taxes, gift taxes, general sales taxes, and excise taxes cannot be deducted under this section.

B.   Property Taxes, Assessments, and Apportionment of Taxes.

For personal property taxes to be deductible, they must be ad valorem (assessed in relation to the value of the property). As a general rule, assessments are not deductible and are added to the adjusted basis of the property.

Real estate taxes are apportioned between the buyer and seller on the basis of the number of days the property was held by each. This apportionment is required without regard to whether the tax is paid by the buyer or seller.

C.   State and Local Income Taxes.

State and local taxes are deductible in the year paid by a cash basis taxpayer. Withholding and actual payments are deductible under this rule, and state and local tax refunds are income, providing there was a tax benefit in the prior year.

State and local income taxes incurred in a trade or business or for the production of income are deductions for AGI, not itemized deductions.

D.   Filing Requirements. Schedule A of Form 1040 is used to report deductible state and local taxes.

III.   INTEREST

A.   Taxpayers are allowed a deduction within limits for the following kinds of interest:

Trade or business interest

Investment interest

Interest on passive activities

Qualified home mortgage interest

The deduction for personal interest is being phased-out on the following schedule:

	Percentage Allowed
1987	65%
1988	40%
1989	20%
1990	10%

1991 and after, no deduction

B. Pre-1987 interest paid on funds borrowed for purchasing or holding investment property is deductible to the extent of $10,000 plus net investment income. Disallowed interest may be carried over and deducted in future years. For tax years 1987-1990, investment interest expense in excess of net investment income plus the same percentages listed above times $10,000 is allowed. After 1990, investment interest will only be deductible to the extent of net investment income.

C. Mortgage interest is deductible without percentage limits on a taxpayer's first and second residence for acquisition indebtedness up to a maximum of $1,000,000. The deductible interest on home equity borrowing is deductible on debt up to $100,000 ($50,000, if married filing separately). Special rules apply for debt acquired before October 13, 1987 (see text).

D. Restrictions on Deductibility and Timing Considerations. Interest is deductible if the related debt represents an obligation for which the taxpayer is liable. A taxpayer is not allowed a deduction for interest paid for someone else. The law limits the deduction for prepaid interest to "points" on a principal residence. All other prepaid interest must be capitalized and amortized over the life of the loan.

E. Classification of Timing Expense. Interest expense can be either a deduction for or a deduction from adjusted gross income, depending on whether the loan is for business, investment, or personal purposes. Deductions for interest charges on personal indebtedness are reported as an itemized deduction on Schedule A of Form 1040.

IV. CHARITABLE CONTRIBUTIONS

A. The Code permits the deduction of contributions made to qualified charitable organizations. The deduction is justified as a social consideration in the tax law.

B. Criteria of a Gift. To qualify as a charitable contribution, the gift must be made to a qualified organization. The major elements needed for a gift to be deductible are a donative intent, an absence of consideration, and acceptance by the donee.

C.   A qualified organization is:

A state or possession of the United States, or any subdivision thereof

An organization operated exclusively for religious, charitable, scientific, literary, or educational purpose or for the prevention of cruelty to children or animals

A veterans' organization

A fraternal organization operating under the lodge system

A cemetery

D.   Time of Payment. Charitable contributions are deductible in the year paid for both cash and accrual basis taxpayers. However, an accrual basis corporation can pledge a contribution at the end of the year and deduct it if the amount is paid within two and one-half months of the close of the tax year.

E.   As a general rule contributions of property are deducted at the fair market value of the property. Taxpayers must have one of the following to substantiate each charitable contribution of money:

A canceled check, or

A receipt from the donee, or

Other reliable written evidence.

For contributions of property less than $500, the taxpayer must have a receipt showing the donee, date, location, description of the property, fair market value, and certain other items. For gifts of over $500 the taxpayer must complete Form 8283 (either Part A or B).

F.   Limitations on Charitable Deductions.

There are limitations placed on the amount of charitable contributions. For individuals, the general A.G.I. limitations are:

50 percent for property contributions to certain public charities, all private operating foundations, and certain private nonoperating foundations (see text).

30 percent for contributions of cash and ordinary income property to private nonoperating foundations and contributions of appreciated capital gain property to 50 percent organizations. If the capital gain property is reduced by any appreciation on the property, then the 50

percent limit applies.

20 percent for contributions to private nonoperating foundations of capital gain property.

If ordinary income property is contributed, the deduction is equal to the fair market value of the property less the amount of ordinary income which would have been reported if the property were sold.

Contributions of services are not allowed as a deduction under Section 170 of the Code. Out-of-pocket expenses are allowed if there is no significant element of personal pleasure, recreation, or vacation in the travel.

Generally, contributions may be carried over for the next five years. However, capital gain property that is reduced by appreciation is not allowed as a carryover.

Contributions made during the carryover years are deducted before carryover amounts are applied.

If a contribution to a college or university carries the right to purchase athletic tickets, then 80% of the amount of the contribution is deductible.

V.   MISCELLANEOUS DEDUCTIONS

    A.   Taxpayers are allowed certain miscellaneous deductions if they exceed two percent of AGI. Examples of such deductions are:

           Moving expenses
           Professional dues
           Uniforms
           Tax return preparation fees
           Job hunting expenses
           Safe-deposit box fees
           Investment expenses
           Appraisals for casualty losses, donated property, etc.
           Hobby loss expenses

Miscellaneous deductions not subject to the two percent limitation are:

           Gambling losses
           Certain handicapped work expenses
           Certain casualty and theft losses
           Certain unrecovered annuity investments

TEST FOR SELF-EVALUATION

True or False

Indicate which of the following statements are true or false by circling the correct answers.

T   F   1.   For medical expenses to be deductible, they must be for the taxpayer, spouse or dependents.

T   F   2.   The term "medical care expenditure" would include an expense that has therapeutic benefits.

T   F   3.   Nursing home expenditures are always deductible as medical expenses.

T   F   4.   Under certain circumstances, capital expenditures can be deducted as medical expenses.

T   F   5.   Special schools for the mentally or physically handicapped may be deductible as a medical expense.

T   F   6.   For nonself-employed taxpayers, 100 percent of medical insurance premiums are subject to the 7.5 percent limitation on adjusted gross income.

T   F   7.   The term "medicine and drugs" does not include toothpaste, shaving lotion, deodorants, and hand lotions.

T   F   8.   Birth control pills, if prescribed by a physician, are considered medicine and are deductible.

T   F   9.   All medicine and drugs are deductible.

T   F   10. If a taxpayer is reimbursed for medical expenses that were paid in a previous year, he or she must always include that amount in income.

T   F   11. All amounts paid to a government are deductible under Section 164 as a tax.

T   F   12. A tax is "an enforced contribution exacted under legislative authority in the exercise of taxing power, and imposed and collected for raising revenue to be used for public or governmental purposes."

T   F   13. State, local, and foreign income taxes are deductible for Federal tax purposes.

T   F   14. For personal property taxes to be deductible, they must be ad valorem, that is assessed in relation to the value of the property.

T   F   15. Real property taxes include taxes assessed for local benefits such as new streets and sidewalks.

T F 16. Real property taxes are apportioned between the buyer and seller on the basis of the number of days each held the property.

T F 17. State income taxes are always deducted on the accrual method.

T F 18. For 1989 only 20 percent of personal interest is deductible by taxpayers.

T F 19. If cash contributions of $3,000 or more are made to one organization, then the name and amount must be reported on the taxpayer's return.

T F 20. Property donated to a charity is generally valued at fair market value at the time of the gift.

T F 21. Any charitable contribution is deductible for tax purposes.

T F 22. Interest on a principle residence mortgage is not deductible.

T F 23. For 1989, the investment interest limitation is the excess investment interest over net investment income plus 20% of $10,000.

T F 24. The interest deduction is always a deduction for adjusted gross income.

T F 25. The estate and gift taxes are deductible for income tax purposes.

Fill-in-the-Blanks

Complete the following statements with the appropriate word(s) or amount(s).

1. Interest has been defined by the Supreme Court as _____ for the use or forbearance of money.

2. For an interest payment to be deductible, the payment must be the taxpayer's _____.

3. The tax law requires that prepaid interest except for "points" on a personal residence be _____ and allocated to the subsequent periods to which the interest payments relate.

4. Excess annual contributions to public charities subject to the 50 percent and 20 percent limitations are carried forward for _____ years.

5. Fees paid to mortgage loan companies for finding, placing, or processing a mortgage loan are called _____.

6. For a charitable contribution to be deductible, the gift must be made to a

_____ organization.

7.   Property donated to a charity is generally valued at fair _____ value.

8.   The maximum limitation on charitable contributions for individuals is
        _____ percent of adjusted gross income.

Multiple Choice

Choose the best answer for each of the following questions.

_____ 1.   Steve Linberg borrows $150,000 at 10% interest on January 3, 1989. The
            proceeds are used to purchase $100,000 worth of raw land and $50,000
            worth of stock in Exxon. During 1989 the stock pays dividends of $2,500.
            Steve has expenses on this investment property of $500. Of the $15,000
            (10% of $150,000) of interest paid in 1989, how much is deductible?
            a. -0-
            b. $12,000
            c. $4,000
            d. $15,000
            e. Some other amount

_____ 2.   During 1989 Mary Adams had adjusted gross income of $30,000 in a year in
            which she paid the following medical expenses:

                    Medical insurance   560
                    Dentist's charges   600
                    Physicians' charges   1,000
                    Drugs   100
                    Hospital costs   400

            What is Mary's medical expense deduction?
            a. -0-
            b. $2,660
            c. $410
            d. $1,160
            e. Some other amount

_____ 3.   During the current year, T paid $65 for California license plates for his
            automobile. California plates are sold at a fee of $23 plus $2 per hundred
            dollar valuation of the automobile. How much, if any, may T claim as a
            deduction?
            a. -0-
            b. $25
            c. $42
            d. $67

e. Some other amount

For Questions 4 through 8, indicate the amount of charitable deductions T would be allowed in each of the independent situations.

_____ 4.   In 1989 T donated an art object to Goodwill Industries, a qualified charity. The art object cost T $2,000 five months ago and has a fair market value of $3,000 on the date of donation.
a. -0-
b. $2,000
c. $2,500
d. $3,000
e. Some other amount

_____ 5.   Assume the same situation as in Question 4, except the art object possesses a fair market value of $1,800 (not $3,000) on the date of donation.
a. -0-
b. $1,800
c. $2,000
d. $1,900
e. Some other amount

_____ 6.   T donated shares of Texaco stock to his church in satisfaction of last year's church pledge. The stocks cost T $3,200 two years ago and possessed a fair market value of $2,700 on the date of donation.
a. -0-
b. $2,700
c. $3,200
d. $2,950
e. Some other amount

_____ 7.   T donated $650 of his time as a painter and paint with a cost basis to him of $200 paint to help fix up his church. How much can he deduct?
a. -0-
b. $850
c. $650
d. $200
e. Some other amount

_____ 8.   T works for the American Red Cross for free in each month during the current year. He would normally charge $400 per month for the type work performed. What is T's charitable deduction?
a. -0-
b. $400
c. $4,800
d. Some other amount

_____ 9.   What is the maximum amount of property contribution that a taxpayer may

give a qualified organization without completing Form 8283?
a. -0-
b. $200
c. $499
d. $3,000
e. Some other amount

_____ 10. Pat Sbarbaro is a cash basis taxpayer who had $1,000 of state income tax withheld from her salary in 1989. In addition she had a refund from her 1988 state income taxes of $250. During 1989 Pat also made estimated state payments of $600. For 1989, Pat's state income tax deduction is:
a. -0-
b. $1,350
c. $1,000
d. $1,600
e. Some other amount

_____ 11. Gene Hallner owns his own home which he bought several years ago. His original mortgage, which was used to buy the house, is $150,000. In the current year he obtains a home equity loan on the house of $90,000. The interest on the original mortgage is $15,000 and on the new loan is $10,000. The fair market value of the house is $325,000. How much of this interest is deductible as "qualified home mortgage" interest?
a. $-0-
b. $10,000
c. $15,000
d. $25,000
e. Some other amount

_____ 12. Which of the following items will not qualify for a medical expense deduction?
a. Eyeglasses
b. Birth control pills
c. A trip to Arizona for the general improvement of health
d. Transportation to and from a doctor's office
e. None of the above

_____ 13. The prepaid interest rules of Section 461(g) apply to all prepaid interest payments except which of the following?
a. "Points" on a rental house
b. Construction loans
c. Bank auto loans
d. "Points" paid by a buyer on a personal residence
e. None of the above

_____ 14. Big Booster gives $1,000 to his alma mater's athletic department. Such a contribution gives him four football tickets worth $200. How much is Big's charitable contribution deduction?

a.   -0-
b. $1,000
c. $800
d. $640
e. Some other amount

Eric Ross, who is single and has no dependents, had adjusted gross income of $80,000 in 1989, comprised of the following:

Salary	$74,000
Net investment income	6,000

During 1989, uninsured art objects owned by Eric, with a basis of $50,000 and a fair market value of $70,000, sustained casualty fire damage reducing the fair market value to $60,000. Also during 1989, Eric made the following payments:

Interest on margin account at stockbroker	$18,000
Real estate taxes on condo-minium owned by Eric's mother, in which Eric resides	3,000
State and city gasoline taxes	180
Medical insurance premiums	300
Unreimbursed dental expenses	4,500
Contribution to political committee of elected public official	500

Eric elected to itemize his deductions for 1989. (CPA adapted)

_____   15.   How much can Eric claim as taxes in itemized deductions on his 1989 return?
a. $0
b. $180
c. $3,000
d. $3,180

_____   16.   How much can Eric claim in his itemized deductions for medical and dental expenses on his 1989 return?
a. $2,400
b. $800
c. $300
d. $-0-

_____   17.   How much can Eric claim in his itemized deductions for the casualty loss on his 1989 return?
a. $0

b. $1,900
c. $2,000
d. $9,900

Problem

1.   Ted and Joyce Skekel had the following incomes and expenses for 1989:

Adjusted gross income	$31,500
Medical insurance	500
Doctor bills	1,000
Prescription drugs	200
Hospital bills	1,000
Medical insurance reimbursement	1,200
State income tax	950
Real estate taxes	775
Home mortgage interest	7,150
Personal interest	625
Contribution to church (by check)	450
Tax return preparation fee	225
Professional dues	600
Contribution of used goods to Goodwill	150
Contribution carryover from 1988	625

They file a joint return. Calculate Ted and Joyce's itemized deductions using the worksheet below.

Medicine and drugs   _____

Other medical   _____

Insurance reimbursement   (_____)

Total   _____

Less 7.5% of A.G.I.   (_____)

Medical Deduction   _____

Taxes   _____

Interest   _____

Contributions   _____

Miscellaneous   _____

Total Deductions   _____

Code Section Recognition

Indicate, by number, the appropriate Code Section where the following items are found.

_____ 1. Disallowance of personal expenditures.

_____ 2. Medical expense deduction.

_____ 3. Deduction for taxes.

_____ 4. The interest deduction.

_____ 5. Deduction for charitable contributions.

SOLUTIONS TO CHAPTER 11

True or False

1. True   (p. 11-2)

2. True   (p. 11-2)

3. False   The expenditure must be primarily for medical reasons. (p. 11-3)

4. True   (p. 11-4)

5. True   (p. 11-3)

6. True   (p. 11-5)

7. True   (p. 11-3)

8. True   (p. 11-3)

9. False   Only prescription drugs and insulin are deductible. (p. 11-3)

10. False   It is income only to the extent of a tax benefit. (p. 11-7)

11. False   Fees are not deductible. (p. 11-8)

12. True   (p. 11-8)

13. True   (p. 11-9)

14. True   (p. 11-9)

15. False   Assessments usually increase the basis of the property. (p. 11-10)

16. True   (p. 11-10)

17. False   Individuals deduct state income taxes on the cash method. (p. 11-11)

18. True   (p. 11-13)

19. True   (p. 11-21)

20. True   (p. 11-21)

21. False   There are limits equal to 50%, 30% and 20% of AGI. (p. 11-22)

22. False   Interest on mortgages is deductible. (p. 11-15)

23. True   (p. 11-13)

24. False   Personal interest is a deduction from AGI. (p. 11-18)

25. False   Estate and gift taxes are not deductible. (p. 11-9)

Fill-in-the-Blanks

1. compensation (p. 11-12)

2. obligation (p. 11-17)

3. capitalized (p. 11-17)

4. five (p. 11-22)

5. "points" (p. 11-16)

6. qualified (p. 11-19)

7. market (p. 11-22)

8. 50 (p. 11-22)

Multiple Choice

1. C ($2,500 - 500) + 20%($10,000) = $4,000. (p. 11-13)

2. C

Drugs	100
Insurance	560
Dentists	600
Physicians	1,000
Hospitals	400
	2,660
Less 7.5% (AGI)	(2,250)
Medical deduction	$410 (p. 11-3)

3. C $65 - 23 = $42. (p. 11-8)

4. B $3,000 - (3,000 - 2,000) = $2,000 ordinary income property. (p. 11-22)

5. B $1,800 - 0 = $1,800. (p. 11-22)

6. B Fair market value is used if the stock does not meet any exceptions. (p. 11-23)

7. D Donation of service is not deductible (p. 11-24)

8. A Donation of free rent (service) is not deductible. (p. 11-23)

9. C (p. 11-21)

10. D $1,000 + 600 = $1,600 (p. 11-11)

11. D All the debt qualifies (p. 11-15)

12. C (p. 11-3)

13. D (p. 11-30)

14. D ($1,000 -$200) x 80% = $640   (p. 11-19)

15. A A taxpayer must own real estate to deduct any taxes on it. (p. 11-9)

16. D $4,500 + $300 - 7.5%($80,000) = $-0-   (p. 11-3)

17. B $10,000 - $100 - 10%($80,000) = $1,900 (see previous chapter)

Problem

1.   Medicine and drugs $200

       Other medical
       $500 + $1000 + $1000   2,500

Insurance reimbursement	(1,200)	
Total	1,500	
Less 7.5% of A.G.I.	(2,363)	
Medical Deduction		-0-
Taxes $950 + $775		1,725
Interest $7,150 + (20% x $625)		7,275
Contributions $450 + $150 + $625		1,225
Miscellaneous $225 + $600 - 2% AGI		195
Total Deductions		10,420

Code Section Recognition

1. Section 262

2. Section 213

3. Section 164

4. Section 163

5. Section 170

12

ALTERNATIVE MINIMUM TAX

CHAPTER HIGHLIGHTS

This chapter deals with those situations where there is an alternative computation of tax liability for individuals and corporations. The purpose of the alternative minimum tax is to prevent taxpayers from reducing their tax liability below certain levels. In general, the alternative minimum tax is a special tax on "loopholes" that keeps taxpayers from using several tax preferences in combination to avoid most of their tax liability.

I. THE INDIVIDUAL ALTERNATIVE MINIMUM TAX

    A.   The alternative minimum tax (AMT) must be paid if it produces a greater tax liability than an individual taxpayer would otherwise pay. This "extra" tax prevents wealthy taxpayers from completely avoiding the Federal income tax through the use of tax preferences.

    B.   The first step in the calculation of the AMT is the determination of alternative minimum taxable income (AMTI). AMTI is defined as:

           Taxable income
           Plus: Positive AMT adjustments
           Minus: Negative AMT adjustments
           Equals: Taxable income after AMT adjustments
           Plus: Tax preferences
           Equals: Alternative minimum taxable income

As shown in the AMTI formula, taxable income is increased by positive adjustments and decreased by negative adjustments. Many of the positive adjustments arise because of timing differences related to the deductions for regular tax purposes. When these timing differences are reversed, negative adjustments are made.

C.   The AMT adjustments include:

> Circulation expenditures
> Certain depreciation on post-1986 real property
> Certain depreciation on post-1986 personal property
> Research and experimental expenditures
> Passive activity losses
> Passive farm losses
> Use of completed contract accounting
> Alternative NOL deduction
> Certain itemized deductions
> The standard deduction

D.   The AMT tax preferences are always an addition to taxable income. Tax preferences include the following:

> Percentage depletion
> Intangible drilling cost
> Charitable contributions of appreciated property
> Interest on certain private activity bonds
> Incentive stock options

E.   The complete formula for computing the alternative minimum tax is as follows:

> Regular taxable income
> Plus or minus: Adjustments
> Plus: Tax Preferences
> Equals: Alternative minimum taxable income
> Minus: Exemption
> Equals: Alternative minimum tax base
> Times: 21% rate
> Equals: Tentative minimum tax before foreign tax credit
> Minus: Alternative minimum tax foreign tax credit
> Equals: Tentative minimum tax
> Minus: Regular tax liability
> Equals: Alternative minimum tax

D.   AMT Credit. To provide equity for taxpayers when timing differences reverse, the regular tax liability may be reduced by a tax credit for prior years' minimum tax liability attributable to timing differences. The credit may be carried over indefinitely, on a FIFO basis.

E.   The alternative minimum tax exemption is equal to $40,000 for married taxpayers filing joint returns, $30,000 for single taxpayers, and $20,000 for married taxpayers filing separate returns. The 25 percent phase-out of the exemption credit begins when alternative minimum taxable income exceeds the following levels:

$112,500 for single taxpayers

$150,000 for married taxpayers filing jointly

$75,000 for married taxpayers filing separately

II.   THE CORPORATE ALTERNATIVE MINIMUM TAX

A.   The corporate alternative minimum tax is similar to the individual AMT. However, corporations have additional adjustments and tax preferences that do not apply to individuals and the AMT rate is 20% instead of 21%. The corporate AMT tax formula is:

Regular taxable income (before NOLs)
Plus/minus: AMT adjustments
Plus: Tax preferences
Equals: AMT before NOL
Minus: AMT NOL (limited to 90%)
Equals: Alternative minimum taxable income (AMTI)
Minus: Exemption
Equals: Alternative minimum tax base
Times: 20%
Equals: AMT before AMT foreign tax credit
Minus: AMT foreign tax credit
Equals: Tentative AMT
Minus: Regular tax before less regular foreign tax credit
Alternative minimum tax

B.   Corporate AMT adjustments include the following:

Certain accelerated depreciation of post-1986 real property

Certain excess mining exploration costs

Certain long-term contract timing differences

A portion of business untaxed reported profits (BURP)

The BURP adjustment is equal to 50% of the difference between pretax book income and AMTI. After 1989 current earnings and profits will replace book income in determining the BURP adjustment.

C.   The common corporate AMT preferences include:

      Amortization of pollution control facilities

      Pre-1987 excess accelerated depreciation on realty

      Certain tax-exempt interest on private activity bonds

      Excess percentage depletion

      Certain intangible drilling costs

      Untaxed appreciation on property donated to charity

D.   The exemption amount for corporations is $40,000, reduced by 25% of the amount by which AMTI exceeds $150,000.

TEST FOR SELF-EVALUATION

True or False

Indicate which of the following statements are true or false by circling the correct answers.

T   F   1.   The alternative minimum tax is beneficial to most individual taxpayers making over $100,000 per year.

T   F   2.   For 1989, the rate for the individual alternative minimum tax is 21 percent.

T   F   3.   The AMT exemption for single taxpayers is $30,000.

T   F   4.   The AMT exemption is reduced 25 cents on the dollar above specified amounts.

T   F   5.   Casualty losses are allowed in calculating alternative minimum taxable income for individuals.

T   F   6.   Tentative AMT less the regular tax liability is the AMT due.

T   F   7.   Net appreciation on contributed capital gains property is not subject to tax under the AMT.

T   F   8.   The alternative tax net operating loss cannot offset more than 90% of alternative minimum taxable income.

T   F   9.   The difference between ACRS depreciation and ADS (alternative depreciation system) is a timing difference adjustment for AMT purposes.

T   F   10. Intangible drilling costs in excess of 50% of net income from oil, gas, and geothermal properties is an AMT tax preference.

T   F   11. For AMT purposes, the cost of certified pollution control facilities placed in service after 1986 must be depreciated over the ADS class life.

T   F   12. Interest on a home mortgage is deductible in calculating the alternative minimum tax.

T   F   13. The corporate AMT tax rate is 25%.

T   F   14. The business untaxed reported profits (BURP) adjustment for the corporate AMT is equal to 50% of the difference between book income and taxable income.

T   F   15. Losses on passive activities acquired after October 22, 1986 are not deductible in computing either the regular income or the AMT.

T   F   16.   Taxpayers are required to use the percentage-of-completion method for AMT computation for long-term contracts.

T   F   17.   For individual AMT calculation, medical expenses are deductible to the extent they exceed 7.5 percent of AGI.

T   F   18.   Consumer interest is not deductible for the individual alternative minimum tax.

T   F   19.   An individual's regular tax liability may be reduced by a credit for prior years' minimum tax liability attributable to timing differences.

T   F   20.   The corporate AMT exemption is $40,000 reduced by 25% of the excess of AMT over $100,000.

T   F   21.   The corporate AMT NOL is limited to 90 percent of the corporation's AMTI.

Fill-in-the-Blanks

Complete the following statements with the appropriate word(s) or amount(s).

1.   The individual alternative minimum tax rate for 1989 is _____ percent.

2.   The corporate AMT foreign tax credit is limited to _____ percent of AMT liability before the AMT foreign tax credit.

3.   After 1989, the business untaxed reported profits adjustments for the corporate AMT will be based on _____ and _____, not pretax book income.

4.   Form _____ is the individual AMT form.

5.   The individual AMT credit may be carried forward _____.

6.   The alternative minimum tax exemption for married taxpayers filing jointly is $_____ for 1989.

Multiple Choice

Choose the best answer for each of the following questions.

_____   1.   For 1989, Carolyn Glasner's taxable income is $300,000. She has tax preferences of $75,000 and positive adjustments of $40,000. What is Carolyn's alternative minimum taxable income?

a. $300,000
b. $375,000
c. $415,000
d. $340,000
e. Some other amount

_____ 2. For question number 1, what is Carolyn's alternative minimum tax?
a.   -0-
b. $87,150
c. $63,000
d. $78,750
e. Some other amount

_____ 3. Which of the following is not allowed as a deduction for the alternative minimum tax?
a. Gambling losses
b. State income taxes
c. Charitable contributions
d. Casualty losses

_____ 4. The Carol Smith is single and has AMTI of $140,000. What is Carol's exemption for the AMT?
a.   -0-
b. $20,000
c. $23,125
d. $30,000
e. Some other amount

_____ 5. On nonresidential real property the AMT depreciation (ADS) is based on a life of how many years?
a. 27.5
b. 31.5
c. 35
d. 40
e. None of the above

_____ 6. In 1989, T incurs mine exploration costs of $200,000 which is deducted for regular income tax purposes. What is T's adjustment for AMTI for 1989?
a.   -0-
b. Positive $200,000
c. Positive $180,000
d. Negative $160,000
e. Some other amount

_____ 7. For question number 6, what is T's adjustment for 1990?
a.   -0-
b. Negative $20,000
c. Negative $40,000

     d. Positive $200,000
     e. Some other amount

_____ 8.   For 1989 T corporation's pretax book income is $400,000 and the corporation has a $100,000 loss for tax purposes. What is T's business untaxed reported profits AMT adjustment?
     a. -0-
     b. $300,000
     c. $500,000
     d. $250,000
     e. Some other amount

_____ 9.   In 1989, T incurred a net operating loss of $200,000. T had no AMT adjustments, but deducted tax preferences of $30,000. What is T's AMT NOL carryover into 1990?
     a. -0-
     b. $170,000
     c. $200,000
     d. $30,000
     e. Some other amount

_____ 10.   T, whose AGI is $70,000, incurred medical expenses of $10,000 during the year. What is T's adjustment, if any, for the individual AMT?
     a. -0-
     b. Negative $1,750
     c. Positive $1,750
     d. Negative $7,000
     e. Some other amount

Code Section Recognition

Indicate, by number, the appropriate Code Section where each of the following items are found.

_____ 1. Alternative minimum tax.

_____ 2. The tax preferences.

_____ 3. The alternative minimum tax adjustments.

SOLUTIONS TO CHAPTER 12

True or False

1. False The AMT is a penalty type tax on wealthy taxpayers. (p. 12-3)

2. True   (p. 12-22)

3. True   (p. 12-21)

4. True   (p. 12-22)

5. True   (p. 12-14)

6. True   (p. 12-21)

7. False It is subject to tax. (p. 12-5)

8. True   (p. 12-25)

9. True   (p. 12-4)

10. False It is in excess of 65%. (p. 12-5)

11. True   (p. 12-7)

12. True   (p. 12-15)

13. False The rate is 20%. (p. 12-29)

14. True   (p. 12-27)

15. True   (p. 12-9)

16. True   (p. 12-12)

17. False The percent is 10%.   (p. 12-14)

18. True   (p. 12-15)

19. True   (p. 12-4)

20. False It is over $150,000. (p. 12-29)

21. True   (p. 12-26)

Fill-in-the-Blanks

1. 21% (p. 12-22)

2. 90% (p. 12-16)

3. earnings, profits (p. 12-27)

4. 6251 (p. App. B)

5. indefinitely (p. 12-23)

6. $40,000 (12-21)

Multiple Choice

1. C $300,000 + $115,000 = $415,000   (p. 12-21)

2. B $415,000 x 21% = $87,150   (p. 12-21)

3. B (p. 12-14)

4. C $30,000 - 25%($140,000 - $112,500) = $23,125 (p. 12-21)

5. D (p. 12-6)

6. C $200,000 - ($200,000/10years) = $180,000 (p. 12-8)

7. B 0 - $20,000 = ($20,000) (p. 12-8)

8. D $400,000 - (-$100,000) = $500,000 x 50% = $250,000 (p. 12-27)

9. B $200,000 - $30,000 = $170,000   (p. 12-13)

10. C [$10,000 - 7.5%(70,000)] - [$10,000 - 10%($70,000)] = $1,750 (p. 12-14)

Code Section Recognition

1. Section 55

2. Section 57

3. Section 56

13

TAX CREDITS AND PAYMENT PROCEDURES

CHAPTER HIGHLIGHTS

This chapter discusses various tax credits currently allowed by the tax law and payment procedures for withholding as well as for self-employed taxpayers.

I.   SPECIFIC BUSINESS RELATED TAX CREDIT PROVISIONS

   A.   Investment Tax Credit.

      The investment tax credit (ITC) was designed to spur investment in capital goods. It is comprised of these components: the regular ITC, the credit for rehabilitation expenditures, and the business energy credit. The regular ITC was repealed for most tangible property placed in service after 1985. The latter two components are discussed later.

      If ITC property is prematurely disposed of or ceases to be qualified ITC property, a percentage of the investment credit previously taken will be recaptured. The portion that is recaptured is added to the taxpayer's regular tax liability for the recapture year. Recapture is triggered by the following events if they take place before the required holding period:

         disposition of property through sale, exchange, or sale and lease-back transactions retirement or abandonment of property or conversion to personal use

gifts of ITC property

transfers to partnerships and corporations unless certain conditions are met

like-kind exchanges (with certain exceptions)

The following events are exceptions to the recapture rule:

a transfer by reason of death

a transfer under certain tax-free reorganizations

a liquidation of a subsidiary corporation where the assets are transferred to the parent without a change in basis

a transfer of property between spouses or incident to divorce

Investment tax credits that were earned before 1986 may be carried forward and used in tax years beginning before January 1, 1987. Any ITC carried forward into years after July 1, 1987 must be reduced by a specified percentage.

B.   Tax Credit for Rehabilitation Expenditures.

For tax years after 1981 taxpayers are allowed a credit for rehabilitating industrial and commercial buildings. The credit is 10 percent for nonresidential buildings other than historical structures originally placed in service before 1936 and 20 percent for certified historic structures. To qualify for the credit, the expenditure must exceed the greater of the adjusted basis of the property before the rehabilitation or $5,000.

The rehabilitation credit must be recaptured if the property is disposed of prematurely or if it ceases to be qualifying property.

C.   Three business energy credits remain through December 31, 1989 to encourage the conservation of natural resources and to develop alternate energy sources. These are the credits for solar energy property (10%), geothermal (10%), and ocean thermal property (15%).

D.   Jobs Credit.

Taxpayers may elect to take a jobs credit for tax years after 1978 and before 1990. The jobs credit is 40 percent of the first $6,000 of wages per employee for the first year of employment. Eligible employees include certain disadvantaged individuals (e.g. youth from low-income families, ex-convicts, and handicapped individuals). The wage expense deduction is reduced by the amount of credit claimed.

A special credit is allowed for qualified summer youth employees. The maximum eligible wages for this credit are $3,000 per employee at a tax credit rate of 40 percent.

E.   Incremental Research Activities Credit.

To encourage research and experimental development, taxpayers are allowed a 20 percent credit for qualifying incremental expenditures. The credit only applies to expenditures which exceed the average amount of expenditures for the base period (usually the three preceding tax years). The base period expenses may not be less than 50 percent of the expenses in the determination year.

The following conditions must be met for the expenditure to qualify:

The expenditure must qualify under Sec 174

It must be technological in nature

The research must be intended to be useful in the development of a new or improved business component of the taxpayer

A business component is any product, process, computer software, technique, formula, or invention held for sale, lease, or license, or used by the taxpayer in a trade or business.

The credit is treated as a general business credit and therefore may be subject to limitation. However any unused credit may be carried back three years and forward 15 years.

F.   Basic Research Credit. Corporations are allowed an additional 20 percent credit for basic research expenditures paid to a qualified research organization in excess of a base amount.

G.   Low-Income Housing Credit. Owners of qualified low-income housing projects are allowed a credit based on the qualified basis of the property. The credit is currently 9 percent for newly constructed and rehabilitated property.

II.   OTHER TAX CREDITS

A.   Earned Income Credit.

The earned income credit is designed to help certain low income taxpayers.

For 1988, the credit is 14 percent of the first $6,240 in wages, reduced by 10 percent of adjusted gross income (or, if greater, earned income) over $9,850. To qualify the individual must meet one of the following conditions:

Married and entitled to an exemption for a child

Surviving spouse with a child who qualifies as a dependent

Head of household with an unmarried child who does not need to be a dependent or with a married child who does need to be a dependent.

The earned income credit is a form of negative income tax because a taxpayer can receive a refundable credit even if no tax is due.

B.   Tax Credit for Elderly or Disabled Taxpayers.

To qualify for the elderly credit, the taxpayer must be 65 years old, or if under 65 must be retired with disability income from a public or private employer because of the disability. The credit is 15 percent of $5,000 (single taxpayers or one spouse over 65), $7,500 (married with both spouses over 65), or $3,750 (married filing separately). The credit is reduced by social security, railroad retirement, and one-half of adjusted gross income over certain amounts ($7,500 for single taxpayers, $10,000 married filing jointly, and $5,000 for married filing separately).

C.   Foreign Tax Credit.

Individual and corporate taxpayers may claim a tax credit for foreign income tax paid on income earned and subject to tax in a country or U.S. possession. Unused foreign tax credits may be carried back two years and forward five years.

The foreign tax credit equals the lesser of the foreign taxes actually paid or the limitation computed using the following formula:

$$\frac{\text{Foreign income}}{\text{Total taxable income}} \times \text{U.S. tax liability}$$

D.   Credit for Child and Dependent Care Expenses.

Taxpayers are allowed a credit for child and dependent care expenses. The credit is 30 percent of expenses reduced by one percent for every $2,000 (or fraction thereof) of AGI over $10,000, but not below 20 percent. The maximum qualifying expenses in any one year are $2,400 for one qualifying individual and $4,800 for two or more individuals. For married taxpayers, the expenses are limited to the spouse with the least amount of earned income. A taxpayer qualifies for the credit if he or she maintains a household for either of the following:

> a dependent child under age 13

> a dependent or spouse who is physically or mentally incapacitated

Special rules allow students to qualify for the credit. A spouse who is a full-time student is deemed to have earned income of $200 per month for one qualifying individual or $400 per month if there are two or more qualifying individuals in the household.

E.   Credit for Mortgage Interest Paid.

Qualified home buyers are allowed to claim a tax credit for a portion of mortgage interest paid. The credit is the product of the certificate rate and the mortgage interest paid. The certificate rate must be at least 10 percent, but not more than 50 percent. If the credit rate exceeds 20 percent the credit is limited to $2,000 per year. Any interest deduction is reduced by the credit claimed.

III.   PRIORITY OF CREDITS

A.   Nonrefundable credits are those that are not refunded if they exceed the taxpayer's tax liability. Refundable credits are those such as the earned income credit which are refunded even if the amount exceeds the taxpayer's tax liability.

The order in which credits are offset against tax liability is specified in the Code. This order can be important since certain credits are not subject to carryover provisions and will be lost if not offset against current tax liability. The specific order of nonrefundable credits is as follows:

> Nonrefundable personal credits

>> child care credit

>> elderly and disabled credit

>> mortgage certificate credit

> Foreign tax credit(s)

> Orphan drugs testing credit

> Nonconventional source fuel credit

General business credits, the sum of the following

investment credit

jobs credit

alcohol fuels credit

research activities credit

low-income housing credit

B.   General Business Credits.

The maximum general business credit in any one year is the taxpayer's net income tax reduced by the greater of the tentative minimum tax or 25 percent of the net regular tax liability over $25,000. Unused general business credits are carried back three years and carried forward fifteen years. If more than one carryover credit is available in a tax year, the FIFO method is applied to the carrybacks, carryovers, and presently earned credits.

IV. PAYMENT PROCEDURES

A.   Procedures Applicable to Employers.

Employers are required to withhold Federal income tax, FICA, and other amounts from employees' paychecks. The IRS publishes a list of which employees and wages require Federal withholding. The procedure involves the following three steps.

1)   Have the employee complete Form W-4.

2)   Determine the employee's payroll period.

3)   Compute the amount to be withheld using the wage bracket table or the percentage method.

The percentage method of calculating withholding requires the following procedures:

a)   Multiply the amount of one allowance (see text) by the employee's total allowances.

b)   Reduce the employee's wages by the amount in step a.

c)   Use the results in step b. to compute the withholding from the proper percentage-method table (see text).

Reporting and payment procedures require that the employer file the following forms with the IRS:

Form SS-4 provides the employer with an identification number which must be used on all other forms filed with the government.

Form W-2 is a summary of each employee's wages and the amounts withheld. The Form W-2 must be furnished to the employee no later than January 31 of the following year.

Form W-3 is a summary of withholdings for all employees and is filed along with a copy of each Form W-2.

Form 940 is used for the employer's annual accounting for FUTA.

Form 941 must be filed quarterly summarizing income tax and FICA withholdings. Any balance due over prior remittances for withholdings must accompany this form.

Form 8109 (Federal Tax Deposits) accompanies the monthly or eighth monthly deposits of withholding when such deposits are required (see text).

B.   Withholding on Pensions.

Income tax withholding for pension payments is mandatory under the tax law unless the taxpayer elects to have no tax withheld. Periodic payments are subject to the same withholding rates as wages, while nonperiodic payments are subject to a flat 10 percent rate.

C.   Backup Withholding.

Certain taxpayers may be subject to "backup withholding" on interest and dividend payments. The backup withholding is designed to make sure that taxpayers report all their investment income. For example backup withholding applies if a taxpayer does not give his or her identification number to a bank so that any income can be reported on Form 1099.

D.   Procedures Applicable to Self-employed Persons.

Taxpayers who are in certain situations or who are self-employed must file a declaration of estimated tax (Form 1040ES). These are installment payments due on April 15, June 15, September 15 of the current year and January 15 of the following year. The required payment is the lesser of the following amounts:

90 percent of the current year's tax

100 percent of last year's tax

90 percent of the current year's tax, including the alternative minimum tax and self-employment tax on an annualized basis.

No payment is required if the estimated tax is under $500. An underpayment occurs when any installment is less than 25 percent of the required annual payment. The penalty for underpayment is based on the average prime rate for the most recent quarter and is calculated on a quarterly basis.

E.   The Self-Employment (SE) Tax.

Self-employed taxpayers are required to pay a self-employment tax, which is for Social Security. Individuals with net earnings from self-employment of $400 or more are subject to this tax. For 1989 the SE tax is 13.02 percent of the first $48,000 of SE income. Beginning in 1990, the rate will increase to 15.30 percent, but taxpayers will be allowed an income tax deduction for one-half of the self-employment tax paid. The maximum income base is reduced by any wages the taxpayer has that are subject to the regular Social Security tax (FICA). Schedule SE is used to calculate the self-employment tax.

TEST FOR SELF-EVALUATION

True or False

Indicate which of the following statements are true or false by circling the correct answers.

T F 1. In general, the investment tax credit has been repealed for tax years after 1985.

T F 2. The basic research credit is 25 percent for tax years after 1986.

T F 3. The highest rate for the low-income housing credit is nine percent.

T F 4. If investment credit property is prematurely disposed of or ceases to qualify as investment property, the investment credit which was previously taken must be recaptured in whole or in part.

T F 5. A transfer of property by reason of death will not cause the recapture of investment credit.

T F 6. For 1988, the earned income credit is 14 percent of the first $6,240 of earned income, reduced by 10 percent of adjusted gross income (or, if greater, earned income) over $9,850.

T F 7. A married individual must file a joint return to receive the benefits of the earned income credit.

T F 8. The earned income credit is a form of negative income tax and can be refunded even if no tax is due.

T F 9. To be eligible for the earned income credit, an individual must maintain a household which is the principal abode of a dependent relative.

T F 10. The tax credit for the elderly is 20 percent of the Section 37 amount, reduced by social security, railroad retirement benefits, and certain pensions.

T F 11. The maximum dependent care credit for three qualifying children is $800.

T F 12. A spouse may qualify for the dependent care credit.

T F 13. Transfers of property do not qualify for the 20 percent basic research credit.

T F 14. The maximum amount of general business credits than can be taken in one year is the taxpayer's net income tax reduced by the greater of tentative minimum tax or 25% of net regular tax over $25,000.

T F 15. If an employee has no regular payroll period, then he or she is considered to be paid on a daily basis.

T F 16. The wage bracket method of withholding calculation requires more computation than the percentage method.

T F 17. Employers can always wait until the end of their taxable year before filing the required form for payroll withholding, and they do not have to deposit the withholding until the end of the year.

T F 18. The penalty for underpayment of tax can be avoided if quarterly payments (including amount withheld) are equal to or exceed the prior year's tax liability.

T F 19. Individuals with net earnings from self-employment of $200 or more are subject to the self-employment tax.

T F 20. The backup withholding rate is 20 percent.

Fill-in-the-Blanks

Complete the following statements with the appropriate word(s) or amount(s).

1.   The purpose of the foreign tax credit is to mitigate _____ taxation.

2.   Taxpayers are required to compute the foreign tax credit based on an _____ limitation.

3.   The maximum child and dependent care credit is equal to 30 percent of the employment related expenses up to _____ for one qualifying individual and _____ for two or more qualifying individuals.

4.   A full-time student is deemed to have earned income of _____ per month for one qualifying individual for purposes of the child care credit.

5.   The regular jobs credit is equal to 40 percent of the first _____ of wages per eligible employee for the first year of employment.

6.   For 1989, individuals with net earnings from self-employment of $400 or more, are subject to a self-employment tax which is 13.02 percent of income up to _____.

7.   For 1989, the net self-employment tax rate on individuals is _____ percent.

8.   Form _____ is the Employer's Quarterly Federal Tax return.

Multiple Choice

Choose the best answer for each of the following questions.

_____ 1.   T and his wife, W, pay $3,000 to keep their son, T Jr., in a day care center. T Jr. is five years old. T's earnings are $12,000 and W's earnings are $15,000, What is the child care credit T and W can claim on a joint return?
a. -0-
b. $480
c. $504
d. $900
e. None of the above

_____ 2.   Given the same situation as in Question 1, except W's earnings are only $1,500, what is the child care credit T and W can claim on a joint return?
a. -0-
b. $315
c. $504
d. $420
e. None of the above

_____ 3.   T is 68 years old and single. He has adjusted gross income of $5,000 and does not receive any social security. What is T's elderly tax credit?
a. -0-
b. $375
c. $750
d. None of the above

_____ 4.   Given the same situation as in Question 3, except T's adjusted gross income is $13,000, what is T's elderly tax credit?
a. -0-
b. $750.00
c. $337.50
d. None of the above

_____ 5.   T maintains a household for her child, who is 13 years old. T's adjusted gross income is $5,000, all from salary. How much is T's 1989 earned income credit?
a. -0-
b. $700
c. $400
d. $300

e. None of the above

_____ 6.   Cary Corporation has $110,000 worth of incremental research expenditures. If Cary is in the 34 percent bracket, what are the tax benefits to Cary from the above expenditures?
a. -0-
b. $20,000
c. $37,400
d. $59,400
e. None of the above

_____ 7.   In 1989, Karen Reed spends $200,000 to build a qualified low-income housing project. What is Karen's credit, assuming the full credit for the first year?
a. $-0-
b. $4,000
c. $5,000
d. $18,000
e. Some other amount

_____ 8.   The basic research credit rate is:
a. 10%
b. 15%
c. 20%
d. 22%
e. Some other amount

_____ 9.   Sheila spends $60,000 to rehabilitate a building originally place in service in 1910. The building is not a historic structure. What is Sheila's rehabilitation credit on the building?
a. $-0-
b. $6,000
c. $9,000
d. $12,000
e. Some other amount

_____ 10.   Same as the above question, what is Sheila's rehabilitation credit if the building is a historic structure?
a. $-0-
b. $6,000
c. $9,000
d. $12,000
e. Some other amount

_____ 11.   A taxpayer had net self-employment income of $20,000 and wages from a part-time job (subject to FICA) of $6,000. What is T's self-employment tax for 1989?
a. $2,860

b. $2,604
c. $2,460
d. $2,820
e. Some other amount

_____ 12. Which of the following taxpayers would not be subject to the imposition of a penalty for the underpayment of estimated tax?
a. The taxpayer did not have the cash to make the payments
b. The taxpayer's estimated payments this year exceed his tax liability last year
c. The taxpayer's CPA forgets to fill out the appropriate forms and send them to the taxpayer
d. The estimated payments this year are equal to 70% of the tax liability
e. None of the above

_____ 13. Which of the following forms is the Employer's Quarterly Federal Tax Return?
a. SS-4
b. W-2
c. 940
d. 941
e. None of the above

_____ 14. Joyce Smith is married and earns a salary of $2,750.00 monthly. If she claims two exemptions, how much must be withheld from her salary using the wage bracket tables found in the text?
a. $327.00
b. $346.00
c. $315.00
d. $321.00
e. Some other amount

_____ 15. Adrian Wong is married and earns a salary of $2,000 per month. If he claims two exemptions, calculate Adrian's withholding using the percentage method.
a. $330.47
b. $405.28
c. $209.94
d. $376.12
e. Some other amount

_____ 16. Backup withholding applies in the following situations except.
a. The taxpayer does not give his or her identification number
b. The taxpayer fails to certify that he or she is not subject to backup withholding
c. The IRS notifies a bank that the taxpayer's identification number is incorrect
d. Interest earned on money in a foreign bank

_____ 17.   Bill and Betty Brown have one child, Bobby, who is 6 years old. Bill's earnings are $15,000 and Betty's are $14,000. Other income includes interest on a savings account at San Diego Federal Savings and Loan of $450. The Brown's paid $2,600 to the Tiny Tot Day Care Center to keep Bobby so they both could work. What is the Browns' child care credit?

   a.   -0-
   b. $480
   c. $520
   d. $2,600
   e.   Some other amount

Code Section Recognition

Indicate, by number, the appropriate Code Section where the following items are found.

_____ 1.   Investment credit.

_____ 2.   Research and experimental credit.

_____ 3.   Child care credit.

_____ 4.   Earned income credit.

SOLUTIONS TO CHAPTER 13

True or False

1.   True   (p. 13-3)

2.   False (p. 13-15) The credit is 20%.

3.   True   (p. 13-16)

4.   True   (p. 13-6)

5.   True   (p. 13-7)

6.   True   (p. 13-17)

7.   True   (p. 13-17)

8.   True   (p. 13-17)

9.   False Children of divorced parents don't always have to be dependents. (p. 13-17)

10. False   The credit is 15 percent. (p. 13-18)

11. False   The maximum credit is 30% x $4,800 = $1,440. (p. 13-21)

12. True   (p. 13-20)

13. True   (p. 13-15)

14. True   (p. 13-25)

15. True   (p. 13-32)

16. False   The wage bracket method is where the amount is simply looked up. (p. 13-32)

17. False   Employers must deposit withholding at least quarterly. (p. 13-36)

18. True   (p. 13-39)

19. False   Self-employment income of $400 or more is subject to tax. (p. 13-41)

20. True   (p. 13-38)

Fill-in-the-Blanks

1. double (p. 13-19)

2. overall (p. 13-19)

3. $2,400, $4,800 (p. 13-21)

4. $200 (p. 13-21)

5. $6,000 (p. 13-11)

6. $48,000 (p. 13-41)

7. 13.02% (p. 13-41)

8. 941 (p. 13-36)

Multiple Choice

1. C   Credit from text: 21% of $2,400 (maximum) = $504 (p. 13-21)

2. D   28% of $1,500 = $420. (p. 13-21)

3. C   15% of $5,000 = $750. (p. 13-18)

4. C   15% of ($5,000 - (($13,000-7,500)/2)) = $337.50. (p. 13-18)

5. B   14% of $5,000 = $700. (p. 13-17)

6. D   (20% x $110,000) - (34% x $110,000) = **59,400**   (p. 13-13)

7. D $200,000 x 9% = $18,000   (p. 13-16)

8. C   (p. 13-15)

9. B $60,000 x 10% = $6,000   (p. 13-9)

10. D $60,000 x 20% = $12,000   (p. 13-9)

11. B $20,000 x 13.02% = 2,604   (p. 13-41)

12. B   (p. 13-39)

13. D   (p. 13-36)

14. D   See table in text. (p. 13-33)

15. C   15% x ($2,000.00 - (2 x $166.67) - $267) = $274.99   (p. 13-35)

16. D   (p. 13-38)

17. B $2,400 x 20% = $480.   (p. 13-22)

Code Section Recognition

1. Section 46

2. Section 41

3. Section 21

4. Section 32

14

PROPERTY TRANSACTIONS: DETERMINATION OF GAIN OR LOSS AND BASIS CONSIDERATIONS

CHAPTER HIGHLIGHTS

When a taxpayer disposes of property, the following four questions should be answered:

Is there a realized gain or loss?
If so, is the gain or loss recognized?
If the gain or loss is recognized, is it ordinary or capital?
What is the basis of any replacement property?

This chapter and the next deal with the first two questions above -- the determination of realized and recognized gain or loss. Chapters 16 and 17 address the third and fourth questions -- the classification of gain or loss as either ordinary or capital and the determination of the basis of any replacement property.

I.   DETERMINATION OF GAIN OR LOSS

    A.   Realized Gain or Loss.

        The realized gain or loss is the difference between the amount realized and the adjusted basis of the property.

        The term "sale or other disposition" is defined broadly in the tax law. The term includes virtually all dispositions of property such as trade-ins, casualties, condemnations, and bond retirements.

The "amount realized" from the sale or other disposition of property is the sum of money received plus the fair market value of other property received, reduced by the costs of transferring the property. The amount realized includes any liability (including nonrecourse debt) on the property assumed by the buyer.

The "adjusted basis" of the property disposed of is its original cost basis adjusted to the date of disposition. The adjustments consist of adding capital additions and subtracting capital recoveries. Capital additions include the cost of capital improvements and betterments made to the property, amortization of bond discounts, and any liability on the property that is assumed by the buyer. The major capital recoveries are depreciation, certain corporate distributions, and amortization of bond premiums.

The basis in property must be reduced by the amount of any deductible casualty or theft loss. The basis is also reduced by any insurance received, but the insurance may cause the recognition of gain which will cause the basis to increase.

B.   Recognized Gain or Loss. Recognized gain is the amount of the realized gain that is included in the taxpayer's gross income. A recognized loss is deductible for tax purposes. As a general rule, the entire gain or loss realized will be recognized unless specific relief is found in the Code.

C.   Nonrecognition of Gain or Loss.

In certain cases, realized gain or loss is not recognized for tax purposes. Several such exceptions include nontaxable exchanges, losses on the sale, exchange, or condemnation of personal use assets, gains on the sale of a personal residence by taxpayers 55 years old or older, and certain transactions between related parties.

Losses realized on the sale, exchange, or condemnation of personal use property are not recognized for tax purposes, whereas gain realized on such property is generally fully taxable.

D.   Recovery of Capital Doctrine.

The recovery of capital doctrine states that a taxpayer is entitled to recover the cost or other basis of property acquired and is not taxed on that amount. The cost of depreciable property is recovered through annual depreciation deductions and the basis is reduced by the amount of the depreciation taken.

The relationship between the recovery of capital doctrine and the concepts of realized and recognized gain or loss can be summarized as follows:

A realized gain (or loss) that is never recognized results in the permanent recovery of more (or less) than the taxpayer's cost or other basis for tax purposes.

When recognition of a realized gain (or loss) is postponed, a temporary recovery of more (or less) than the taxpayer's cost or other basis results for tax purposes.

II.   BASIS CONSIDERATIONS

    A.   Determination of Cost Basis.

The basis of property is generally its cost, where cost is the amount paid for the property in cash or other property. The basis of property acquired in a "bargain purchase" is its fair market value.

The Regulations require that taxpayers must adequately identify stock that is sold. If the stock cannot be identified, the IRS will assume FIFO for determining the basis of the shares sold.

When a taxpayer acquires multiple assets in a lump-sum purchase, it is necessary to allocate the total cost among the individual assets. This allocation is on the basis of the relative fair market value of the individual assets acquired.

Shares of common or preferred stock received as nontaxable stock dividends must be allocated a part of the basis of the common stock owned. This allocation is done on the basis of relative fair market value.

If a taxpayer owns stock on which nontaxable rights to purchase additional stock are distributed, he may elect to allocate part of his stock basis to the stock rights received if the fair market value of such rights is less than 15 percent of the fair market value of the stock. If the value of the rights is 15 percent or more of the fair market value of the stock, then the rights must be allocated part of the basis using relative fair market values. The holding period of nontaxable rights received includes the holding period of the stock on which the rights were distributed. However, if the rights are exercised, the holding period of the new stock begins the day the rights are exercised.

    B.   Gift Basis.

When the property owned by a taxpayer is received by gift, there is no cost basis, so a basis must be assigned to the asset. If the gift property was acquired before 1921, its basis is the fair market value on the date of gift. For gifts after 1920, the basis for dispositions that result in a gain is the donor's adjusted basis. If the property is disposed of at a loss, the basis to the donee is the lower of the donor's adjusted basis or fair market value on the date of the gift. This post-1921 gift property is referred to as "dual basis" property.

An adjustment to the basis of property acquired by gift is made for any gift tax paid. For gifts before 1977, the full amount of the gift tax is added to the donor's basis up to the fair market value of the property. The following formula is used to calculate the donee's gain basis for gifts after 1976:

Donee's gain basis = Donor's adjusted basis +

$$\frac{\text{Unrealized appreciation}}{\text{Fair market value}} \times \text{Gift tax paid}$$

The holding period of property acquired by gift begins on the date the property was acquired by the donor if the gain basis rule applies. Otherwise, if the loss basis rule applies, the holding period starts on the date of the gift.

C.   Property Acquired from a Decedent.

The basis of property acquired from a decedent is generally its fair market value at the date of death or the alternate valuation date. The alternate valuation date is six months after the date of death and may be elected only if the value of the gross estate and estate tax liability will be reduced.

The holding period for property acquired from a decedent is always long-term.

The basis of community property at the time of death of one spouse becomes the fair market value of the entire amount of the property, not just the decedent's share.

D.   Disallowed Losses.

Under Section 267, the realized losses from sales or exchanges of property, directly or indirectly, between certain related parties are not recognized. If property is acquired in such a transaction, the basis is cost. However, if a subsequent sale or other disposition of the property results in a realized gain, the amount of the gain is reduced by the loss which was previously disallowed.

The most common related party transactions are those between family members, and those between an individual and a corporation in which the individual owns directly or indirectly more than 50 percent of the stock.

If a taxpayer acquires stock or securities in a "wash sale" under Section 1091, any loss will be disallowed. The basis in the replacement stock or securities will be the cost plus any disallowed loss. A wash sale occurs when a taxpayer sells or exchanges stock or securities and within 30 days before or after such sale or exchange acquires substantially identical stock or securities. If the taxpayer acquires less than the number of shares sold in a wash sale any loss must be prorated on the basis of the number of shares acquired relative to the number of shares sold.

Recognized loss on "tax straddles", such as buy and sell orders in the same commodity, is limited to the amount that realized loss exceeds realized gain on the offsetting position. Nonrecognized losses are treated as having occurred in the following taxable year.

E.   Conversion of Property from Personal to Business or Income-Producing Use.

The basis for loss and depreciation for property converted from personal to business or income-producing use is the lower of the property's adjusted basis or fair market value on the date of conversion. The basis for gain is the adjusted basis on the date of conversion.

Depreciation is calculated for tax purposes using the basis for loss. The basis for gain, however, must also be adjusted for depreciation to determine the gain or loss on disposition.

TEST FOR SELF-EVALUATION

True or False

Indicate which of the following statements are true or false by circling the correct answers.

T F 1.   A realized gain and a recognized gain are the same thing.

T F 2.   Trade-ins are not dispositions and would not cause a gain or loss to be recognized.

T F 3.   The amount realized from a sale or disposition includes property received at fair market value.

T F 4.   The amount realized from a sale or disposition of property does not include any liability assumed by the buyer.

T F 5.   The term fair market value is defined by the courts as the price at which property will change hands between a willing seller and a willing buyer when neither is compelled to sell nor buy.

T F 6.   The amount realized is reduced by the cost to transfer the property.

T F 7.   The adjusted basis of property is the original basis plus capital recoveries, less capital additions.

T F 8.   Depreciation is an example of capital recovery.

T F 9.   The Code assumes all gains that are realized will be recognized unless otherwise stated.

T F 10.   A realized loss from the sale or disposition of a personal asset is not recognized for tax purposes.

T F 11.   Under the cost recovery doctrine, a taxpayer may recover the cost of property acquired and will be taxed on that amount.

T F 12.   The cost of depreciable property is recovered through annual depreciation deductions.

T F 13.   The basis of property is generally its cost, which is paid for by cash or other property.

T F 14.   The basis of property acquired in a bargain purchase is its cost.

T F 15.   If stock lots cannot be identified, the Regulations make a LIFO presumption.

T   F   16.   A lump sum cost is allocated on the basis of relative fair market values of the individual assets acquired.

T   F   17.   For gifts acquired before 1921, the basis for income tax purposes to the donee is the fair market value at the date of the gift.

T   F   18.   If stock rights are exercised, the holding period of the newly acquired stock begins with the date the rights are exercised.

T   F   19.   The basis of property converted to business use is always fair market value on the date of conversion.

T   F   20.   The wash sale provision applies to both gains and losses.

T   F   21.   In a wash sale, the disallowed loss is added to the basis of the replacement security.

T   F   22.   As a general rule, the relief of a liability is an amount realized.

Fill-in-the-Blanks

Complete the following statements with the appropriate word(s).

1.   For gifts after 1920, the basis for gain is the same as the donor's adjusted _____.

2.   For gifts after 1920, the basis for loss is the lesser of the donor's adjusted basis or fair _____ value on the date of the gift.

3.   For a gift made before 1977, the gift tax paid is _____ to the donor's basis up to the fair market value of the property.

4.   If a gift is made after 1976, the gift taxes paid that are due to the net unrealized _____ on the gift are added to the basis of the gift property.

5.   The basis of property acquired from a decedent is its fair market value at the date of _____ or the alternative valuation date.

6.   In a wash sale, the realized loss that is not recognized is _____ to the basis of the replacement stock.

7.   If property is converted from personal to business or income-producing use, the basis for loss and depreciation is the lesser of the property's adjusted _____ or fair market value on the date of conversion, while the basis for gain is the adjusted basis on the date of _____.

Multiple Choice

Choose the best answer for each of the following questions.

_____ 1.   In 1974, D acquired Texaco stock at a cost of $300,000. This stock was
              worth $275,000 on the date of D's death, March 1, 1989. If the securities
              are sold by D's heirs, the basis for determining gain or loss under Section
              1014 is:
              a. -0-
              b. $275,000
              c. $300,000
              d. $400.000
              e. Some other amount

_____ 2.   Under the Internal Revenue Code, the holding period for property acquired
              from a decedent is always:
              a. Long-term
              b. Short-term
              c. Determined by the date acquired by the decedent
              d. Determined by the date of death
              e. Some other amount

_____ 3.   On January 2, 1989, T converts his house into rental property. The basis of
              the house is $60,000 and its fair market value on the date of conversion is
              $48,000. T's basis for depreciation is:
              a. -0-
              b. $48,000
              c. $60,000
              d. $12,000
              e. Some other amount

_____ 4.   Assume the same situation as in Question 3. T's basis for gain in the event
              the property is later sold would be:
              a. $48,000 less any depreciation
              b. $60,000 less any depreciation
              c. $48,000
              d. Some other amount

_____ 5.   Assume the same situation as in Question 3. T's basis for loss in the event
              the property is later sold would be:
              a. $48,000 less any depreciation
              b. $60,000 less any depreciation
              c. $60,000
              d. Some other amount

_____ 6.   On July 1, 1989, T sells 100 shares of Texaco stock (basis of $4,000) for
              $3,500. On July 18, 1989, he purchases 50 shares for $1,800. T's recognized

loss on the sale is:
a. -0-
b. $500
c. $250
d. Some other amount

_____ 7. Assume the same situation as in Question 6. T's basis in the 50 shares purchased on July 18, 1989, would be:
a. -0-
b. $1,800
c. $2,300
d. $2,050
e. Some other amount

_____ 8. John Deaux, of Lake Charles, Louisiana, sold some common stock acquired two years ago to his brother, Don, at the current market price of $6,000. John's basis in the stock is $8,000. He should report:
a. Neither a gain nor a loss
b. A long-term capital loss of $2,000
c. An ordinary loss of $2,000
d. A short-term capital loss of $2,000
e. Some other amount

_____ 9. Assume the same situation as in Question 8. The stock market recovered rapidly and later Don Deaux sold the stock to an unrelated third party for $9,000. This recognized gain would be:
a. -0-
b. $3,000
c. $1,000
d. $2,000
e. Some other amount

_____ 10. During 1989, T received a gift of property with a fair market value of $8,000. The property had an adjusted basis to the donor of $8,500. There was no gift tax paid on the transfer. If T sold the property for $8,700, the gain or (loss) would be:
a. $200
b. $700
c. $500
d. Some other amount

_____ 11. Assume the same situation as in Question 10, except the property is sold for $7,500. What is the gain or (loss)?
a. $500 gain
b. $500 loss
c. $1,000 loss
d. Some other amount

_____ 12. Assume the same situation as in Question 10, except that the property is sold
          for $8,200. What is the gain or (loss)?
          a. No gain or loss
          b. $300 loss
          c. $200 gain
          d. Some other amount

_____ 13. T sells his house with a basis of $40,000 for $50,000 in cash. The buyer
          assumes T's mortgage of $60,000. The amount of gain on this transaction is:
          a. -0-
          b. $10,000
          c. $20,000
          d. $70,000
          e. Some other amount

_____ 14. T buys an automobile from her employer for $8,000. The fair market value
          of the car is $12,000 and its basis to the employer is $14,000. T's basis in
          the automobile is:
          a. $4,000
          b. $8,000
          c. $12,000
          d. $14,000
          e. Some other amount

_____ 15. T has a "straddle" in silver futures. In 1989 he sells his short position for a
          $5,000 loss. He has an unrealized gain of $5,000 in the offsetting position
          which is not liquidated. What is T's recognized loss?
          a. -0-
          b. $5,000
          c. $10,000
          d. $15,000
          e. Some other amount

_____ 16. An asset used in a trade or business is damaged by a fire. The adjusted
          basis of the asset before the fire is $25,000 and the fair market value is
          $15,000 after the fire. The amount of the casualty loss deduction is $10,000.
          What is the adjusted basis of the asset?
          a. -0-
          b. $10,000
          c. $15,000
          d. $25,000
          e. Some other amount.

_____ 17. Van Ballew purchases a rental house and land for $90,000 in a depressed
          real estate market. Appraisals place the value of the house at $70,000 and
          the land at $30,000 (a total of $100,000). What is Van's basis in the house?
          a. $63,000
          b. $70,000

   c. $90,000
   d. $100,000
   e. Some other amount.

_____ 18.   On March 1, 1989, Harry Beech received a gift of income-producing real estate having a donor's adjusted basis of $50,000 at the date of the gift. Fair market value of the property at the date of gift was $40,000. Beech sold the property for $46,000 on August 1, 1989. How much gain or loss should Beech report for 1989?
   a. No gain or loss
   b. $6,000 short-term capital gain
   c. $4,000 short-term capital loss
   d. $4,000 ordinary loss   (CPA adapted)

Use the following information for the next three questions.

On March 1, 1989, Lois Rice learned that she was bequeathed 1,000 shares of Elin Corp. common stock under the will of her uncle, Pat Prevor. Pat had paid $5,000 for the Elin stock in 1981. Fair market value of Elin stock on March 1, 1989, the date of Pat's death, was $8,000. Lois sold the Elin stock for $9,000 on May 1, 1989, the date that the executor distributed the stock to her. (CPA adapted)

_____ 19.   How much should Lois include in her 1989 individual income tax return for the inheritance of the 1,000 shares of Elin stock which she received from Pat's estate?
   a. $0
   b. $5,000
   c. $8,000
   d. $9,000

_____ 20.   Lois' basis for gain or loss on the sale of the Elin stock is:
   a. $5,000
   b. $8,000
   c. $9,000
   d. $0

_____ 21.   Lois should treat the 1,000 shares of Elin stock as a:
   a. Short-term Section 1231 asset
   b. Long-term Section 1231 asset
   c. Short-term capital asset
   d. Long-term capital asset.

Code Section Recognition

Indicate, by number, the appropriate Code Section where the following items are found.

_____ 1. Cost basis.

_____ 2. Adjustments to basis.

_____ 3. Basis of property acquired from a decedent.

_____ 4. Gift basis.

_____ 5. Wash sales.

_____ 6. Disallowed loss basis.

SOLUTIONS TO CHAPTER 14

True or False

1. False Recognized is for tax purposes only. (p. 14-6)

2. False Trade-ins are dispositions. (p. 14-2)

3. True (p. 14-3)

4. False Liabilities are an amount realized. (p. 14-3)

5. True (p. 14-3)

6. True (p. 14-3)

7. False The adj. basis is basis less capital recoveries, plus capital additions. (p. 14-4)

8. True (p. 14-4)

9. True (p. 14-6)

10. True (p. 14-6)

11. False Taxpayers are not taxed on capital recoveries. (p. 14-7)

12. True (p. 14-7)

13. True (p. 14-8)

14. False The basis of property acquired in a bargain purchase is FMV. (p. 14-8)

15. False The Regulations assume FIFO. (p. 14-9)

16. True (p. 14-9)

17. True (p. 14-12)

18. True (p. 14-12)

19. False The basis of converted property is the original basis, not FMV. (p. 14-20)

20. False The wash sale provision only applies to losses. (p. 14-19)

21. True (p. 14-19)

22. True (p. 14-3)

Fill-in-the-Blanks

1. basis (p. 14-12)

2. market (p. 14-12)

3. added (p. 14-14)

4. appreciation (p. 14-13)

5. death (p. 14-15)

6. added (p. 14-19)

7. basis, conversion (p. 14-21)

Multiple Choice

1. B (p. 14-15)

2. A (p. 14-17)

3. B The basis for depreciation is the lesser of the adjusted basis or FMV. (p. 14-21)

4. B (p. 14-21)

5. A (p. 14-21)

6. C $3,500 - 4,000 = ($500), less 50% wash sale = ($250) allowed. (p. 14-19)

7. D $1,800 + 250 = $2,050. (p. 14-19)

8. A (p. 14-17)

9. C $9,000-6,000 = $3,000, less (2,000) disallowed loss = 1,000 recognized gain (p. 14-18)

10. A $8,700 - 8,500 = $200. (p. 14-12)

11. B $7,500 - 8,000 = ($500). (p. 14-12)

12. A (p. 14-13)

13. D $50,000 + 60,000 - 40,000 = $70,000. (p. 14-2, 3)

14. C (p. 14-8)

15. A The recognized loss is limited to the excess of loss over unrealized gain. (p. 14-20)

16. C $25,000 - $10,000 = $15,000 (p. 14-5)

17. A ($70,000/$100,000) x $90,000 = $63,000 (p. 14-9)

18. A (p. 14-13)

19. A (p. 14-15), previous chapter.

20. B (p. 14-15)

21. D (p. 14-17)

Code Section Recognition

1. Section 1012

2. Section 1016

3. Section 1014

4. Section 1015

5. Section 1091

6. Section 267

15

PROPERTY TRANSACTIONS: NONTAXABLE EXCHANGES

CHAPTER HIGHLIGHTS

Certain exchanges are not recognized for tax purposes. In general, new property is viewed as substantially a continuation of an old investment, so the taxpayer is in the same relative economic position. This chapter discusses several of the major types of transactions which receive nontaxable exchange treatment. Chapter 20 covers nontaxable contributions for partnership or corporate formation.

I.   LIKE-KIND EXCHANGES -- SECTION 1031

Under Section 1031, gain or loss on a like-kind exchange will not be recognized if property held for investment or for productive use in a trade or business is exchanged for like-kind property. This provision is mandatory, rather than elective.

A.   Like-Kind Property. Although like-kind property is broadly defined, one important restriction is that real property must be exchanged for other real property and personalty must be exchanged for personalty. Real property includes rental buildings, office and store buildings, manufacturing plants, and land. Personalty consists primarily of machines, equipment, trucks, automobiles, furniture and fixtures. Livestock of different sexes is not considered to be like-kind property.

B.   Exchange Requirement. To qualify for the like-kind treatment, property must be part of an exchange, not a sale and repurchase. In certain situa-

must be part of an exchange, not a sale and repurchase. In certain situations, taxpayers may want to avoid Section 1031 in order to receive a higher basis for depreciation purposes or to recognize a realized loss.

C.   Boot. On a like-kind exchange, gain realized will be recognized to the extent of boot received. However, the receipt of boot will not trigger the recognition of realized loss. Boot paid in a like-kind exchange has no effect on the recognition of realized gains or losses.

D.   Basis of Property Received.   The basis of like-kind property received is:

> Adjusted basis of like-kind property surrendered
> +Adjusted basis of boot given
> +Gain Recognized
> -Fair market value of boot received
> -<u>Loss</u> <u>recognized</u>
> **=Basis of like-kind property received**

The holding period of the property surrendered in exchange carries over and "tacks on" to the holding period of the like-kind property received. Depreciation recapture potential also carries over.

The amount of any liability assumed by the transferee is treated as boot received by the transferor for purposes of computing basis.

II.   INVOLUNTARY CONVERSIONS -- SECTION 1033

A.   General Scheme. The second major nonrecognition provision deals with involuntary conversions. Under Section 1033, a taxpayer who suffers an involuntary conversion may postpone recognition of gain realized from the conversion if certain conditions are met. In general, gain is recognized to the extent that the amount realized is not reinvested in replacement property.

B.   Involuntary Conversion Defined. An involuntary conversion is the result of destruction (complete or partial), theft, seizure, requisition, condemnation, or the sale or exchange under threat or eminence of requisition or condemnation of the taxpayer's property. Most involuntary conversions are casualties or condemnations.

C.   Computing the Amount Realized. The amount realized from a condemnation of property usually includes only the amount received as compensation for the property. It does not generally include amounts designated as severance damages, which occurs when only part of the property is condemned.

D.   Replacement Property. The replacement property for an involuntary conversion must be similar or related in service or use. To qualify, owner-investors must meet the taxpayer use test and owner-users must pass the functional use test for replacement property. Business or investment real property is subject to the broader replacement rules for like-kind exchanges, which means that the taxpayer has more flexibility in replacing the property.

E. Time Limitation on Replacement. A taxpayer has two years after the close of the tax year in which any gain is realized to replace the property. For condemnations of trade or investment real property the taxpayer has three years instead of two.

F. Nonrecognition of Gain.

If the conversion is directly into conversion property then the taxpayer must not recognize any gain. The taxpayer's basis carries over to the new property.

If the conversion is into money, a taxpayer may elect to postpone the gain or recognize it. The basis of the replacement property purchased is its cost less any postponed gain, and the holding period includes that of the converted property if postponement of the gain is elected.

Section 1033 does not modify the general rules for loss recognition. Therefore losses from involuntary conversions of business or income producing property are recognized, whereas conversion losses related to personal use assets are not recognized.

G. Involuntary Conversion of a Personal Residence. An involuntary conversion of a personal residence can have several tax treatments. In a loss situation, if the conversion is a condemnation, the loss realized is not recognized. If the conversion is a casualty, the taxpayer may recognize the loss subject to the casualty loss limitations. In a gain situation, if the conversion is a condemnation, the gain can be postponed under Section 1033 or Section 1034. If the conversion is a casualty, the gain can be postponed only under Section 1033.

H. Reporting Considerations. Supporting details should be included with the taxpayer's return in the year a gain is realized, and also in the year the property is replaced. If the property is not replaced within the time allotted, or it is replaced at a lower cost than anticipated, an amended return must be filed for the year the gain was realized.

III. SALE OF A RESIDENCE -- SECTION 1034

A loss on the sale of a personal residence cannot be recognized. However, gain is taxable unless the taxpayer purchases (or constructs) a qualified new residence within the required time.

A.   Replacement Period. For nonrecognition to apply, the old residence must be replaced with a new residence within a period beginning two years before and ending two years after the date of sale of the old residence.

B.   Principal Residence. To qualify for nonrecognition under Section 1034, both the old and new residences must be the taxpayer's principal residences. However, temporarily renting out the old or new residence does not necessarily terminate its status as the taxpayer's principal residence.

C.   Nonrecognition of Gain Requirements.

The gain from the sale of an old residence is not recognized if a taxpayer reinvests an amount at least equal to the adjusted sales price of the old residence. Realized gain is recognized to the extent that the taxpayer does not reinvest the adjusted sales price in a new residence. The adjusted sales price is the amount realized less any qualified fixing-up expenses. The amount realized is the selling price less selling expenses.

Fixing-up expenses are those personal expenses incurred by the taxpayer in getting the old residence ready for sale including ordinary repairs, painting, wallpapering, etc. They must be incurred during the 90 day period ending on the date of the contract to sell, must be paid within 30 days of sale, and must not be capital expenditures. While fixing-up expenses may reduce the amount of gain to be recognized, they are not deductible, unlike selling expenses, in computing the amount of gain to be realized.

D.   Basis of the New Residence. The basis of the new residence is its cost reduced by any nonrecognized gain. The cost of the new residence includes any qualified capital expenditures incurred within the replacement period. If there is any postponed gain, the holding period of the old residence attaches to the new residence.

E.   Reporting Procedures. The taxpayer must report the details of the sale transaction on Form 2119 in the year gain is realized. If the old residence is not replaced within the allotted time period, or recognized gain results, an amended return must be filed for the year in which the sale took place.

IV.   SALE OF A RESIDENCE -- SECTION 121

A.   Taxpayers 55 years old or over who sell or exchange their principal residence may elect to exclude up to $125,000 ($62,500 for married filing separately) of realized gain from the sale or exchange. The election can only be made once. To qualify for this election, the residence must have been the taxpayer's principal residence for three of the previous five years. If the residence is jointly owned by a husband and wife and a joint return is filed, only one spouse must meet the requirements.

B. Relationship to Other Provisions. Taxpayers may treat an involuntary conversion of a principal residence as a sale for purposes of Section 121. If a qualified new residence is purchased, any gain not excluded under Section 121 can be postponed under Section 1033 or Section 1034.

C. Making or Revoking the Election. The election not to recognize gain under this Section may be made or revoked at any time before the statute of limitations expires. The election is made on Form 2119.

V. OTHER NONRECOGNITION PROVISIONS

A. Exchanges of Stock for Property. No gain or loss is recognized by a corporation dealing in its own stock, including treasury stock.

B. Certain Exchanges of Insurance Policies. Under Section 1035 of the Code certain insurance contracts qualify for nonrecognition of gain or loss when exchanged.

C. Exchange of Stock of the Same Corporation. No gain or loss is recognized by a shareholder from the exchange of common stock for common stock, or preferred stock for preferred stock of the same corporation. An exchange of common stock for preferred stock is generally a taxable event.

D. Reacquisitions of Real Property. When property sold on the installment basis is repossessed only limited gain may be recognized and no loss may be recognized.

E. Under Section 1041, transfers of property between spouses or former spouses incident to divorce or during marriage are nontaxable events. The basis of the property is carried over to the recipient.

F. Under Section 1042, if a taxpayer has realized gain on securities sold to an employee stock ownership plan (ESOP) or a worker-owned cooperative, such gain will not be recognized if qualified replacement property is acquired within a specified time period.

TEST FOR SELF-EVALUATION

True or False

Indicate which of the following statements are true or false by circling the correct answers.

T F 1.   Raw land held for investment would not qualify for a Section 1031 like-kind exchange.

T F 2.   A store building could be exchanged for a delivery truck and qualify for a like-kind exchange.

T F 3.   In a like-kind exchange, gain realized will be recognized to the extent boot is received.

T F 4.   The Section 1031 like-kind provision is elective, not mandatory.

T F 5.   If a liability is assumed in a like-kind exchange, it will be treated as boot paid.

T F 6.   The replacement period on the sale and purchase of a new personal residence is 24 months.

T F 7.   The holding period of like-kind property starts the day the exchange took place.

T F 8.   Involuntary conversion under Section 1033 applies to gains and not to losses.

T F 9.   The Section 1033 involuntary conversion provision is always elective.

T F 10. In an involuntary conversion, gain is recognized to the extent that the proceeds are not reinvested in property that is similar or related in service or use.

T F 11. Livestock destroyed because of disease will qualify for an involuntary conversion.

T F 12. Section 1033 applies to condemnation payments if they are designated as severance damages.

T F 13. Owner-investors must conform to the functional use test to postpone gain under Section 1033.

T F 14. To qualify for nonrecognition under Section 1033, taxpayers have two years from the date property is involuntarily converted to replace it.

T F 15. Involuntary conversions that are a casualty to a personal residence can be recognized subject to the personal casualty loss limitations.

T F 16. If a conversion on a personal residence is from a casualty, gains can only be postponed under the involuntary conversion provision of Section 1033.

T F 17. A realized loss from the sale of a personal residence can be recognized for tax purposes.

T F 18. Section 1034 is mandatory, not elective.

T F 19. To qualify for the $125,000 exclusion on the sale of a personal residence, the taxpayer must be at least 65 years old.

T F 20. If gain is deferred on a personal residence, the basis of the new residence is its cost.

Fill-in-the-Blanks

Complete the following statements with the appropriate word(s) or amount(s).

1. Under Section 1034, if a new residence is purchased, the replacement period is _____ years from the date of sale of the old residence.

2. A taxpayer must physically _____ a new residence within the required replacement period.

3. Gain realized from the sale of an old residence is not recognized if the taxpayer reinvests an amount at least equal to the _____ sales price of the old residence.

4. The adjusted sales price is the amount realized less the _____ expenses.

5. Fixing-up expenses must be incurred for work performed during the _____ day period ending on the date of sale, and be paid within _____ days after the date of sale, and not be capital expenditures.

6. The basis of a new residence purchased under Section 1034 is its cost less _____ gain.

7. Taxpayers 55 years or over who sell or exchange their personal residences may elect to exclude up to _____ of realized gain.

8. To qualify under Section 121, a residence has to be a personal residence for _____ of the last _____ years.

Multiple Choice

Choose the best answer for each of the following questions.

_____ 1.   On May 11, 1989, Vern Odmark, age 40, sold his personal residence for
             $120,000. The house had been purchased several years ago at a cost of
             $88,000. To be able to sell it, Vern painted the house in April 1989, at a
             cost of $2,000, which he paid in April. On June 12, 1989 Vern purchased a
             duplex for $220,000. He rented one-half of the duplex and used the other
             half as a personal residence. For 1989 Vern should report a recognized gain
             of:
             a. -0-
             b. $4,000
             c. $8,000
             d. $16,000
             e. Some other amount

_____ 2.   During the current year, T and X exchange real estate investments. T gives
             up property with an adjusted basis of $250,000 (fair market value of
             $300,000), which is subject to a mortgage of $50,000 (assumed by X). In
             return for this property, T received property with a fair market value of
             $225,000 and $25,000 cash. What is T's realized gain?
             a. -0-
             b. $50,000
             c. $75,000
             d. $100,000
             e. Some other amount

_____ 3.   Assuming the same situation as in Question 2, what is T's recognized gain
             on the new property?
             a. -0-
             b. $50,000
             c. $75,000
             d. $100,000
             e. Some other amount

_____ 4.   Assuming the same situation as in Question 2, what is T's basis in the new
             property?
             a. $225,000
             b. $250,000
             c. $275,000
             d. Some other amount

_____ 5.   T's building, which has an adjusted basis of $100,000, is destroyed by fire
             in 1989. During 1989, T receives insurance for the loss of $250,000. T
             invests $160,000 in a qualified replacement building. How long does T have
             to make the new investment to come within the nonrecognition provision of

Section 1033?
a. December 31, 1989
b. December 31, 1990
c. December 31, 1991
d. December 31, 1992
e. None of the above

_____ 6. Assuming the same situation as in Question 5, what is T's realized gain?
a. -0-
b. $90,000
c. $60,000
d. $150,000
e. Some other amount

_____ 7. Assuming the same situation as in Question 5, what is T's recognized gain?
a. -0-
b. $150,000
c. $90,000
d. $60,000
e. Some other amount

_____ 8. T is 60 years old and sells her personal residence for $180,000 (adjusted basis of $50,000). If T elects Section 121 and does not replace the residence, she would have a recognized gain of:
a. -0-
b. $5,000
c. $130,000
d. $55,000
e. Some other amount

_____ 9. Which of the following exchanges would not qualify for like-kind treatment under Section 1031?
a. Land held as an investment for a rental house
b. A three-ton Ford truck for a four-ton Dodge truck
c. A personal automobile for a business automobile
d. A computer for a copy machine, both used in a business
e. All of the above would qualify

_____ 10. Three years ago T acquired a capital asset for $10,000 which is worth $20,000 today. This property was exchanged for another capital asset worth $20,000, in a qualified Section 1031 exchange. Five months later the new property was sold for $28,000. On this sale T should report:
a. $10,000 long-term capital gain
b. $10,000 short-term capital gain
c. $18,000 long-term capital gain
d. $8,000 short-term capital gain
e. None of the above

losses, and the Section 1033 involuntary conversion provision applies to:
a. Gains only
b. Losses only
c. Gains and losses
d. Capital gains only
e. None of the above

_____ 12. Indicate which of the following conversions would not qualify for involuntary conversion treatment under Section 1033:
a. A personal residence burns down
b. Inventory is damaged by a flood
c. A taxpayer sells his house because it is on a flood plain
d. Livestock is destroyed by disease
e. None of the above

_____ 13. The Section 1033 involuntary conversion provision is:
a. Always elective
b. Never elective
c. Mandatory for direct conversions
d. Mandatory for conversions into money
e. None of the above

_____ 14. Which of the following does not qualify as selling expenses under Section 1034?
a. Title transfer fees
b. Painting a house to make it ready for sale
c. Real estate commissions
d. Advertising the property for sale
e. All of the above qualify

_____ 15. If a qualified taxpayer elects Section 121 on the sale of his or her personal residence, he or she may:
a. Still use Section 1034
b. Not use Section 1034
c. Not use Section 1033
d. Still use Section 1033
e. None of the above

_____ 16. In May of 1989, Jim Williamson sold his residence for $140,000 and realized a gain of $60,000. On June 15, 1989 he moved into his new residence. This new residence is sold in November 1989 for $160,000 for a realized gain of $30,000 and Jim occupies his new (a third) residence which cost $170,000. During 1989 Jim should recognize a gain of:
a. -0-
b. $60,000
c. $30,000
d. $130,000
e. Some other amount

_____ 17.   Ray Ballew transfers a house to his ex-wife in a divorce settlement. The house has a basis to Ray of $70,000 and a fair market value of $120,000 on the date of the transfer. From this transaction Ray should recognize a gain of:

    a. $-0-
    b. $50,000
    c. $70,000
    d. $120,000
    e. Some other amount.

_____ 18.   On July 1, 1989 Louis Herr exchanged an office building having a fair market value of $400,000, for cash of $80,000 plus an apartment building having a fair market value of $320,000. Herr's adjusted basis for the office building was $250,000. How much gain should Herr recognize in his 1989 income tax return?

    a. $-0-
    b. $80,000
    c. $150,000
    d. $330,000   (CPA adapted)

Problem

1.   Maureen Motsinger, age 28, sells her personal residence on July 1, 1989 for $68,000. Selling expenses amount to $4,100. She pays qualified fixing-up expenses of $2,000. Her basis in the old residence is $42,000. On June 19, 1989 she purchases and occupies a new residence at a cost of $72,000. Calculate Maureen's realized gain, recognized gain, and the adjusted basis of her new residence using the following worksheet.

1.   a.   Amount Realized   _____

       Adjusted Basis   (_____)

       Realized Gain   _____

    b.   Adjusted Sales Price   _____

       Cost of New Residence   (_____)

       Recognized Gain   _____

    c.   Cost of New Residence   _____

       Unrecognized Gain   (_____)

       Basis of New Residence   _____

Code Section Recognition

Indicate, by number, the appropriate Code Section where each of the following items are found.

_____ 1.   Like-kind exchanges.

_____ 2.   Involuntary conversions.

_____ 3.   Sale of a personal residence.

_____ 4.   Exclusion on sale of a residence for certain taxpayers 55 years old or over.

SOLUTIONS TO CHAPTER 15

True or False

1.   False   Realty held for investment would qualify for a like-kind exchange. (p. 15-3)

2.   False   Real estate cannot be exchanged for personal property. (p. 15-3)

3.   True   (p. 15-4)

4.   False   Section 1031 is not elective. (p. 15-3)

5.   True   (p. 15-5)

6.   True   (p. 15-16)

7.   False   The holding period starts when the original property was acquired. (p. 15-7)

8.   True   (p. 15-9)

9.   False   For direct conversion,Section 1033 is mandatory. (p. 15-13)

10.   True   (p. 15-9)

11.   True   (p. 15-10)

12.   False   Section 1033 does not apply to severance damages. (p. 15-10)

13.   False   Owner-investors must conform to the taxpayer use test. (p. 15-10)

14.   False   Taxpayers have until two years after the close of the tax year in which gain was realized. The time may be up to a maximum of two years and 364 days. (p. 15-11)

15. True   (p. 15-14)

16. True   (p. 15-15)

17. False   Losses on personal assets are not deductible. (p. 15-15)

18. True   (p. 15-15)

19. False   The taxpayer must be at least 55 years old. (p. 15-21)

20. False   The basis is cost less nonrecognized gain. (p. 15-20)

Fill-in-the-Blanks

1. two (p. 15-16)

2. occupy (p. 15-16)

3. adjusted (p. 15-18)

4. fixing-up (p. 15-18)

5. ninety, thirty (p. 15-18)

6. unrecognized (p. 15-20)

7. $125,000 (p. 15-21)

8. three, five (p. 15-21)

Multiple Choice

1. C $120,000 - 2,000 = $118,000 Adjusted sales price
        $120,000 - $88,000 = $32,000 gain realized
        $118,000 - ($220,000/2) = $8,000 gain recognized   (p. 15-19)

2. B $225,000 + 25,000 + 50,000 - 250,000 = $50,000. (p. 15-4)

3. B   Lesser of gain realized $50,000 or boot received $75,000. (p. 15-4)

4. A $250,000 + 0 + 50,000 - 75,000 = $225,000. (p. 15-6)

5. C   (p. 15-11)

6. D $250,000 - 100,000 = $150,000. (p. 15-13)

7. C $250,000 - 160,000 = $90,000. (p. 15-14)

8. B $180,000 - 50,000 = $130,000 - 125,000 = $5,000. (p. 15-21)

9. C (p. 15-3)

10. C $28,000 - 10,000 = $18,000 LTCG. (p. 15-7)

11. A (p. 15-9)

12. C (p. 15-9)

13. C (p. 15-13)

14. B (p. 15-18)

15. A (p. 15-22)

16. C If a taxpayer acquired more than one house during the replacement period, gain is postponed from the first house to the third house. Any gain on the middle house is recognized. (p. 15-16)

17. A For divorces after July 1984 transfers are nontaxable. (p. 15-25)

18. B Gain is recognized to the extent of boot received. (p. 15-4)

Problem

1.   a.   Amount Realized $63,900
              Adjusted Basis   (42,000)
              Realized Gain $21,900

      b.   Adjusted Sales Price $61,900
              Cost of New Residence   (72,000)
              Recognized Gain   -0-

      c.   Cost of New Residence $72,000
              Unrecognized Gain   (21,900)
              Basis of New Residence $50,100

Code Section Recognition

1. Section 1031

2. Section 1033

3. Section 1034

4. Section 121

16

PROPERTY TRANSACTIONS: CAPITAL GAINS AND LOSSES

CHAPTER HIGHLIGHTS

This chapter discusses the tax treatment of capital assets. Congress enacted the historical favorable capital gain provision to encourage the formation of capital investment and to alleviate the adverse effect caused by the recognition in one year of gain generated over a longer period. For tax years after 1986, preferential rates are no longer applicable. However, in future years, Congress can reinstate the preferential capital gains tax rate.

I.   GENERAL CONSIDERATIONS

    A.   Capital gain or loss reporting arises from the sale or exchange of a capital asset. Although, currently, the tax on a net capital gain is the same as the tax on ordinary income, the tax law requires careful separation of capital gains and losses from other gains and losses. The reason for the difference is that taxable income may vary significantly when both ordinary and capital gains and losses are present. For example, there is a $3,000 annual limit on capital losses while there is no dollar limit on ordinary losses.

    B.   General Scheme of Taxation. Gains and losses that are recognized must be properly classified. The following three characteristics determine proper classification:

        Tax status of the property (capital assets, Section 1231 assets, or ordinary assets)

Manner of the property's disposition (sale, exchange, casualty, theft, or condemnation)

Holding period of the property (short-term or long-term).

II.   CAPITAL ASSETS

A.   Definition of a Capital Asset.

Section 1221 defines what is not a capital asset. A capital asset is all property held by the taxpayer (whether or not connected with his or her trade or business) but does not include:

inventory or property held primarily for sale to customers in the ordinary course of business

accounts and notes receivable

depreciable property or real estate used in a business.

certain copyrights, literary, musical, or artistic compositions, letters or memoranda

certain U.S. Government publications

The most common capital assets held by an individual are items such as a personal residence, automobile, or investment property (land, stock, bonds, etc.). Since losses on the sale or exchange of personal use property are not recognized, the taxpayer need only be concerned with the capital gain treatment of such property.

B.   Effect of Judicial Action. The courts have held that motive must be determined to distinguish a capital from an ordinary asset. Capital asset determination by the courts hinges on whether the assets is held for investment purposes (capital assets) or business purposes (ordinary assets).

C.   Statutory Expansions. There are several expansions to the definition of capital assets found in Section 1221.

Dealers in securities must identify which securities are held for investment purposes and which are considered to be part of their inventory. To receive capital gain treatment on a sale, securities held for investment must be identified as such on the date of acquisition. Losses are considered capital losses if at any time the securities have been identified as being held for investment.

Under Section 1237, if certain rules are met, investors in real estate can avoid dealer status. See text for requirements and limitations.

Lump-sum distributions of an employee's pension or profit sharing plan are taxed in the current year. Under certain circumstances part of the gain may be taxed as a capital gain. See chapter 19.

Nonbusiness bad debts are always treated as short-term capital losses.

III. SALE OR EXCHANGE

A.   The recognition of a capital gain or loss requires a sale or exchange of a capital asset. The term "sale or exchange" is used in the Code but is not defined. A sale usually involves the receipt of money or the assumption of liabilities for property, and an exchange involves the transfer of property for other property.

B.   Worthless securities which are capital assets are deemed to have become worthless on the last day of the taxable year.

C.   Special Rule: Retirement of Corporate Obligations. As a general rule, collection of a debt does not constitute a sale or exchange, so it does not qualify for capital gain treatment for tax purposes. However, under Section 1232, the retirement of corporate and certain governmental obligations is considered to be an exchange and therefore usually qualifies for capital gain or loss treatment.

D.   Original Issue Discount. Bonds that are issued at less than maturity value may have an "original issue discount" (OID). If OID exists it must generally be amortized over the life of the bond. Once the OID is amortized the bond holder's basis in the bond will be its face value, thus there will be no gain on the redemption of the bond by the issuer.

E.   Options.

The sale or exchange of an option to buy or sell property will generally produce capital gain or loss if the property is (or would be) a capital asset in the hands of the option holder.

If an option holder fails to exercise an option, the lapse is considered a sale or exchange on the option expiration date. If the option is exercised, the amount paid for the option is added to the selling price of the property. The grantee then has a larger basis, and the grantor has a larger gain.

F.   Patents. Under Section 1235, inventors are given long-term capital gain treatment on patents. To qualify for this provision, a holder must transfer substantially all rights to a patent. A holder is the creator or inventor, and anyone who purchases the patent rights from the creator, except the creator's employer and certain related parties. To constitute "substantially all rights", the patent rights must not be limited geographically or in duration.

G.   Franchises. The transfer of a franchise, trademark, or trade name is not considered a sale or exchange of a capital asset if the transferor retains any significant power, right, or continuing interest concerning the subject matter of the franchise, trade-mark, or trade name. The transferee can deduct the amounts paid in a manner consistent with the tax treatment to the transferor. This section does not apply to professional sports franchises.

H.   Lease Cancellation Payments. Payment received by a lessee for cancellation of a lease is treated as a capital gain if the lease is a capital or Section 1231 asset. Generally, a lease would be a capital asset if the property is used for personal use and an ordinary asset if the property is used in a traded or business. Payment received by a lessor for lease cancellation is always ordinary income because it is deemed to be in lieu of rental payment.

IV.   HOLDING PERIOD

A.   Property acquired after December 31, 1987 must be held more than one year to be long-term property.

B.   Review of Special Holding Period Rules.

The holding period of property received in a nontaxable exchange includes the holding period of the asset exchanged if such property was a capital or Section 1231 asset.

The holding period of an asset received in a nontaxable transaction (e.g. a gift) where the basis carries over will generally include the holding period of the former owner. The holding period for inherited property is treated as long-term no matter how long the property is actually held. Taxpayers who acquire property in a disallowed loss transaction do not carry over the holding period or the basis.

C.   Short Sales.

A short sale is a form of speculation where a taxpayer sells borrowed property (usually stock) and later repays the lender with substantially identical property.

For short sales, the holding period of the property (except substantially identical property) sold is determined by the length of time the seller held the property used to repay the lender when closing the short sale.

V.   CAPITAL GAINS AND LOSSES OF NONCORPORATE TAXPAYERS

   A.   Treatment of Capital Gains.

         The first step in computing net capital gain is to net all long-term capital gains and losses and all short-term capital gains and losses. Next, taxpayers computes their net capital gain or loss by combining the net long-term and net short-term gains and losses. If the net gain is short-term, the gain is included in ordinary income. For tax years after 1986, if the net gain is long-term, then the taxpayer includes the long-term gain in ordinary income, currently subject to a 33 percent maximum rate.

   B.   Treatment of Capital Losses.

         If a taxpayer has a net capital loss for a year, that loss could be limited. Net capital losses are deductible dollar-for-dollar. However, the maximum deduction against ordinary income cannot exceed $3,000 per year. Any unused losses are carried forward and keep their original character as long-term or short-term. These losses can be carried forward indefinitely.

   C.   Capital gains and losses are reported on Schedule D of Form 1040.

VI.   CAPITAL GAINS AND LOSSES OF CORPORATE TAXPAYERS

   The treatment of capital gains and losses for corporations differs from that of individuals in the following areas:

   A.   An alternative tax rate of 34 percent was allowed in computing the tax on capital gains. Since the maximum corporate rate is 34 percent, for ordinary income, there is nothing to be gained from the alternative capital gain tax rate for current tax years.

   B.   Capital losses offset capital gains. No deduction is allowed against ordinary income.

   C.   There is a five year carryover and a three year carryback for net capital losses. Corporate carryovers and carrybacks are always short-term, regardless of their original nature.

TEST FOR SELF-EVALUATION

True or False

Indicate which of the following statements are true or false by circling the correct answers.

T F 1.   Inventory or stock used in a trade or business are not capital assets as defined in Section 1221.

T F 2.   A depreciable building used in a taxpayer's trade or business is not a capital asset.

T F 3.   Accounts and notes receivable acquired in the ordinary course of a trade or business or from the sale of inventory are not capital assets.

T F 4.   The taxpayer's use is important in determining whether an asset is an ordinary or capital asset.

T F 5.   Dealers in securities will always have ordinary gains and losses on the sale of securities.

T F 6.   Under Section 1237, investors in real estate who engage in limited development activities can be allowed capital gains treatment.

T F 7.   Taxable lump-sum distributions from a qualified pension and profit-sharing plan are ordinary income (subject to certain phase-out rules).

T F 8.   Nonbusiness bad debts are treated as long-term capital losses.

T F 9.   The term "sale or exchange" is defined in the Internal Revenue Code.

T F 10. Worthless securities are treated as a loss from the sale or exchange of a capital asset on the last day of the taxable year.

T F 11. The retirement of a corporate bond is considered an exchange and therefore is usually subject to capital gain or loss treatment.

T F 12. If an option lapses, it is considered to be a sale or exchange on the last day of the taxable year.

T F 13. If an option is exercised, the amount paid is added to the purchase price of the property subject to the option.

T F 14. The holder of a patent is entitled to long-term capital gain treatment if he or she transfers substantially all the rights to the patent.

T F 15. The sale of a franchise always generates long-term capital gain under Section 1253.

T   F   16.   Lease cancellation payment received by a lessee is capital gain if the lease is a capital or Section 1231 asset.

T   F   17.   Lease cancellation payment received by a lessor is always long-term capital gain.

T   F   18.   Unused capital losses for non-corporate taxpayers can be carried forward indefinitely.

T   F   19.   Capital losses for corporate taxpayers are deductible 100% against ordinary income, subject to the annual limitation.

T   F   20.   For 1989, the maximum deduction against ordinary income for a capital loss is $3,000.

T   F   21.   A truck used in a taxpayer's trade or business is a capital asset.

T   F   22.   For capital assets acquired after 1987 the long-term holding period is more than a year.

T   F   23.   The holding period of property "sold short" is determined by the length of time the seller held the property used to close the short sale.

T   F   24.   Corporate capital losses carryback three years and forward five years and all carryovers are treated as short-term, regardless of the original nature.

Fill-in-the-Blanks

Complete the following statements with the appropriate word(s) or amount(s).

1.   For 1989 the required holding period for a long-term capital gain is more than _____ year.

2.   The holding period of property received in a nontaxable exchange _____ the holding period of the former asset.

3.   In a short sale, the holding period of the property sold short is determined by the length of time the seller held the property used to _____ the lender when closing the short sale.

4.   Net gains from short-term capital transactions are taxed as ordinary _____.

5.   For 1989 the maximum capital loss that can be deducted against other income is

_____.

6.   Unused capital losses of individuals can be carried forward for an
        _____ time period.

Multiple Choice

Choose the best answer for each of the following questions.

_____ 1.   In 1989 T incurs a short-term capital loss of $5,000. T's gross income for
            1989 (not including the loss) is $20,000. If T is single, her adjusted gross
            income for 1989 is:
            a. $20,000
            b. $19,000
            c. $18,000
            d. $17,000
            e. Some other amount

_____ 2.   Assuming the same situation as in Question 1, what is T's short-term capital
            loss carryover for 1990?
            a. $1,000
            b. $2,000
            c. $3,000
            d. $4,000
            e. Some other amount

_____ 3.   Tasty Taco sells franchises to independent operators. In 1989 it sold a
            franchise to Pen Wilson for $70,000 plus 3 percent of sales. Tasty Taco
            retains significant rights to control management. If Pen's 1989 sales
            amounted to $100,000, Tasty Taco would include in its computation of 1989
            taxable income:
            a. Long-term capital gain of $73,000
            b. Long-term capital gain of $70,000, ordinary income of $3,000
            c. Ordinary income of $73,000
            d. Ordinary income of $70,000, long-term capital gain of $3,000
            e. Some other amount

_____ 4.   Which of the following is a capital asset?
            a. Inventory
            b. Texaco stock owned by an investor
            c. Accounts receivable
            d. Land used in a trade or business
            e. None of the above

_____ 5.   T owns a tract of land and subdivides it for sale. In 1989 she sells five lots
            for $10,000 each and has a basis of $6,000 in each lot. Her total selling
            expenses are $2,000 and she meets the requirements of Section 1237. T

should report for 1989:
a. Capital gain of $18,000
b. Capital gain of $500, ordinary income of $17,500
c. Capital gain of $17,500, ordinary income of $500
d. Ordinary income of $18,000
e. Some other amount

_____ 6. T invents a machine which he patents. The patent is assigned to a manu-facturer in 1989 for $100,000, plus a $5 per machine royalty. During 1989 1,000 machines are sold. Assuming T transferred substantially all the rights, he should report for 1989:
a. Long-term capital gain of $105,000
b. Long-term capital gain of $100,000, ordinary income of $5,000
c. Long-term capital gain of $5,000, ordinary income of $100,000
d. Ordinary income of $105,000
e. Some other amount

_____ 7. To receive long-term capital gains treatment for 1989, an asset has to be held:
a. One year or more
b. Nine months or more
c. More than one year
d. More than six months
e. None of the above

_____ 8. During 1989 T has net long-term capital gains of $12,000 and net short-term capital gains of $8,000. These gains would increase T's adjusted gross income by:
a. $20,000
b. $12,800
c. $12,000
d. $8,000
e. Some other amount

_____ 9. During 1989 T, an individual, has a long-term capital loss of $14,000. The maximum amount of deduction from this loss against ordinary income is:
a. -0-
b. $1,000
c. $2,000
d. $3,000
e. Some other amount

_____ 10. Assuming the same situation as in Question 9, what is T's carryover to 1990 if he uses the maximum deduction?
a. $11,000
b. $14,000
c. $8,000
d. $10,000

    e. Some other amount

_____ 11. For 1989 T has net long-term capital gains of $20,000 and net short-term
           capital losses of $8,000. What is T's long-term capital gain deduction?
           a. $7,200
           b. $12,000
           c. $-0-
           d. $4,800
           e. Some other amount

_____ 12. In December 1989, T receives a lump-sum distribution from a qualified
           pension plan of $52,000, T contributed $12,000 to the plan and the employer
           contributed the rest. If T was in the plan a total of 8 years, he should
           report:
           a. Long-term capital gain of $24,000, ordinary income of $16,000
           b. Long-term capital gain of $10,000, ordinary income of $30,000
           c. Long-term capital gain of $40,000
           d. Ordinary income of $40,000
           e. Some other amount

_____ 13. T Corporation issues bonds at 95 percent of the face amount. The bonds are
           due in ten years. Which of the following is true?
           a. The bonds are not issued at an original discount
           b. The bonds are issued at original discount
           c. These bonds are capital assets to T Corporation
           d. The bond holders can only be individuals
           e. None of the above

_____ 14. T buys an option on vacant land. He pays $4,000 for an option to purchase
           land for three years at $100,000. After six months T sells the option for
           $9,000. From this transaction, T would recognize:
           a. LTCG of $5,000
           b. STCG of $5,000
           c. STCG of $9,000
           d. STCG of $109,000
           e. Some other amount.

_____ 15. Same as number 14, except T fails to exercise the option after the three year
           period. What is T's recognized gain or loss?
           a. LTCG of $4,000
           b. STCG of $4,000
           c. LTCL of $4,000
           d. STCL of $4,000
           e. Some other amount

Problem

1.   During 1989 Pat Felde had the following stock transactions:

Description	Acquired	Sold	Price	Basis
100 shs Exxon	2/01/85	11/05/89	$6,000	$2,500
100 shs ATT	6/11/89	10/03/89	$4,000	$4,500
100 shs IBM	3/12/89	8/22/89	$6,000	$5,200
100 shs GM	5/12/81	9/15/89	$8,000	$5,000
100 shs Ford	9/15/78	12/01/89	$6,000	$7,000

Calculate Pat's net amount included or deducted in adjusted gross income for 1989.

Net short-term capital gain or loss   _____

Net long-term capital gain or loss   _____

Net capital position   _____

Amount included in income   _____

Code Section Recognition

Indicate, by number, the appropriate Code Section where each of the following items are found.

_____ 1. Definition of a capital asset.

_____ 2. Limited sales of real property.

_____ 3. Worthless securities.

_____ 4. Options.

_____ 5. Patents.

_____ 6. Short sales.

SOLUTIONS TO CHAPTER 16

True or False

1. True   (p. 16-3)

2. True   (p. 16-3)

3. True   (p. 16-3)

4. True   (p. 16-5)

5. False Dealers may designate which of their securities are inventory and held for investment. (p. 16-6)

6. True   (p. 16-6)

7. True   (p. 16-8)

8. False Nonbusiness bad debts are treated as short-term capital losses. (p. 16-8)

9. False The term is not defined in the Code. (p. 16-8)

10. True   (p. 16-8)

11. True   (p. 16-9)

12. False It is a sale or exchange on the day it lapses. (p. 16-9)

13. True   (p. 16-10)

14. True   (p. 16-12)

15. False Franchises usually produce ordinary income on sale. (p. 16-13)

16. True   (p. 16-14)

17. False Lease cancellation payment received by a lessor is ordinary income. (p. 16-14)

18. True   (p. 16-24)

19. False Corporate capital losses are not deductible against other income. (p. 16-27)

20. True   (p. 16-24)

21. False Assets used in a trade or business are not capital assets, they are Section 1231 assets. (p. 16-3)

22. True   (p. 16-15)

23. True   (p. 16-17)

24. True   (p. 16-27)

Fill-in-the-Blanks

1. one (p. 16-15)

2. includes (p. 16-15)

3. repay (p. 16-17)

4. income (p. 16-21)

5. $3,000 (p. 16-20)

6. indefinite (p. 16-24)

Multiple Choice

1. D $20,000 - 3,000 (maximum) = $17,000. (p. 16-24)

2. B $5,000 - 3,000 = $2,000. (p. 16-24)

3. C $70,000 + 3% (100,000) = $73,000 ordinary income. (p. 16-13)

4. B   (p. 16-3)

5. A   5 x $10,000 = $50,000 - 2,000 - (5 x 6,000) = $18,000. (p. 16-7)

6. A $100,000 + ($5 x 1,000) = $105,000. (p. 16-12)

7. C   (p. 16-15)

8. A   (p. 16-20)

9. D   (p. 16-24)

10. A $14,000 - 3,000 = $11,000. (p. 16-24)

11. C   (p. 16-21)

12. D $52,000 - 12,000 = $40,000 ordinary income. (p. 16-8)

13. B   1/4% x 10 Years = 2.5%, the maximum discount is exceeded. (p. 16-9)

14. B   ($9,000 - $4,000) = $5,000 STCG   (p. 16-10)

15. C   (p. 16-10)

Problem

1.   Net short-term capital gain or loss
               ATT   ($500)
               IBM   800 $300

        Net Long-term capital gain or loss
               Exxon   3,500
               GM   3,000
               Ford   (1,000) $5,500

        Net capital position   5,800

        Amount included in income $5,800

Code Section Recognition

1.   Section 1221

2.   Section 1237

3.   Section 165

4.   Section 1234

5.   Section 1235

6.   Section 1233

17

PROPERTY TRANSACTIONS: SECTION 1231 AND RECAPTURE PROVISIONS

CHAPTER HIGHLIGHTS

This chapter summarizes Code Section 1231 which grants favorable long-term capital gain treatment on the sale or exchange or involuntary conversion of certain non-capital assets. Also covered are recapture provisions which provide that certain gains which would qualify for capital gain treatment, or would not be recognized, are to be treated as ordinary income.

I. SECTION 1231 ASSETS

    A. Relationship to Capital Asset Definition.

        Section 1231 assets are not capital assets because they are excluded under Section 1221(2). The concept of Section 1231 assets was enacted by Congress in 1942 to ease the burden of taxation on the sale of business assets and to help the war effort.

        Section 1231 provides that net gains on Section 1231 property are treated as long-term capital gains, and net losses are subject to ordinary loss treatment.

    B. Section 1231 property includes the following:

        depreciable or real property used in a business

timber, coal, or domestic iron ore to which Section 631 applies

livestock, held for draft, breeding, dairy, or sporting purposes

unharvested crops on land used in a business

certain nonpersonal use capital assets

C.   The following property is not Section 1231 property:

property held less than the long-term holding period

property where casualty losses exceed casualty gains for the taxable year

inventory and property held primarily for sale to customers

copyrights; literary, musical, or artistic compositions; certain government publications.

D.   The long-term holding period for assets obtained after 1987 is more than one year. For assets acquired before 1988 the holding period was more than six months.

E.   The general procedure for calculating Section 1231 gains and losses is as follows:

--Net all long-term casualty gains and losses of nonpersonal use property.

If the casualty gains exceed the losses, combine the excess with other Section 1231 gains.

If the casualty losses exceed casualty gains exclude all losses and gains from further Section 1231 computations. All casualty gains are then considered ordinary income and casualty losses are deductible for AGI if business related or from AGI if not.

--Net all Section 1231 gains (including casualty gains, if any) and losses.

If the gains exceed the losses, the excess is treated as long-term capital gain.

If the losses exceed the gains, all gains are ordinary income and all losses are fully deductible.

For tax years after 1984, net Section 1231 gains must be offset by non-recaptured Section 1231 losses for the previous five years under the "lookback" rule.

II.   SECTION 1245 RECAPTURE

A.   Congress enacted Section 1245 to prevent taxpayers from receiving the dual benefits of depreciation deductions which offset ordinary income and then receiving long-term capital gain treatment when the property is sold under Section 1231. Under this provision, gain on disposition of Section 1245 assets should be treated as ordinary income to the extent of depreciation taken since January 1, 1962. Any excess gain is either Section 1231 gain or casualty gain if the property was disposed of in a casualty event.

B.   Section 1245 property includes all depreciable personal property. Depreciation taken on livestock after 1969 is included. Buildings and their structural components are subject to Section 1245 if they are nonresidential and accelerated cost recovery (ACRS) is used. The following special property is also Section 1245 property.

> amortizable personal property such as patents, copyrights, leaseholds, and professional sports contracts
>
> amortization of reforestation and cost to remove handicap barriers
>
> amounts expensed under Section 179
>
> elevators and escalators acquired before January 1, 1987
>
> certain depreciable tangible real property
>
> amortization taken on pollution control facilities, railroad grading and tunnel boring equipment, on-the-job training and child care facilities
>
> agricultural and horticultural structures and petroleum storage facilities
>
> 15-year, 18-year, or 19-year nonresidential realty on which ACRS was taken, although it is technically not Section 1245 property.

III. SECTION 1250 RECAPTURE

A.   Section 1250 is similar to Section 1245, but Section 1250 only recaptures *additional* depreciation on real property. This additional amount is the accelerated depreciation taken in excess of straight-line.

B.   Generally, Section 1250 property is depreciable real property that is not subject to Section 1245. It applies to the following property for which accelerated deprecation was used:

Residential real estate acquired before 1987

Nonresidential real estate acquired before 1981

Real property used outside the United States

Certain government-financed or low-income housing

C.   For Section 1250 property, other than residential rental property, the follow-ing general rules apply:

Post-1969 amount recaptured is depreciation taken in excess of straight-line after 1969.

If property is held one year or less, all depreciation taken is recap-tured.

Special rules apply to dispositions of substantially improved Section 1250 property.

D.   For tax years after 1980 and before 1987 (ACRS property):

Nonresidential property (office buildings etc.) is subject to Section 1245 recapture if the ACRS statutory method is used (i.e. all the depreciation is recaptured).

Residential real property (apartments etc.). The recaptured amount is the depreciation claimed over what would have been allowed if straight-line were used.

E.   For tax years after 1986:

For real property acquired after 1986 only straight-line depreciation can be used therefore there is no Section 1250 recapture (except for property held less than one year).

IV.   CONSIDERATIONS COMMON TO SECTIONS 1245 AND 1250.

There are several special rules that apply in the following circumstances:

A.   For a gift of property, the recapture potential carries over to the donee.

B.   If property is transferred by death the recapture does not carry to the heir.

C.   For a charitable transfer, the recapture potential reduces the amount of the charitable deduction under Section 170.

D.   For tax-free transactions in which the adjusted basis of the property carries over to the transferee, recapture potential also carries over. Section 351 tax-free incorporations fall into this category.

E.   Gains recognized under the like-kind exchange or involuntary conversion provision are subject to recapture as ordinary income under Sections 1245 and 1250.

F.   For installment sales, recapture gain is recognized in the year of sale. Furthermore, all gain is ordinary income until recapture potential is fully absorbed.

G.   For a property dividend subject to recapture, gain must be recognized by the distributing corporation to the extent of the recapture.

V.   SPECIAL RECAPTURE PROVISIONS

A.   Corporations selling depreciable realty will be subject to an "ordinary gain adjustment." This adjustment is equal to 20 percent of the excess Section 1245 potential recapture over Section 1250 recapture. Section 1231 gain is converted to ordinary income to the extent of this adjustment.

B.   Property eligible for the investment tax credit before 1986 sometimes required reduction to the basis. This reduction is subject to Section 1245 recapture. However, if part of the investment credit taken is recaptured, one-half of the recapture is added back to the property's basis before computing gain or loss.

C.   If a sale or exchange of depreciable property is between spouses or between an individual and a controlled corporation, any gain recognized is ordinary income. Depreciable means subject to depreciation in the hands of the transferee. Recapture under Sections 1245 and 1250 is applied before recapture under the related party provisions.

D.   Low-income Housing. Section 1250 recaptures the low-income housing rapid amortization under Section 167(k).

E.   Intangible drilling and development costs are recaptured on the sale or disposition of such property, if such costs were expensed instead of capitalized. The amount of the recapture is subject to recapture as follows:

         For property acquired before 1987, the IDC expensed after 1975 in excess of what cost depletion would have been had the IDC been capitalized.

         For properties acquired after 1986, the IDC is expensed.

VI.   PASSIVE LOSS ACTIVITIES

When a passive activity is disposed of, any suspended losses of the activity are offset against any gain from the disposition. Any remaining gain is offset against current and/or suspended losses of other passive activities. If any gain remains it is treated as a normal property disposition.

VII.   REPORTING PROCEDURES

Form 4797 is used to report noncapital gains and losses, including Section 1231 gains and losses, and Sections 1245 and 1250 gains. Form 4684, which is used for reporting casualties and thefts, should be completed first since a resulting net gain will impact the computation of Section 1231 gains and losses.

TEST FOR SELF-EVALUATION

True or False

Indicate which of the following statements are true or false by circling the correct answers.

T   F   1.   Section 1231 assets are the same as capital assets under Section 1221.

T   F   2.   A contract to cut timber owned more than one year is a Section 1231 asset.

T   F   3.   The primary tax advantage of a Section 1231 asset is that gains are ordinary income and losses are capital losses.

T   F   4.   All livestock must be held for at least 24 months to qualify as a Section 1231 asset.

T   F   5.   Inventory is not a Section 1231 asset.

T   F   6.   Net gains from casualty and theft are Section 1231 gains.

T   F   7.   Section 1245 applies to depreciable personalty and requires that all depreciation be recaptured if the gain realized exceeds the recapture.

T   F   8.   Depreciation on elevators and escalators acquired before 1987 is recaptured under Section 1245.

T   F   9.   Professional baseball and football players contracts are not Section 1245 property.

T   F   10. All depreciation on pre-1987 residential Section 1250 property is recaptured to the extent of gain on disposition.

T   F   11. Any net gain from the disposal of Section 1245 property that is not recaptured is either Section 1231 gain or casualty gain.

T   F   12. For gifts subject to recapture, the donor must recapture, not the donee.

T   F   13. For a charitable transfer, the recapture potential reduces the amount of the charitable contribution deduction under Section 170.

T   F   14. Generally, if the adjusted basis in a transaction carries over to the transferee, the recapture potential also carries over.

T   F   15. For an installment sale, capital gain applies first, then recapture under Sections 1245 and 1250.

T F 16. Intangible drilling costs that are expensed are recaptured to the lesser of gain realized or IDC over cost depletion.

T F 17. For tax years after 1984 Section 1231 gains are offset by nonrecaptured Section 1231 losses from the previous 6 years.

T F 18. All depreciation on post-1986 non-residential rental property is recaptured.

T F 19. A gift transaction triggers recapture under Section 1245, but not under Section 1250.

T F 20. Chickens that are held for 12 months are Section 1231 assets.

T F 21. For real property acquired after 1986 there can be no Section 1250 recapture because depreciation is limited to straight-line.

T F 22. Suspended passive losses are first offset against any gain from the disposition of the passive activity.

T F 23. Section 1245 recapture is often referred to as partial recapture while Section 11250 recapture is referred to as full recapture.

T F 24. For Section 1245 recapture it does not matter which method of depreciation is used.

Fill-in-the-Blanks

Complete the following statements with the appropriate word(s) or amount(s).

1. Sections 1245 and 1250 recapture rules _____ all other Code sections.

2. Section 1239 applies to a sale or exchange between spouses or between an individual and his or her _____ corporation.

3. For control purposes of Section 1239, the taxpayer must own _____ percent of the corporation's outstanding stock.

4. Intangible drilling and development costs that are paid or incurred after 1975 are recaptured if such costs were _____ instead of capitalized.

Multiple Choice

Choose the best answer for each of the following questions.

_____ 1. Which of the following is not a Section 1231 asset for 1989?

     a. A delivery truck owned 5 months
     b. Timber owned two years
     c. An apartment owned five years
     d. Unharvested crops used on land in a trade or business
     e. All of the above are Section 1231 assets

_____ 2. To qualify as a Section 1231 asset, cattle and horses must be held at least:
     a. 6 months
     b. 12 months
     c. 18 months
     d. 24 months
     e. None of the above

_____ 3. Mr. I.C. Ewe sold Exxon stock (owned 10 years) for a $25,000 gain in 1989. In addition, he had a loss of $10,000 on the sale of one acre of land used in his trade or business. The land was purchased five years ago. Mr. Ewe's net gain from the sale or exchange of capital assets for 1989 will be:
     a. -0-
     b. $5,000
     c. $10,000
     d. $25,000
     e. Some other amount

_____ 4. On January 6, 1989, Isadora Xena sold Section 1245 business equipment. She had purchased this equipment for $5,000 three years ago and had claimed straight-line ACRS depreciation of $2,500 on it. If the selling price was $4,000, Ms. Xena should recognize:
     a. Section 1231 gain of $1,500
     b. Section 1245 gain of $1,500
     c. Section 1231 loss of $500
     d. Section 1245 loss of $500
     e. Some other amount

_____ 5. Assume the same situation as in Question 4, except that the selling price was $2,000. Ms. Xena should recognize:
     a. Section 1245 loss of $500
     b. Section 1231 loss of $500
     c. Section 1245 loss of $2,000
     d. Section 1231 loss of $2,000
     e. Some other amount

_____ 6. Assume the same situation as in Question 4, except that the selling price was $5,500. Ms. Xena should report:
     a. Section 1245 gain of $3,000
     b. Section 1231 gain of $3,000
     c. Section 1245 gain of $2,500, Section 1231 gain of $500
     d. Section 1245 gain of $500, Section 1231 gain of $2,500
     e. Some other amount

_____ 7.   Becky Smith acquired residential real property on January 1, 1986 at a cost
            of $200,000. She used the accelerated method of cost recovery under ACRS.
            The asset is sold on January 1, 1989 for $240,000. For 1986, 1987, and 1988
            the cost recovery allowed was $62,000. Straight-line would have yielded
            $40,000. What is Becky's recapture under Section 1250?
            a. -0-
            b. $22,000
            c. $40,000
            d. $62,000
            e. Some other amount

_____ 8.   T owns 100 percent of T Corporation. In 1989 she sells a truck (basis of
            $6,000) to T Corporation for $7,500. She should report:
            a. A capital gain of $1,500
            b. A capital loss of $1,500
            c. Ordinary income of $1,500
            d. No gain or loss
            e. Some other amount

_____ 9.   In the current year, T donates Section 1245 property to Goodwill Industries
            with a fair market value of $20,000 and an adjusted basis of $12,000. If the
            property is subject to $4,000 of Section 1245 recapture potential, T's char-
            itable contribution deduction is:
            a. $20,000
            b. $12,000
            c. $8,000
            d. $16,000
            e. Some other amount

_____ 10.   T Corporation distributes a property dividend of property subject to recap-
            ture potential. If the recapture potential is $500 and the property's fair
            market value exceeds the adjusted basis by $800, T Corporation should
            recognize:
            a. $500 ordinary income
            b. $800 ordinary income
            c. $300 ordinary income
            d. No recognized gain or loss
            e. Some other amount

_____ 11.   In 1989, Jim Dox has a net Section 1231 gain of $12,000 on property that he
            sold. During 1986, Jim reported a Section 1231 loss of $7,000, which has not
            been recaptured. Jim did not have any other Section 1231 gains or losses
            during the past five years. What is Jim's ordinary income from the above
            transactions for 1989?
            a. $-0-
            b. $12,000
            c. $7,000

____   d. $5,000

       e. Some other amount

____ 12. In 1989, Z Corporation has Section 1245 gain of $100,000 and Section 1250 recapture of $40,000. The Section 291 ordinary gain adjustment would be:

       a. -0-

       b. $12,000

       c. $6,000

       d. $15,000

       e. Some other amount.

____ 13. Jim Waugh acquired non-residential realty three years ago for $200,000. His ACRS deductions for the past three years has been $62,000, which gives him an adjusted basis of $138,000. In 1989, Jim sells the property for $240,000, for a gain of $102,000. Jim should report:

       a. $102,000 Section 1231 gain.

       b. $102,000 ordinary income.

       c. $40,000 Section 1231 gain and $62,000 ordinary income.

       d. $40,000 ordinary income and $62,000 Section 1231 gain.

       e. Some other amount.

____ 14. Jerry Canning has a passive activity with a suspended loss of $10,000. In the current year he disposes of the activity for a net long-term capital gain of $23,000. In the current year he has a profit of $3,000 from the activity. What is Jerry's reportable long-term gain from this disposition?

       a. $-0-

       b. $13,000

       c. $20,000

       d. $23,000

       e. Some other amount

Problem

1. Sid Tekel owns a Section 1245 asset that was acquired two years ago at a cost of $8,500, and on which he claimed ACRS depreciation of $1,700. In 1989 Sid sells this asset for $10,250. Besides the Section 1245 asset, he disposes of a residential Section 1250 asset for $102,500 in 1989. This asset originally cost $80,000 and he has claimed accelerated depreciation of $13,500 since 1979. Straight-line depreciation would have been $8,750 on this asset. Sid did not have any Section 1231 loss in prior years. Calculate Sid's gain or loss and ordinary income recapture (if any).

	Sec. 1245 Asset	Section 1250 Asset
Sales price		
Adjusted basis		
Gain realized		
Recapture potential		
Ordinary income		
Section 1231 gain		

Code Section Recognition

Indicate, by number, the appropriate Code Section where the following items are found.

_____ 1. Depreciable assets used in a trade or business.

_____ 2. Recapture on depreciable real estate.

_____ 3. Recapture on depreciable personalty.

_____ 4. Gain on depreciable property between "related" parties.

SOLUTIONS TO CHAPTER 17

True or False

1. False   Capital assets and Section 1231 assets are not the same. (p. 17-2)

2. True   (p. 17-4)

3. False   Gains are capital gains and losses are ordinary. (p. 17-2)

4. False   Livestock other than cattle and horses only has to be held 12 months. (p. 17-5)

5. True   (p. 17-4)

6. True   (p. 17-5)

7. True   (p. 17-11)

8. True   (p. 17-13)

9. False   Sports contracts are Section 1245 property. (p. 17-13)

10. False   Only the excess over straight-line is recaptured. (p. 17-15)

11. True   (p. 17-12)

12. False   Recapture passes to the donee. (p. 17-18)

13. True   (p. 17-19)

14. True   (p. 17-19)

15. False   In an installment sale, recapture comes first. (p. 17-20)

16. True   (p. 17-24)

17. False   The previous 5 years, not 6 years (p. 17-7)

18. False   There is no recapture because only straight-line can be used. (p. 17-17)

19. False   Gifts do not cause recapture under Section 1250 or 1245. (p. 17-18)

20. False   Poultry is excluded from the definition of Section 1231 assets. (p. 17-5)

21. True   (p. 17-17)

22. True   (p. 17-25)

23. False   (p. 17-12, 17-15)

24. True   (p. 17-12)

Fill-in-the-Blanks

1. override (p. 17-20)

2. controlled (p. 17-22)

3. 50 (p. 17-23)

4. expensed (p. 17-24)

Multiple Choice

1. A (p. 17-4)

2. D (p. 17-5)

3. D (p. 17-2)

4. B $5,000 - 2,500 = $2,500 adjusted basis. $4,000 - 2,500 = $1,500 gain realized, which
      is less than the depreciation. Therefore the realized gain is all Section 1245 gain.
      (p. 17-12)

5. B $2,000 - 2,500 = ($500) Section 1231 loss. (p. 17-12)

6. C $5,500 - 2,500 = $3,000 gain realized, of which $2,500 is Section 1245 gain and $500
      is Section 1231 gain. (p. 17-13)

7. B $240,000 - 138,000 (basis) = $102,000 realized
      $62,000 - 40,000 = $22,000 recapture. (p. 17-17)

8. C $7,500 - 6,000 = $1,500 ordinary income because of Section 1239. (p. 17-23)

9. D $20,000 - 4,000 = $16,000. (p. 17-19)

10. A (p. 17-20)

11. C (p. 17-7)

12. B 20% x (100,000 - 40,000) (p. 17-21)

13. C All the depreciation is recaptured for ACRS nonresidential real property (p. 17-16)

14. B $23,000 - $10,000 = $13,000   (p. 17-25)

Problem

1.

	Sec. 1245 Asset	Sec. 1250 Asset
Sales price	$10,250	$102,500
Adjusted basis	(6,800)	(66,500)
Gain realized	3,450	36,000
Recapture potential	1,700	4,750 Note (1)
Ordinary income	1,700	4,750
Section 1231 Gain	$1,750	$31,250

Note (1) $13,500 - $8,750

Code Section Recognition

1. Section 1231

2. Section 1250

3. Section 1245

4. Section 1239

18

ACCOUNTING PERIODS AND METHODS

CHAPTER HIGHLIGHTS

This chapter discusses some of the options available to taxpayers in choosing accounting methods and periods. The cash, accrual, and hybrid methods are covered along with the special treatments available for long-term construction contracts, installment contracts, and inventory valuation.

I. ACCOUNTING PERIODS

A. In general, taxpayers may use a calendar year or a fiscal year in filing a tax return. Most individual taxpayers use a calendar year. However, certain corporate and noncorporate taxpayers may elect to use a fiscal year ending on the last day of any month. If certain conditions are met, taxpayers may use the 52-53 week year so that their year always ends on the same day of the week.

Partnerships and S corporations can elect an otherwise impermissible tax year if any one of the following conditions are met:

A business purpose for the year can be demonstrated.

The deferral is not more than three months and the entity agrees to make "required tax payments."

The entity retains the same tax year it had in 1987 and agrees to make the "required tax payments."

The required tax payments are computed by applying the highest individual tax rate plus one percent to an estimate of the deferral period income.

Personal Service Corporations (PSCs) can retain or use a fiscal year if one of the following applies:

A business purpose can be demonstrated, or

The deferral is not more than three months and the required minimum payments are made to the shareholders during the deferral period, or

The same fiscal year is retained that was used in 1987, and the required minimum payments are made.

See the text for the calculation of the required minimum payments for a PSC corporation.

B.   Changes in the Accounting Period. To change an accounting period a tax payer must have the consent of the IRS. The IRS will not usually grant a change unless the taxpayer can establish a substantial business purpose for the change. If the taxpayer has a NOL for the short period, the IRS may require that the loss be carried forward for six years.

C.   Taxable Periods of Less Than One Year. A short year is a period of less than 12 months. A taxpayer may have a short year for the first tax reporting period, the final income tax return, or a change in the tax year. Due to the progressive tax rate structure, the short period tax must be "annualized" if it is due to a change in the tax year.

The tax is computed on the amount of the annualized income and then converted to a short period tax. The conversion is made using the following formula:

$$\text{Tax on short period} \times \frac{\text{\# of months in short period}}{12}$$

D.   Mitigating the Annual Accounting Period Concept.

There are several provisions in the tax law designed to give taxpayers relief from the bunching of income because of arbitrary accounting periods. An example of such relief is the net operating loss carryover.

Under the "claim of right" doctrine an amount is includible in income on actual or constructive receipt if the taxpayer has an unrestricted claim to the amount, even if the taxpayer's right to the income is disputed. If the taxpayer is later required to repay such income, a deduction is allowed in the year of greater tax benefit for amounts exceeding $3,000.

II. ACCOUNTING METHODS

A. Permissible Methods.

The Code requires taxpayers to report taxable income under the method of accounting regularly used by the taxpayer in keeping his or her books, provided the method is consistently employed and clearly reflects income. The tax law recognizes three methods: (1) cash receipts and disbursements, (2) accrual, and (3) hybrid (a combination of cash and accrual).

Taxpayers for whom inventories are a significant income producing factor must use the accrual method in computing sales and cost of goods sold. Special methods are also permitted for installment sales and long-term contracts which are discussed later in this chapter.

B. Cash Receipts and Disbursements Method. Under the cash method, income is recognized when the taxpayer actually or constructively receives cash, and deductions are taken in the year of payment. There are exceptions to these rules for cash basis taxpayers. For example, capital expenditures and prepaid items such as interest cannot be deducted in the current period. Also, an accrual basis taxpayer who receives prepaid income (e.g. rent) in advance must usually recognize the income on a cash basis.

C. Accrual Method. The accrual method of accounting requires that income be recognized when: (1) all events have occurred which fix the rights to receive such income, and (2) the amount can be determined with reasonable accuracy. An expense is deductible for the year in which all events have occurred which determine the fact of liability and "economic performance" has occurred. In the case of services or property to be provided, economic performance occurs in the year the services or property are actually provided. There are several exceptions to the economic performance test such as bad debts, etc. See text for details.

D. Hybrid Method. A hybrid method involves the use of both cash and accrual accounting. It is common for a taxpayer to report cost of goods sold on the accrual method and other items of income and deductions on the cash method.

E.   Change of Method.

Taxpayers make an election to use an accounting method when they file an initial tax return and use a particular method. Taxpayers who later want to change a method must obtain the permission of the IRS.

A correction of errors such as incorrect posting, omissions of income or deductions, or incorrect calculation of tax liability does not constitute a change in accounting method. An error may be corrected by filing an amended return.

Permission from the IRS is necessary to change an erroneous method of accounting to a correct method.

The IRS may require a taxpayer to change accounting methods to clearly reflect income. If the amount of the necessary adjustment exceeds $3,000, certain averaging techniques are available to prevent the bunching of income.

To voluntarily change accounting methods, the taxpayer must file a request for a change within the first 180 days after the beginning of the taxable year of the desired change. Any adjustment due to a change in method is required to be spread over future periods.

III.   SPECIAL ACCOUNTING METHODS

A.   Installment Method. The installment method allows taxpayers to recognize gains but not losses. Gains are recognized from the sale of property when installments are collected.

The installment method may not be used for any of the following:

Gains on property held in the ordinary course of business.

Depreciation recapture under Sections 1245 or 1250.

Gains on stocks or securities traded on an established market.

Exceptions to the first item generally include the following:

Timeshare units

Residential lots

Any property used or produced by farming

As a general rules, those activities that are eligible must use the installment method.   Limitations for electing out of the installment method are discussed later.

The recognized gain for installment sales is computed by using the following formula:

$$\frac{\text{Total gain}}{\text{Contact price}} \times \text{Collections} = \text{Recognized gain}$$

Total gain is the selling price reduced by selling expenses and the adjusted basis of the property. The selling price is the amount received by the seller, including receivables from the buyer and liabilities assumed by the buyer. Contract price is generally the amount the seller will receive, other than interest, from the buyer. Collections are payments received in the tax year, less any interest income.

If the installment sale contract does not provide for interest of an amount at least equal to the Federal rate and meets the other requirements of Section 483, then interest will be imputed at the Federal rate. The Federal rate is the rate the Federal government pays to borrow money and is published semi-annually by the IRS. The imputed interest reduces the selling price and increases the percentage relationship of the payment in the year of sale to the total selling price. Special rules apply for imputing interest on installment contracts with contingent payment elements.

Sales to related parties are limited by Section 453(e) of the Code. This provision separates transactions regarding related parties into a "first" and "second" disposition. If the second disposition takes place within two years of the first disposition, then some of the gain on the first disposition may be recognized. See text for examples.

The Code places the related seller of depreciable property on the accrual method of accounting for purposes of timing and recognition. The gift of an installment note is a taxable disposition.

B.   Dispositions of Installment Obligations. If installment notes are disposed of, gain must be recognized on the unrecognized portion of the note. Exceptions to this rule include transfers to controlled corporations, contributions to partnerships, and transfers due to the death of the taxpayer. Borrowing against installment notes causes tax recognition in most cases. In some cases taxpayers may be required to make interest payments on amounts deferred by using the installment method. See text for rules.

C.   Repossession of Property. Generally, on repossessions of property, taxpayers have a recognize gain on the transaction. The gain or loss is equal to the FMV of the property received (reduced by repossession expenses) less the unrecovered basis. However, on the repossession of real property, the gain recognize from the repossession cannot exceed the total cash collected (other than interest) by the seller less the gain previously recognized from collections.

D.   Electing Out of the Installment Method.

An election not to use the installment method is made by reporting the gain under the taxpayer's usual accounting method on a timely filed return. A cash basis taxpayer cannot realize less than the value of the property less the cash down payment. This allows a cash basis taxpayer to report gain or loss as an accrual basis taxpayer.

If the taxpayer elects out of the installment method, permission from the IRS is required to revoke the election.

E.   Long-term Contracts.

Generally a taxpayer must accumulate all of the direct and indirect costs incurred under a contract. Mixed service cost must be allocated to production. For example, fringe benefit costs would be allocated as follows:

$$\frac{\text{Labor on the contract}}{\text{Total salaries and labor}} \times \text{Total cost of fringe benefits}$$

Taxpayers can use one of the following three methods for contracts:

The completed contract method

The percentage of completion method

The percentage of completion-- capitalized cost method.

The completed contract method is limited and can be use only on certain real estate construction contracts (see text). All other contractors must use either the percentage of completion method or the percentage of completion-capitalized cost method.

IV.   INVENTORIES

A.   Determining Inventory Cost.

The cost of inventory is the invoice price less any discounts, plus freight, and other handling costs. The cost of goods manufactured must be determined using the uniform capitalization rules. Taxpayers may use standard cost to value inventory if the cost variances are not significant. Inventory may be valued at the lower of cost or market except for LIFO inventories.

Taxpayers using LIFO must value inventory at cost.

Taxpayers may use specific identification, FIFO, LIFO, or average cost methods of inventory valuation for tax purposes. A taxpayer may use any of these methods, but the method selected must be used consistently from year to year.

B.   The LIFO Election.

A taxpayer may adopt LIFO by using the method in the tax return for the year of change and attaching the proper form for the change. Once the election is made, it cannot be revoked unless the IRS gives permission. The change will usually be granted if the request is filed timely and the taxpayer agrees to a ten year spread on any positive adjustments.

TEST FOR SELF-EVALUATION

True or False

Indicate which of the following statements are true or false by circling the correct answers.

T   F   1.   If certain conditions are met, a taxpayer may adopt a 52-53 week fiscal year.

T   F   2.   For an accrual taxpayer to take a deduction, the "all events test" including economic performance must be met.

T   F   3.   If taxpayers do not keep adequate books and records, they are required to use a calendar tax year.

T   F   4.   The Internal Revenue Service will automatically grant requests for changes to fiscal years from calendar years.

T   F   5.   All short years must have the tax calculated on an annualized basis.

T   F   6.   The standard deduction will be allowed in calculating short-period income.

T   F   7.   The Code requires that taxable income be computed under the method of accounting regularly used by a taxpayer in keeping books, provided the method clearly reflects income.

T   F   8.   Taxpayers who have more than one trade or business must use the same method of accounting for each trade or business.

T   F   9.   A cash basis taxpayer must include in income all amounts actually or constructively received as cash or its equivalent.

T   F   10.   Expenses for a cash basis taxpayer must usually be paid before they are allowed as a deduction for tax purposes.

T   F   11.   All cash expenses of a cash basis taxpayer are deductible when paid.

T   F   12.   An accrual basis taxpayer has to recognize income when it is earned.

T   F   13.   As a general rule, reserves for expenses of an accrual basis taxpayer are allowed as a deduction.

T   F   14.   A hybrid accounting method uses elements of both cash and accrual methods.

T   F   15.   The correction of an error in a tax return is usually considered a change in accounting method.

T F 16.   A taxpayer may file a request for a change in accounting method at any time during the tax year.

T F 17.   A transfer at death causes installment notes to be recognized in full.

T F 18.   Long-term contracts must always recognize income under the percentage of completion method.

T F 19.   Under the percentage of completion-capitalized cost method for long-term contracts, 90 percent of the items produced must use the percentage of completion method.

T F 20.   The installment method of reporting is not allowed for depreciation recapture under Sections 1245 or Section 1250.

T F 21.   Sales of real property must have a selling price of more than $1,000 to qualify for the installment sale election.

T F 22.   Internal Revenue Service permission is required to adopt LIFO inventory for tax purposes.

T F 23.   In periods of inflation, LIFO inventory produces a lower tax liability than FIFO inventory.

T F 24.   Lower of cost or market inventory cannot be used for tax purposes.

T F 25.   Direct costing is an acceptable method for calculating taxable income.

T F 26.   The contract price in an installment sale is generally the total amount (except interest) the seller will collect from the purchaser.

T F 27.   Partnerships, S corporations, or Personal Service Corporations can never elect a fiscal year for tax years after 1986.

T F 28.   The S corporation required tax payment is due by April 15th of each tax year.

T F 29.   The IRS applies an objective gross receipts test to determine if an entity has a natural business year. Under this test, 25% if the gross receipts must be realized in the final two months of the tax year for three consecutive years.

T F 30.   Taxpayers are required to pay interest on deferred taxes from an installment sale if outstanding obligations exceed $5,000,000 at the close of the year.

T F 31.   Generally, the gain recognized from the repossession of real property cannot exceed the total cash collected (other than interest) by the seller less the gain previously recognized from collections.

Fill-in-the-Blanks

Complete the following statements with the appropriate word(s) or amount(s).

1.   The IRS may require a NOL from a "short year" to be carried forward _____ years.

2.   The contract price in an installment sale is generally the total amount (excluding interest) the seller will ultimately _____ from the purchaser.

3.   If an installment contract has a stated interest rate of less than _____ percent of the Federal rate, the IRS will impute interest at the Federal rate.

4.   The cost of goods produced or manufactured by the taxpayer must be determined by using the uniform _____ rules of inventory costing.

5.   Inventories may be valued at the lower of cost or market except for _____ inventories.

6.   Taxpayers using LIFO must value inventory at _____.

7.   During a period of rising prices, LIFO will generally produce a lower ending inventory and a _____ cost of goods sold.

8.   Once a LIFO election is made, it _____ be revoked without the permission of the IRS.

Multiple Choice

Choose the best answer for each of the following questions.

_____   1.   X Corporation, a calendar-year taxpayer, would like to switch to a fiscal year ending June 30, 1989. The last day that X can file the election (Form 1128) is:
a. July 15, 1989
b. August 15, 1989
c. September 15, 1989
d. October 15, 1989
e. None of the above

_____   2.   G Corporation obtained permission to change from a calendar year to a fiscal year ending March 31. For the short period (January 1 to March 31), she had taxable income of $24,000. The annualized income for 1989 would

be:
a. $96,000
b. $6,000
c. $48,000
d. -0-
e. Some other amount

_____ 3. In 1989 T Corporation, an accrual basis taxpayer, declared a $9,000 bonus payable in 1989 to X, its sole shareholder. The bonus was reasonable in amount and the corporation had sufficient cash to pay the bonus in December, although the bonus was actually paid in January 1990. From these transactions, X should report:
a. $9,000 ordinary income in 1990
b. $9,000 long-term capital gain in 1990
c. $9,000 ordinary income in 1989
d. No income in 1989
e. Some other amount

_____ 4. Imputed interest cannot be charged in which of the following examples:
a. A deferred contract on real estate
b. If the interest rate is less than Federal rate
c. A deferred contract with a selling price of $2,500
d. Installment sales of personalty
e. None of the above

_____ 5. The California Limited Publishing Company invests $60,000 in printing 20,000 copies of a book. Twelve thousand copies were sold in the first two years of operation, and none have been sold over the last four years. Regardless, the company expects the books will sell in the future and thus it leaves the price the same ($20 per copy). How much may the taxpayer write off (expense) in the current year?
a. -0-
b. $120,000
c. $240,000
d. $360,000
e. Some other amount

_____ 6. T is a building contractor who agrees to construct a building for $200,000. In 1989 she incurs costs of $90,000 and in 1990 costs of $70,000. An architect estimates the building is 60 percent complete in 1989 and the building is completed in 1990. If T uses the completed contract method for 1989, she should report income of:
a. -0-
b. $30,000
c. $10,000
d. $40,000
e. Some other amount

_____ 7. In January 1989, a husband sells stock to his wife for $100,000, its fair market value. The husband's basis in the stock was $45,000. Under terms of the sale, his wife pays $25,000 down and issues notes for the balance, payable over ten years plus interest at 10 percent. Four months later the wife sells the stock for $105,000. If the husband elects installment sale treatment, how much gain should the husband report in 1989?
   a. -0-
   b. $13,750
   c. $14,250
   d. $55,000
   e. Some other amount

_____ 8. T sells a parcel of real estate (basis of $40,000) for $100,000, receiving $20,000 as a down payment and the buyer's note for the balance, payable over a period of five years at the federal rate interest. The first note payment is due next year. If T uses the installment method under Section 453, how much gain should be reported in the year of sale?
   a. $60,000
   b. $40,000
   c. $12,000
   d. -0-
   e. Some other amount

_____ 9. Assume the same situation as in Question 8. How much gain (excluding interest) should T report in each of the next five years?
   a. $9,600
   b. $16,000
   c. $80,000
   d. $48,000
   e. Some other amount

_____ 10. T sold land (basis of $12,000) to X for $20,000, receiving a down payment of $5,000 and notes for $5,000 per year for the next three years, plus interest at the Federal rate. After paying one payment when the balance due is $10,000, X defaults. At the time of repossession, the land is worth $30,000. T's expenses of repossession amount to $2,000. What is T's recognized gain on the repossession?
   a. -0-
   b. $10,000
   c. $12,000
   d. $2,000
   e. Some other amount

_____ 11. In 1989 T uses the lower of cost or market and FIFO inventory method. The FIFO cost of the ending inventory was $40,000 and its market value was $34,000. Therefore, the ending inventory for 1989 was $34,000. In 1990 T switched to LIFO inventory. How much income, if any, must T recognize for 1990?

a. -0-
b. $2,000 ordinary income
c. $2,000 long-term capital gain
d. $2,000 long-term capital loss
e. Some other amount

_____ 12. Carol Venable's corporation (a personal service corporation) paid her a salary of $132,000 during the fiscal year ended October 31, 1988. The corporation can continue to use its fiscal year, provided Carol receives a salary of how much during the period November 1 to December 31?
a. $-0-
b. $33,000
c. $22,000
d. $11,000
e. Some other amount

_____ 13. The required tax payments of partnerships and S corporations is being phased in over how many years?
a. Three years
b. Four years
c. Five years
d. Six years
e. Ten years

Problems

1. Jill Richards acquired a duplex in 19X5 which she held as rental property. The original cost of the property was $80,000. During 19X5 Jill spent $14,500 in capital improvements on the property. For tax years 19X5 and 19X6, straight-line depreciation of $11,300 was claimed on the property.

In the current year, 19X7, Jill sold the property for $120,000, receiving $20,000 on March 1st as a cash down payment and the buyer's note for $100,000 at the Federal rate interest. The note is payable at $10,000 per year for ten years, with each payment being due on December 1st, starting with 19X7. Her selling expenses were $6,800. If Jill uses Section 453 installment sale treatment on this transaction, calculate the amount of taxable gain that must be reported during 19X7. Use the following worksheet.

a. Gross sales price   _____

  Adjusted cost   (_____)

  Net profit   _____

b. Gross profit percentage   _____

c. Taxable gain   _____

2.   Tecate limited, a partnership, has a fiscal year ending on October 31, 1991. For the prior fiscal year it has taxable income of $96,000. What is Tecate's required tax payment that is due April 15, 1992.

        $_____

Code Section Recognition

Indicate, by number, the appropriate Code Section where the following items are found.

_____   1.   General rules for methods of accounting.

_____   2.   Changes in accounting periods.

_____   3.   Installment method.

_____   4.   Imputed interest.

_____   5.   General rules for inventories.

SOLUTIONS TO CHAPTER 18

True or False

1.   True   (p. 18-2)

2.   True   (p. 18-12)

3.   True   (p. 18-2)

4.   False   The IRS will grant requests for a substantial business purpose. (p. 18-6)

5.   False   First and last years do not have to be annualized. (p. 18-7)

6. False The standard deduction is not allowed. (p. 18-8)

7. True   (p. 18-10)

8. False Each trade or business may use a different method of accounting. (p. 18-10)

9. True   (p. 18-11)

10. True   (p. 18-11)

11. False Prepaid expenses must be capitalized and amortized. (p. 18-11)

12. True   (p. 18-12)

13. False Reserves are usually not allowed as a deduction. (p. 18-14)

14. True   (p. 18-14)

15. False A correction is not a change in accounting method. (p. 18-15)

16. False The request must be made within the first 180 days of the year. (p. 18-14)

17. False Death does not cause deferred gain to be recognized. (p. 18-28)

18. False In certain cases, long-term contracts may also use the completed contract method subject to the rules under the TRA of 1986. (p. 18-34)

19. True   (p. 18-35)

20. True   (p. 18-19)

21. False There is no limit on the selling price. (p. 18-19)

22. False IRS permission is not needed. (p. 18-41)

23. True   (p. 18-41)

24. False Lower of cost or market can be used for tax purposes. (p. 18-40)

25. False Uniform capitalization rules must be used for tax purposes. (p. 18-39)

26. True   (p. 18-20)

27. False They can elect if certain test are met. (p. 18-3)

28. True   (p. 18-3)

29. True   (p. 18-6)

30. True   (p. 18-38)

31. True   (p. 18-29)

Fill-in-the-Blanks

1. six (p. 18-7)

2. collect (p. 18-20)

3. 100 (p. 18-22)

4. capitalization (p. 18-39)

5. LIFO (p. 18-40)

6. cost (p. 18-40)

7. larger (p. 18-41)

8. cannot (p. 18-41)

Multiple Choice

1. B (p. 18-6)

2. A $24,000 x (12/3) = $96,000   (p. 18-7)

3. C (p. 18-13)

4. C (p. 18-22)

5. A (p. 18-40)

6. A (p. 18-34)

7. D $100,000 - 45,000 = $55,000 realized. Because the wife sold the stock four months later, the entire $55,000 must be recognized by the husband. (p. 18-24)

8. C   ($100,000 - 40,000)/100,000 x 20,000 = $12,000. (p. 18-21)

9. A   ($100,000 - 40,000)/100,000 x 16,000 = $9,600. (p. 18-21)

10. D   ($20,000 - 12,000) - (40% x $10,000) - $2,000 = $2,000   gain on repossession (p. 18-29)

11. B ($40,000 - 34,000)/3 = $2,000 ordinary income. (p. 18-42)

12. C (2/12 x $132,000) = $22,000.   (p. 18-5)

13. B (p. 18-3)

Problems

1.   a.   Gross sales price $120,000

              Adjusted cost:
                   Original cost $80,000
                   Capital improvements   14,500
                   Expense of sale   6,800
                   Depreciation   (11,300)

                                                              90,000

      Net Profit   30,000

      b.   Gross profit percent: $ 30,000/$120,000 = 25 percent

      c.   Amount received in 19X7:

                   Down payment $20,000
                   12/1/X7 payment   10,000

              Total received $30,000
              Gross profit %   x25%

              Taxable gain $7,500   (p. 18-20)

      2.   ($96,000 x 2/12 x 29%) = $4,640. (p. 18-3)

Code Section Recognition

1. Section 446

2. Section 442

3. Section 453

4. Section 483

5. Section 471

19

DEFERRED COMPENSATION

CHAPTER HIGHLIGHTS

This chapter covers various deferred compensation plans which are available to employees and self-employed taxpayers. Deferred compensation means that an employee receives compensation after the services are performed. Contributions to such plans and income on the contributions are generally not taxed to employees until the funds are actually received. Such favorable tax treatment is meant to encourage deferred compensation plans which supplement the Social Security system.

I.   QUALIFIED PENSION PLANS, PROFIT-SHARING, AND STOCK BONUS PLANS

   A.   Types of Plans. The tax law provides substantial benefits for retirement plans that meet certain qualifications. Three types of plans qualify under the law: (1) pension, (2) profit- sharing, and (3) stock bonus.

   A pension plan is a deferred compensation arrangement which provides for systematic payments of retirement benefits to employees who meet the requirements set forth in the plan. Employer contributions are computed on an actuarial basis to be sufficient to provide benefits.

   A profit-sharing plan is an arrangement established and maintained by an employer to provide for employee participation in the company's profits.

   A stock bonus plan is a plan established and maintained by an employer to provide contributions of the employer's stock to the plan. There is no requirement that contributions be dependent on profits.

B.   Qualification Requirements.

To be qualified a plan must meet the following requirements:

Exclusive benefit requirement

Nondiscriminatory rules

Participation and coverage requirements

Vesting rules

Distribution requirements

The plan must be created by an employer for the exclusive benefit of the employees or their beneficiaries. The investment must be of the type that a "prudent person" would make.

The plan must not discriminate in favor of employees who are highly compensated. A plan is not considered discriminatory if contributions and benefits uniformly relate to compensation.

The plan must provide that all employees in the covered group who are 21 years of age are eligible to participate after completing one year of service. Furthermore, the plan must cover a reasonable percentage (generally at least 70%) of the company's employees.

The plan must meet certain vesting requirements for both the employer and employee. The employee must have a non-forfeitable right to the accrued benefits from his own contributions. Benefits from the employer contributions must be non-forfeitable in accordance with one of two minimum vesting schedules.

Uniform distribution rules exist after 1988 for all qualified plans, IRAs, unfunded deferred compensation plans of state and local governments and tax-exempt employers, and tax sheltered custodial accounts and annuities. Distributions must begin no later than April 1 of the calendar year following the calendar year in which the participant attains the age of 70 1/2. This date is not affected by the actual date of retirement or termination. Various penalties exist if the required distribution is not made. See text for rules.

C.   Tax Consequences to the Employee and Employer.

The primary tax benefit of a qualified plan is that the employer contributions to a plan are not subject to income taxation until such amounts are made available or distributed to the employees. In addition, earnings are not taxable until withdrawn.

Employee contributions have been previously subject to taxation, therefore part of the payments from the plan are excluded from income under the annuity rules of Section 72.

Employees who receive a lump-sum distribution from qualified plans are subject to various special rules on the distributions. See text for rules.

D.   Limitations on Contributions to and Benefits from Qualified Plans.

Under a defined contribution plan, the annual addition to an employee's account cannot exceed the smaller of $30,000 or 25 percent of the employee's compensation. If the plan is a defined benefit plan, the benefit payable to an employee is limited to the smaller of $94,023 (in 1988) or 100 percent of the employee's average compensation for the three highest years of employment. For collectively bargained plans with at least 100 participants the annual limitation is the greater of $68,212 or one-half of the $94,023 monetary limit.

The maximum deduction permitted each year for the contributions to profit-sharing and stock bonus plans is 15 percent of the employee's compensation. If both types of plan exist the limit is raised to 25 percent. Any unused contributions can be used in a later year as a carryover credit, subject to certain limitations.

E.   Top-Heavy Plans.

A top-heavy plan is generally one which provides more than 60% of the cumulative benefits to an employer's key employees. Key employees include officers, the ten employees owning the largest interest in an employer, a greater-than-five percent owner of an employer, or an employee with annual compensation greater than $150,000 who owns more than one percent of the employer.

Top-heaviness is determined on an annual basis using different criteria depending on the type of plan.

F.   Cash or Deferred Arrangement Plans.

A Section 401(k) plan allows participants to elect to receive up to $7,313 (in 1988) either cash or have a contribution made on their behalf to a profit sharing or stock bonus plan. The plan may also be a salary reduction agreement. Any pretax amount elected as a contribution is not includible in gross income and all of it is invested in the plan. The employer contributions and earnings on the contributions are tax deferred.

II.   RETIREMENT PLANS FOR SELF-EMPLOYED INDIVIDUALS

Self-employed individuals and their employees are allowed to receive qualified retirement benefits under H.R. 10 or Keogh plans.

A.   Coverage Requirements. Contributions and benefits of a self-employed individual are subject to the general provisions of percentage, ratio, and average benefits applied to other qualified plans.

B.   Contribution Limitations. The maximum annual contribution that may be made to a defined contribution Keogh plan is the smaller of $30,000 or 25 percent of earned income. Earned income is reduced by the Keogh contribution which means that the contribution is limited to 20 percent of income before the contribution. There is a 15 per cent (instead of 25 percent) limit on contributions to profit sharing Keogh plans. Under a defined benefit Keogh plan, the annual benefit payable to an employee is limited to the smaller of $94,023 (in 1988) or 100 percent of the employee's average compensation for the three highest years of employment.

III.   INDIVIDUAL RETIREMENT ACCOUNTS (IRAs)

A.   General Rules.

For tax years after 1981, all taxpayers may have an individual retirement account. The maximum contribution is the smaller of $2,000 ($2,250 for a spousal account) or 100 percent of compensation. If the taxpayer is not covered by another plan, or if the taxpayer's AGI is less than $25,000 for single and $40,000 for married filing jointly, the IRA contribution is deductible. If the taxpayer is covered by another plan, the deduction is phased out 20 cents on the dollar until it is no longer available once AGI reaches $35,000 for single taxpayers and $50,000 for married filing jointly.

Simplified employee plans (SEPs) are available to employers as an alternative to regular qualified plans. The employer may contribute to an IRA the lesser of 15 percent of the employee's earned income or $30,000.

If both spouses work, each may establish a separate IRA. Special rules apply to spouses who establish a spousal IRA before divorce.

A taxpayer may make a contribution to an IRA at any time before the due date (April 15th) of his or her tax return.

Contributions can be made to an IRA anytime before the due date of the individual's tax return and still be claimed as a deduction for that year. A H.R. 10 plan must be established before year end, but contributions may be made up until the due date of the return, as for other qualified plans.

B.   Penalty Taxes for Excess Contributions. There is a cumulative nondeductible 6 percent excise penalty tax imposed on the smaller of any excess contributions or the market value of the plan assets determined at the due date
(including extensions) of the individual's tax return.

C.   Taxation of Benefits. A participant has a zero basis in his or her contributions to an IRA, and once retirement payments are received, they are included in ordinary income. Payments made to a participant before age 59-
1/2 are subject to a nondeductible 10 percent penalty tax on such actual or
constructive payments.

IV.   NONQUALIFIED DEFERRED COMPENSATION PLANS

A.   Underlying Rational for Tax Treatment. Nonqualifed deferred compensation plans allow individuals to defer income taxes on payments to a plan
until they are possibly in a lower tax bracket. Unlike qualified plans, most
deferred compensation plans do not have to meet the discrimination, fund-
ing, coverage and other requirements.

B.   Tax Treatment to the Employer and Employee. In an unfunded NQDC
plan, the employee relies upon the company's promise to make the compensation payment in the future. In this case, the employee is taxed when the
compensation is paid or made available and the employer is allowed a
deduction when the employee recognizes income.

V.   RESTRICTED PROPERTY PLANS

A.   General Provisions. A restricted property plan is an arrangement whereby
an employer transfers property to an employee at no cost or at a bargain
price. The transfer is income to the employee when the property is no
longer subject to substantial risk of forfeiture. The property is included in
income at its fair market value.

B.   Substantial Risk of Forfeiture. A substantial risk of forfeiture exists if a
person's rights to full enjoyment of such property are conditioned on the
future performance, or refraining from the performance, of substantial
services by an individual. An employee may elect within 30 days after the
receipt of restricted property to recognize as ordinary income the excess of
fair market value over the amount paid for the property. Thus, any future
appreciation is taxed at capital gain rates instead of as ordinary income.

C.   Employer Deductions. An employer is allowed a tax deduction for restricted property for the same amount and at the same time that the employee is
required to include the payment in income.

VI.   STOCK OPTIONS

A.   In General. A stock option gives an individual the right to purchase a stated number of shares of stock from a corporation at a certain price within a specified period of time.

B.   Incentive Stock Options.

Incentive stock options (ISO) are designed to help corporations attract management. To qualify for stock option treatment the option holder must be an employee of the corporation from the date the option is granted until three months before the date of exercise.   Under this plan there are no tax consequences when an option is granted or exercised. When the stock is sold, any gain is long-term capital gain to the employee if certain holding period requirements are met.

The excess of fair market value of the share at the date of exercise over the option price is a tax preference item for the alternative minimum tax.

C.   Nonqualified Stock Options.

The fair market value of nonqualified stock options must be included in the employee's income at the date the stock options are granted.

If the fair market value is not ascertainable then the difference between the option price and the fair market value of the stock at the exercise date is ordinary income in the year of exercise.

The corporation will receive a deduction at the same time and in the same amount as the income recognized by the employee.

TEST FOR SELF-EVALUATION

True or False

Indicate which of the following statements are true or false by circling the correct answers.

T   F   1.   The three basic types of qualified plans are pension plans, profit sharing plans, and stock bonus plans.

T   F   2.   Profit sharing plans maintain separate accounts for each participant in the plan.

T   F   3.   A stock bonus plan is a deferred compensation arrangement established to provide contributions of stock other than the employer's stock.

T   F   4.   The two types of qualified pension plans are defined contribution plans and defined benefit plans.

T   F   5.   A defined contribution plan provides a formula which defines the benefits employees are to receive.

T   F   6.   An ESOP is a defined contribution plan that is a qualified stock bonus plan or a stock bonus plan and a money purchase plan, both of which qualify under Section 401(a).

T   F   7.   A qualified plan does not have to be for the exclusive benefit of employees or their beneficiaries.

T   F   8.   The contributions or benefits of a qualified plan may discriminate in favor of employees who are officers, stockholders, or highly compensated.

T   F   9.   In all qualified plans employer contributions must vest immediately.

T   F   10. Employer contributions to qualified plans are not subject to taxation until such amounts are made available or distributed to the employees.

T   F   11. It is possible for a taxpayer to be covered by a qualified plan and also have a Keogh plan to which contributions are made in the current year.

T   F   12. All lump-sum distributions qualify for the special ten-year averaging rule.

T   F   13. The maximum contribution to a defined contribution plan is the smaller of $30,000 or 25 percent of the employee's compensation for 1989.

T   F   14. For all defined benefit plans, the maximum contribution is the smaller of $94,023 or 100 percent of the employee's average compensation for the three highest paid years of employment.

T F 15.   The maximum amount permitted per year for contributions to profit sharing and stock bonus plans is 15 percent of the employee's compensation.

T F 16.   All employees of a company must be covered under its Keogh plan in order for the plan to be qualified.

T F 17.   All individual taxpayers with earned income can qualify for an individual retirement account.

T F 18.   The maximum IRA contribution for an individual taxpayers is $2,000 regardless of how many accounts they have if AGI is less than $25,000.

T F 19.   Employee benefits under a qualified plan must vest under one of three alternative schedules.

T F 20.   Unless special circumstances apply, the earliest age to withdraw funds without penalty from an IRA is 59 1/2 years old.

T F 21.   All IRA contributions of an individual are deductible in tax years after 1986.

Fill-in-the-Blanks

Complete the following statements with the appropriate word(s) or amount(s).

1.   The deduction for an IRA is limited to the smaller of _____ or the individual's taxable compensation from personal services.

2.   In an IRA, a participant has a _____ basis in his or her deductible contributions.

3.   The doctrine of _____ receipt is an important concept relating to the taxability of non-qualified deferred compensation.

4.   In a restricted property plan, if an employee performs services and receives property, the fair market value of the property in excess of any amount paid is _____ in gross income.

5.   If a person's rights to full enjoyment of property are conditioned on future performance, or the refraining from the performance, of substantial services, there is said to be a substantial _____ of forfeiture.

6.   An employee may elect within _____ days after the receipt of restricted property to recognize immediately as ordinary income the excess of fair market value over the amount paid for the property.

7. In a restricted property plan, the employer is allowed a deduction for the same amount and at the same time the employee is required to _____ the compensation in income.

8. If a nonqualified stock option has a readily ascertainable fair market value, the value of the option must be included as ordinary _____ by the employee at the date of the grant.

9. If a nonqualified stock option does not have a readily ascertainable price, the employee's recognized income in the year of _____ is the amount equal to the difference between the fair market value of the stock at the exercise date and the option price.

Multiple Choice

Choose the best answer for each of the following questions.

_____ 1. The qualified pension plan of Grossmont Corporation calls for both the employer and employee to contribute 6% of the employee's compensation to the plan. This plan is a:
  a. Defined benefit plan
  b. Defined contribution plan
  c. Profit sharing plan
  d. Stock bonus plan
  e. None of the above

_____ 2. Brian Shay, age 66, has accumulated $920,000 in a defined contribution plan, $120,000 of which represents his own after-tax contributions. What is the excise tax due, if Brian takes a lump-sum distribution?
  a. -0-
  b. $7,500
  c. $15,525
  d. $12,575
  e. Some other amount

_____ 3. Dee Walsh has completed 6 years of service with her employer. If her pension plan uses "graded vesting," what is Dee's nonforfeitable percentage?
  a. 10%
  b. 40%
  c. 60%
  d. 80%
  e. Some other amount

_____ 4. Assume the same situation as in Question 3. If the plan vests under "cliff vesting," what percentage of the employer's contributions must be vested?

a. 100%
b. 55%
c. 50%
d. 45%
e. Some other amount

_____ 5.   Karen Hreha, receives a $500,000 payment under a golden parachute agreement entered into in 1989. Karen's base amount is $120,000 from her employer corporation. What amount of this payment is not deductible to the corporation under Section 280G?
a. -0-
b. $120,000
c. $360,000
d. $140,000
e. Some other amount

_____ 6.   I.M. Sweet is single and self-employed. During the current year, her adjusted gross income was $14,000, including interest of $12,500 and salary of $1,500. The maximum amount that could be contributed and deducted by Sweet to an IRA is:
a. -0-
b. $1,500
c. $2,000
d. $2,100
e. Some other amount

_____ 7.   Assume the same situation as in Question 6, except the adjusted gross income is all from salary. The maximum amount that could be contributed by Sweet to an IRA is:
a. -0-
b. $1,500
c. $1,200
d. $2,000
e. Some other amount

_____ 8.   I. Shade, C.P.A., is self-employed and has established a Keogh (H.R. 10) plan. The plan states that he will contribute the maximum percentage of earned income to the plan. His self-employment income before any Keogh deduction for 1989 is $190,000. Shade's deduction for this plan is:
a. $47,500
b. $38,000
c. $30,000
d. $90,000
e. Some other amount

_____ 9.   The basic required minimum coverage for a qualified plan for all employees in 1989 is:
a. 25 years old and 3 years of service

b. 21 years old and 1 year of service
c. 18 years old and 3 years of service
d. 21 years old and 3 years of service

_____ 10. During 1988 T was employed by Z Corporation at a salary of $70,000. Z Corporation contributes to a retirement plan for T that allows extra volun-tary Section 401(k) contributions. How much additional income may T contribute to this plan?
a. -0-
b. $7,313
c. $3,000
d. $1,000
e. Some other amount

_____ 11. T Corporation and T, a cash basis employee, enter an employment agreement which provides for an annual salary of $140,000. Of this amount, $120,000 is to be paid currently and $20,000 is to be paid in 10 installments on T's retirement. How much would be taxable to T in the current year?
a. -0-
b. $100,000
c. $120,000
d. $140,000
e. Some other amount

_____ 12. In the current year, T is granted a nonqualified stock option to purchase 200 shares of stock from his employer at $9 per share. On the date the options are issued, the stock was selling on the New York Stock Exchange for $14 per share. For this transaction T should report:
a. $1,000 long-term capital gain
b. $1,000 ordinary income
c. $1,800 ordinary income
d. $1,800 long-term capital gain
e. Some other amount

_____ 13. On March 1, 1988, T is granted a nonqualified stock option for 100 shares of common stock at $12 per share. On that date, there is no readily ascer-tainable fair market value for the stock. T exercised the option on May 1, 1989, when the stock is selling for $20 per share. The stock is sold for $30 in 1992. For 1989, T should recognize:
a. No gain or loss
b. $800 ordinary income
c. $800 long-term capital gain
d. $1,200 ordinary income
e. Some other amount

_____ 14. T is a sole proprietor with six employees. She has offered her employees a SEP IRA, which all six have elected to participate in. W, an employee, has a salary of $18,000 for the current year. In 1989, how much of a contribu-

tion may T make to W's IRA if W is married with a nonworking spouse?
a. -0-
b. $1,500
c. $1,750
d. $2,700
e. Some other amount

_____ 15. In 1987, T is given an option on 100 shares of his employer's stock. The option price and FMV was $75 per share. T exercised the option in 1988 when the price was $125 per share. He sold the stock in 1989 for $200 per share. What is T's reported gain in 1989?
a. -0-
b. $12,500 long-term capital gain
c. $12,500 ordinary income
d. $5,000 long-term capital gain
e. Some other amount

_____ 16. T has $15,000 in a deductible IRA and $5,000 in a nondeductible IRA. In the current year T withdraws $1,000 from the nondeductible IRA. What portion of the withdrawal in included in T's income?
a. $-0-
b. $250
c. $750
d. $1,000
e. Some other amount

_____ 17. In the current year Nancy Bailey is over 70 1/2 years old. Her IRA account has a balance in it of $157,300 as of December 31 of last year. Her life expectancy multiple is 14.3 and she taken out a total of $22,000 from the IRA in prior years. Her required minimum distribution from this IRA is:
a. $-0-
b. $11,000
c. $9,462
d. $135,300
e. $157,300

Code Section Recognition

Indicate, by number, the appropriate Code Section where the following items are found.

_____ 1. Qualified pension, profit-sharing, and stock bonus plans.

_____ 2. Individual retirement accounts trusts.

_____ 3. Top-heavy plans.

_____ 4. Individual retirement accounts deductions.

_____ 5. Restricted property plans.

_____ 6. Incentive stock options.

SOLUTIONS TO CHAPTER 19

True or False

1. True   (p. 19-2)

2. True   (p. 19-4)

3. False A stock bonus plan uses the employer's stock. (p. 19-5)

4. True   (p. 19-3)

5. False A defined contribution plan does not define benefits. (p. 19-3)

6. True   (p. 19-5)

7. False The plan must be for the exclusive benefit of employees. (p. 19-6)

8. False Plans cannot discriminate. (p. 19-7)

9. False Vesting can be over a period of time as prescribed by law. (p. 19-9)

10. True   (p. 19-12)

11. True   (p. 19-22)

12. False Ten-year averaging has been repealed. (p. 19-13)

13. True   (p. 19-16)

14. False For certain collectively bargained plans, lower limits may apply. (p. 19-16)

15. True   (p. 19-18)

16. False Employee coverage must follow corporate rules. (p. 19-21)

17. True   (p. 19-22)

18. False $2,250 can be contributed to a spousal IRA. (p. 19-23)

19. True   (p. 19-9)

20. True   (p. 19-26)

21. False   There are AGI limitations for taxpayers covered under other plan(s).   (p. 19-23)

Fill-in-the-Blanks

1. $2,000 (p. 19-22)

2. zero (p. 19-26)

3. constructive (p. 19-27)

4. includible (p. 19-30)

5. risk   (p. 19-30)

6. thirty (p. 19-31)

7. include (p. 19-32)

8. income (p. 19-35)

9. exercise (p. 19-36)

Multiple Choice

1. B   (p. 19-3)

2. B   ($920,000 - $120,000 - $750,000) x 15% = $7,500   (p. 19-11)

3. D   See table in text. (p. 19-9)

4. A   After 5 years it's 100%.   (p. 19-9)

5. D $500,000 - (3 x $120,000) = $140,000   (p. 19-29)

6. B   Lesser of $2,000 or $1,500. (p. 19-22)

7. D   Lesser of $2,000 or $14,000   (p. 19-22)

8. C   20% x $190,000 = $38,000 ==> max of $30,000. (p. 19-23)

9. B   (p. 19-7)

10. B   (p. 19-20)

11. C (p. 19-20)

12. B ($14 - 9) x 200 = $1,000. (p. 19-33)

13. B ($20 - 12) x 100 = $800. (p. 19-36)

14. D $18,000 x 15% = $2,700. (p. 19-24)

15. B ($200 - 75) x 100 = $12,500 LTCG. (p. 19-33)

16. C ($15,000/$20,000) X $1,000 = $750. (p. 19-27)

17. B $157,300/14.3 = $11,000.   (p. 19-27)

Code Section Recognition

1. Section 401

2. Section 408

3. Section 416

4. Section 219

5. Section 83

6. Section 422A

20

CORPORATIONS AND PARTNERSHIPS

CHAPTER HIGHLIGHTS

This chapter provides a brief overview of the tax provisions applicable to various forms of business organizations, including corporations and partnerships.

I. WHAT IS A CORPORATION?

A. Compliance with State Law. Although important, compliance with state law is not the only requirement to qualify for corporate tax status. The degree of business activity at the corporate level is the key consideration for corporate tax status.

B. The Association Approach. Under the association approach, it is possible for an organization to be taxed as a corporation although it is not a legal corporation. If an association has more corporate than noncorporate characteristics, then it will be taxed as a corporation. The corporate characteristics are:

associates

objective to carry on a business and divide the gains therefrom

continuity of life

centralized management

limited liability

free transferability of interests

According to the Regulations, if an organization has the first two characteristics and three of the last four, it is an association (corporation) for tax
purposes.

II.   INCOME TAX CONSIDERATIONS

A.   Individuals and Corporations Compared.

A business may be conducted as a sole proprietorship, partnership, or corporation. Sole proprietorships and partnerships are not separate taxable entities, so all transactions are reported on the individual tax returns of the
owners. On the other hand, corporations are recognized under the tax law
as regular tax paying entities (except S corporations).

Individual and corporate tax rules vary in several situations. These situations are:

capital gains and losses; carryback and carryover provisions

charitable contributions limitations

net operating losses

special deductions for corporations

Net capital gains of corporate taxpayers are included in ordinary income.
Capital losses for corporations are deductible only against capital gains.
Corporate capital losses carry back three years and forward five years.

Corporate charitable contributions are limited to ten percent of taxable
income, computed without regard to the charitable contribution deduction,
net operating loss carryback or capital loss carrybacks, and the dividends
received deduction.

The net operating loss deduction for a corporation is equal to taxable
income plus any dividends received deduction. The NOL is carried back
three years and forward fifteen years. Corporations can elect to forgo the
carryback period.

B. Deductions Available Only to Corporations.

A corporate taxpayer is allowed a deduction equal to 70, 80, or 100 percent of the amount of dividends received, depending on the amount of stock owned in the dividend paying corporation. If the ownership is less than 20%, then the deduction is 70%; if it is over 20% and less than 80%, then the deduction is 80%; and if it is 80% or more, then the deduction is 100%. The deduction is limited to the appropriate percent of the taxable income computed without regard to certain items. However, there is no income limit if a net operating loss results.

Corporations are entitled to amortize organization expenses over a period of 60 months or more. Organization expenses include legal and accounting services incident to organization, expenses of temporary directors, meeting expenses, and fees paid to the state for incorporation.

C. Determination of Tax Liability.

The corporate tax rates are:

Taxable Income	Tax Rate
0 - $50,000	15%
$25,001 - $75,000	25%
Over $75,000	34%

Corporations have to pay an additional tax on taxable income over $100,000. The additional tax is five percent of taxable income over $100,000 up to a maximum of $11,750 (the tax savings because of the increasing brackets on the first $75,000).

Qualified personal service corporations (PSCs) are taxed at a flat 34 percent of all taxable income. The do not get any benefit from the graduated rate schedule.

D. Filing Requirements.

Generally, corporations file tax returns on Form 1120, however, certain small corporations may file the corporate short Form 1120A. S Corporations use Form 1120S. The return must be filed by the fifteenth day of the third month following the close of the tax year. Unlike individuals, corporations must file a tax return even when they do not have taxable income. Estimated payments must be made quarterly if the tax liability is expected to exceed $500.

E. Reconciliation of Taxable Income and Accounting Income. Corporate taxpayers must reconcile taxable income to financial statement income since these amounts are rarely the same. The reconciliation is done on Schedule

M-1 of Form 1120.

III. FORMING THE CORPORATION

A. Capital Contributions.

The receipt of money or property in exchange for capital stock or as a capital contribution is not income to a corporation. Contributions by nonshareholders are not income to the corporation and a corporation has a zero basis in such contributions.

Debt financing is often more advantageous to a corporation than equity financing since interest payments are deductible and dividend payments are not. In certain instances such as when a corporation issues debt with features similar to capital stock, the IRS may contend that the debt is really a form of stock and disallow the interest deduction.

B. Transfers to Controlled Corporations.

If property is exchanged for stock in a corporation and the shareholders are in control of the corporation after the exchange, any gain on the property is not recognized under Section 351. Gain or loss is postponed by adjusting the basis of the stock and property. The basis of the stock received by the shareholder is the basis of the property transferred plus any gain recognized, less any boot received. The basis of property received by the corporation is the basis in the hands of the transferor plus any gain recognized to the transferors. Gain is recognized to the extent that the shareholder receives boot.

IV. OPERATING THE CORPORATION

A. Dividend Distributions.

Operating the corporation. Corporate distributions of cash or property to shareholders are dividends to the extent the corporation has accumulated or current earnings and profits (E&P). Any distribution over E&P is a nontaxable return of capital and reduces the basis of the stock held by the shareholder. If there is a distribution over E&P and over the stock basis, then it is treated as a capital gain. While E&P serves the same function as retained earnings, numerous differences may arise in its calculation. For example, nontaxable stock dividends would not affect E&P. Distributions of property are valued at fair market value for noncorporate shareholders and the lesser of the basis or the fair market value for corporate shareholders. The basis of the property received by the shareholder is the same as the dividend income reported. In closely-held corporations the IRS may contend that certain economic flows to a shareholder are constructive dividends, and therefore the corporation and shareholder may lose certain tax benefits. Constructive dividends include:

Unreasonable compensation

Excessive rent paid to shareholders
Interest on certain debt to shareholders
Advances to shareholders
Low interest loans
Shareholder use of property
Absorption of personal expenses by the corporation
Bargain purchases of corporate property

B. **Stock Redemptions.** Redemptions of stock in a corporation are treated as dividends under Section 301 unless the redemption can qualify as a sale or exchange under Sections 302 or 303.

V. LIQUIDATING THE CORPORATION

A. **General Rule of Section 331 and Exceptions.** Under Section 331, gain or loss (usually capital) is recognized to the shareholders in a corporate liquidation. However, if the liquidating corporation is a subsidiary, then no gain or loss is recognized on the liquidation.

B. **Basis Determination.** The shareholder's basis in property received in a liquidation is usually its fair market value. The basis of property received from a subsidiary under Section 332 is the basis of the property to the subsidiary unless the basis rules of Section 338 apply. In such a case, the basis of the property to the parent is the parent's basis in the subsidiary's stock.

C. Under the general rule of Section 336, the liquidating corporation recognizes any gain or loss, except in the parent subsidiary situation.

VI. THE S ELECTION

A. **Justification for the Election.** The S Corporation election allows qualified small corporations to elect not to pay the corporate income tax and to pass the income through to its shareholders. To qualify, a corporation must have the following characteristics:

be a domestic corporation

not be a member of an affiliated group

have 35 or fewer shareholders

have as its shareholders only individuals, estates, and certain trusts

not have a nonresident alien shareholder

issue only one class of stock

B.   Operational Rules.

The S Corporation is a reporting entity, not a taxpayer. Taxable income and losses are reported by the shareholders individually.

Certain items pass through to the shareholder of a S Corporation "as is." Examples of items that are passed from the S Corporation to its shareholders without changing identity are:

> Tax-exempt income
> Capital gains and losses
> Section 1231 gains and losses
> Charitable contributions
> Foreign tax credits
> Depletion
> Nonbusiness income and loss under Section 212
> Intangible drilling costs.
> Investment interest and expenses under Sec. 163(d)
> Certain portfolio income
> Passive gains, losses, and credits under Section 469
> Tax preference items

Taxable income of the S Corporation is equal to the net of all items which are not passed through "as is" to the shareholders. The dividends received deduction and net operating loss deduction are not allowed to a S Corporation.

Taxable income and separately stated items are passed through to the shareholders on the last day of the S Corporation's tax year, allocated on a per share and per day of stock ownership basis.

The shareholder's basis in a S Corporation's stock will be increased or decreased by the pass through of income or loss (including the separately stated items). Distributions will decrease the basis of the stock. Losses in excess of the basis are applied against the basis of loans that the shareholders may have made to the corporation, and are then carried forward until there is basis against which to deduct the losses.

VII.   PARTNERSHIPS

A.   Nature of Partnership Taxation. Partnerships are not separate taxable entities. Instead partnership income is passed through to the partners. A partnership tax return is an information return only. It provides the necessary information to determine a partner's income and expenses.

B.   Partnership Formation. Under Section 721 no gain or loss is recognized to a partnership or any of its partners on the transfer of property to a partnership in exchange for a capital interest. If the partner receives money, an interest for services, or transfers property with a liability more than basis, gain may be recognized on the transfer. The partner's basis in his or her partnership interest is the sum of money contributed plus the adjusted basis of other property transferred. A partner's basis is determined without regard to any amount on the partnership books such as the capital or equity account. The partner's basis will be increased or decreased by gains, losses, contributions, withdrawals, etc.

C.   Partnership Operation.

The reporting of partnership income requires that certain transactions be segregated and reported separately. Such items as charitable contributions, capital gains and losses, dividends, etc., must be allocated separately to the partners. Otherwise the taxable income of a partnership is calculated like that of an individual without the following deductions:

          Exemptions
          Deduction for foreign taxes paid
          Net operating losses
          Itemized deductions

Partnership losses pass through to partners and are deductible to the extent of basis. Losses in excess of the basis carry forward and can be used against future income in a manner similar to S corporation losses.

A partner engaging in a transaction with a partnership is regarded as a nonpartner under Section 707 unless the partner's direct or indirect interest is more than 50 percent, or the transaction is between two partnerships in which the same persons own more than 50 percent.

Payments made by a partnership to one of its partners for services rendered or for the use of capital, to the extent they are determined without regard to the partnership income are called guaranteed payments. Such payments are generally deductible by the partnership and must be reported as income by the partner.

TEST FOR SELF-EVALUATION

True or False

Indicate which of the following statements are true or false by circling the correct answers.

T F   1.   All legal corporations will be taxed as a corporation for Federal tax purposes.

T F   2.   It is possible for an organization that is not a legal corporation to be taxed as a corporation for Federal tax purposes.

T F   3.   Sole proprietorships and partnerships are not taxable entities.

T F   4.   The regular corporation is recognized as a taxable entity.

T F   5.   A partner engaging in a transaction with his partnership is generally regarded as a nonpartner or as an outsider. However a loss between a partnership and a 60 percent partner would be disallowed.

T F   6.   Net capital losses of a corporation are deductible against ordinary income.

T F   7.   When carried back or forward, a corporate long-term capital loss becomes a short-term capital loss.

T F   8.   Corporate charitable contributions are limited to 10 percent of taxable income computed without regard to the charitable contribution deduction, NOL and capital loss carrybacks, and the dividends received deduction.

T F   9.   A net operating loss deduction is carried back three years and forward five years.

T F 10.   The dividends received deduction is always 80 percent of dividends received.

T F 11.   The purpose of the dividends received deduction is to prevent triple taxation.

T F 12.   The maximum corporate tax rate is 34 percent (disregarding the 5% surtax); and the rate applies to income over $75,000.

T F 13.   Qualified organizational expenditures under Section 248 may be written off over 50 months or more.

T F 14.   Expenses incident to the printing and sale of stock certificates will not qualify as Section 248 expenses.

T F 15. Each partner must include in income his or her share of partnership income and any guaranteed payments from the partnership whose tax year ends with or within the partner's tax year.

T F 16. A corporate tax return is due on the fifteenth day of the third month following the close of the tax year.

T F 17. The purpose of Schedule M-1 of Form 1120 is to reconcile retained earnings at the end and the beginning of the tax year.

T F 18. The receipt of money or property in exchange for stock produces gain to the recipient corporation.

T F 19. If a corporation has excessive debt in its capital structure and a substantial portion of the debt is held by shareholders, the corporation may have thin capitalization problems.

T F 20. Control for purposes of nonrecognition under Section 351 means stock ownership of at least 80 percent of the total combined voting power and at least 80 percent of the total number of shares of all other classes of stock.

T F 21. Gain will never be recognized on a Section 351 transfer to a controlled corporation.

T F 22. The term "earnings and profits" is defined in the Code.

T F 23. Earnings and profits and retained earnings will always be the same amount.

T F 24. Partnership losses reduce a partner's basis in his partnership interest, but not below zero and any excess is lost to the partner.

T F 25. Since a partnership is not a taxable entity, it does not have to file any income tax return.

Fill-in-the-Blanks

Complete the following statements with the appropriate word(s) or amount(s).

1. A distribution of property to a non corporate shareholder is measured by the _____ of the property on the date of distribution.

2. The additional tax paid by corporations is five percent of taxable income over $100,000 up to a maximum of $_____.

3.   Under Section 331, gain or loss is recognized to the shareholder in a corporate
        _____.

4.   Under the general rule of Section 334, the basis of property received by shareholders in a liquidation is fair market _____.

5.   The maximum number of shareholders in a S Corporation is _____.

6.   Unlike corporations, partnerships are not considered separate taxable
        _____.

7.   A partner's basis in his partnership interest will _____ by additional capital contributions.

8.   Partnership taxable income and distributions are reported on Form _____.

9.   Taxable income of a partnership is computed (with exceptions) in the same manner as the taxable income of an _____.

10.   A partner's deductions for partnership losses are limited to the adjusted
        _____ of his or her partnership interest at the end of the partnership year in which the losses were incurred.

11.   Payments made to partners for services or use of capital, computed without regard to partnership income, are called _____ payments.

Multiple Choice

Choose the best answer for each of the following questions.

_____ 1.   Samuelson Corporation's taxable income for 1989 was $120,000, all from regular operations. Samuelson's tax liability before credits would be:
        a. $57,600
        b. $44,100
        c. $30,050
        d. $26,400
        e. Some other amount

_____ 2.   Which of the following items do not pass through from an S Corporation to its shareholders?
        a. Long-term capital gains
        b. Tax-exempt interest
        c. Wages of employees
        d. Short-term capital gains
        e. Section 1231 losses.

_____ 3.   Which of the following could not be a shareholder in a S Corporation?

    a. Corporation
    b. Individual
    c. Trust
    d. Estate

____ 4. In 1989 Lamden Corporation had gross income of $80,000, including $50,000 of dividends received from domestic corporations of which it owned less than 20 percent of the stock. Lamden had business expenses of $33,000. What is the 1989 dividends received deduction?
    a. -0-
    b. $35,000
    c. $50,000
    d. $32,900
    e. Some other amount

____ 5. In 1989 T Corporation had a net long-term capital loss. If this loss is carried over to T's 1989 income tax return, it will be treated as a:
    a. Ordinary loss
    b. Section 1231 loss
    c. Long-term capital loss
    d. Short-term capital loss
    e. None of the above

____ 6. Xeno Corporation is a closely-held corporation. Its sole shareholder is Philo Xeno. The corporation currently pays Philo a salary of $600,000 per year. A reasonable salary for a person in Philo's position would be $200,000 per year. During an IRS audit, the government will probably contend that there is a constructive dividend of:
    a. $-0-
    b. $200,000
    c. $400,000
    d. $600,000
    e. Some other amount

____ 7. Porter Corporation had taxable income of $100,000 for 1989 without charitable contributions. If during the year it gave $12,000 in cash to a charitable organization, how much may the company deduct?
    a. -0-
    b. $12,000
    c. $10,000
    d. $9,500
    e. Some other amount

____ 8. Sharon Lightner contributes property with a basis of $15,000 and a fair market value of $18,000 to a partnership in exchange for a 25 percent interest therein. Her basis in the partnership interest is:
    a. -0-
    b. $15,000

       c. $18,000
       d. $33,000
       e. Some other amount

_____ 9.   Assume the same situation as in Question 8. What is the basis of the proper-
       ty to the partnership if Sharon recognized no gain or loss?
       a. -0-
       b. $15,000
       c. $18,000
       d. $33,000
       e. Some other amount

_____ 10.   Toole Corporation, a calendar year S Corporation, has taxable income on
       December 31, 1989, of $25,000. If there is one shareholder and she receives
       a cash distribution from Toole of $40,000 on July 1, 1989, how much ordi-
       nary income should she report on her individual return, assuming her basis
       is sufficient to cover any dividend?
       a. $100,000
       b. $60,000
       c. $25,000
       d. $40,000
       e. Some other amount

_____ 11.   T Corporation, an accrual basis calendar year taxpayer, was formed and
       became operational on July 1, 1989. The following expenses were incurred
       during its first year of operation:

           $600   Expenses of organizational meetings
           $300   Fee for state charter
           $300   Expenses for sale of stock

       What is T Corporation's maximum organization expense deduction under
       Section 248 for 1989?
       a. $180
       b. $240
       c. $90
       d. $120
       e. Some other amount

_____ 12.   A and B form AB Corporation. A contributes cash of $50,000 and B con-
       tributes property with a basis of $20,000 and a fair market value of $50,000.
       If A and B own all the stock in AB Corporation, what is B's recognized gain
       on the transfer?
       a. -0-
       b. $30,000
       c. $20,000
       d. $50,000
       e. Some other amount

_____ 13. Assume the same situation as in Question 12. What is B's basis in the stock he receives from AB Corporation?
   a. -0-
   b. $30,000
   c. $50,000
   d. $20,000
   e. Some other amount

_____ 14. Rothe Corporation has E&P of $25,000. In the current year the corporation makes a $60,000 distribution to its only shareholder. The shareholder's basis in his Rothe stock is $20,000. From this distribution the shareholder would have a capital gain of:
   a. $-0-
   b. $15,000
   c. $25,000
   d. $20,000
   e. $45,000

_____ 15. X Corporation's only asset is raw land with an adjusted basis of $80,000 and a fair market value (net of tax on liquidation) of $135,000. T, an individual, owns all the stock (basis of $90,000) in X. X Corporation distributes the land to T in complete liquidation. How much gain or loss should T report?
   a. $10,000 loss
   b. $45,000 gain
   c. $55,000 gain
   d. $10,000 gain
   e. Some other amount

_____ 16. San Diego Medical Group is a qualified personal service corporation for 1989. It has taxable income for the year of $42,000. What is the tax liability for the corporation?
   a. $6,300
   b. $10,500
   c. $14,280
   d. $16,400
   e. Some other amount

Problems

1.   Three persons (A, B, and C) form a closely-held corporation with the following
        investment:

		Basis to Transferor	FMV	Number of Shares
From Ms. A:	Cash	$20,000	$20,000	
	Equipment	$75,000	$80,000	100
From Ms. B:	Equipment	$10,000	$15,000	5
From Mr. C:	Land	$60,000	$50,000	50

Besides the stock, B receives $10,000 in cash. The value of the stock is $1,000 per
share. Based on the above information, complete the answers to the following
questions.

	A	B	C
Realized gain (or loss)	___	___	___
Recognized gain (or loss)	___	___	___
Basis of the property to the corporation (excluding cash)	___	___	___
Stock basis to shareholder	___	___	___

2.   Crown Corporation was formed and began operation on January 1, 1989. The adjusted trial balance as of December 31, 1989, is as follows:

Account	Debit	Credit
Cash	35,000	
Accounts receivable	8,000	
Land	15,000	
Building	50,000	
Accumulated depreciation-building		3,000
Accounts payable		18,000
Common stock		10,000
Revenue		275,000
Interest on certificate of deposit		10,000
Cost of goods sold	95,000	
Compensation of officers	70,000	
Salaries and wages	25,000	
Repairs	6,000	
Depreciation expense	3,000	
State taxes	9,000	
Total	$316,000	$316,000

Based on the above information, calculate Crown's taxable income.

Revenue   _____

Cost of goods sold   (_____)

Gross profit   _____

Other income   _____

Total income   _____

Expenses   (_____)

Taxable income   _____

3.   Bhrionn Corporation reported taxable income of $600,000 on its income tax return before special items. Selected information available from the corporate records is as follows:

$280,000	Provision for Federal income tax
140,000	Book depreciation
85,000	Tax depreciation
100,000	Life insurance proceeds on death of an officer

What is Bhrionn's net income per books?

Net income per books   _____

Adjustments   _____

      _____

      _____

Taxable income   _____

Code Section Recognition

Indicate, by number, the appropriate Code Section where the following items are found.

_____ 1. The dividends received deduction.

_____ 2. Organizational expense deduction.

_____ 3. Transfers to controlled corporations.

_____ 4. Corporate distributions.

_____ 5. Stock redemptions.

_____ 6. General rules for corporate liquidations.

_____ 7. Definition of a S Corporation.

_____ 8. Gain or loss on partnership formations.

_____ 9. Partner/partnership transactions.

SOLUTIONS TO CHAPTER 20

True or False

1. False Some corporations may be treated as partnerships for tax purposes. (p. 20-3)

2. True (p. 20-3)

3. True (p. 20-4)

4. True (p. 20-4)

5. True (p. 20-35)

6. False Capital losses can only offset capital gains. (p. 20-6)

7. True (p. 20-6)

8. True (p. 20-7)

9. False NOLs are carried back three years and forward 15 years. (p. 20-8)

10. False It is 70%, 80%, or 100%. (p. 20-9)

11. True (p. 20-9)

12. True (p. 20-11)

13. False Section 248 expenses may be written off over 60 months or more. (p. 20-11)

14. True (p. 20-11)

15. True (p. 20-34)

16. True (p. 20-13)

17. False Schedule M-1 reconciles taxable income to book income. (p. 20-13)

18. False Receipt of money for its stock is not a gain to a corporation. (p. 20-16)

19. True (p. 20-17)

20. True (p. 20-17)

21. False Gain is recognized to the extent of boot received. (p. 20-18)

22. False E&P is not defined in the Code. (p. 20-20)

23. False   The calculation is not the same. (p. 20-20)

24. False   The excess losses carries forward for each partner. (p. 20-32)

25. False   Partnerships file an information return, the Form 1065. (p. 20-31)

Fill-in-the-Blanks

1. fair market value (p. 20-20)

2. $11,750 (p. 20-11)

3. liquidation (p. 20-23)

4. value (p. 20-23)

5. 35 (p. 20-25)

6. entities (p. 20-31)

7. increase (p. 20-32)

8. 1065 (p. 20-34)

9. individual (p. 20-34)

10. basis (p. 20-35)

11. guaranteed (p. 20-36)

Multiple Choice

1. C   15% ($50,000) + 25% (25,000) + 34% (45,000) +.5% (20,000) = $30,050. (p. 20-11)

2. C (p. 20-27)

3. A (p. 20-25)

4. D   70% x $50,000 = $35,000 general rule;   70% x $47,000 = **$32,900** limitation   (p. 20-9)

5. D (p. 20-6)

6. C $600,000 less $200,000 (p. 20-21)

7. C 10% x $100,000 = $10,000 maximum. (p. 20-7)

8. B (p. 20-32)

9. B (p. 20-32)

10. C (p. 20-28)

11. C ($600 + 300)/60 months x 6 months = $90. (p. 20-11)

12. A (p. 20-18)

13. D (p. 20-18)

14. B Distribution   60,000
       Dividend   (25,000)
       Return of Capital   (20,000)
       Capital gain $15,000   (p. 20-19)

15. B $135,000 - 90,000 = $45,000 Section 331. (p. 20-20)

16. C 34% x $42,000 = $14,280. (p. 20-12)

Problems

1.

	A	B	C
Realized gain (or loss)	5,000	5,000	(10,000)
Recognized gain (or loss)	-0-	5,000	-0-
Basis of the property to the corporation (excluding cash)	75,000	15,000	60,000
Stock basis to shareholder	95,000	5,000	60,000

2.

Revenue	$275,000
Cost of goods sold	(95,000)
Gross profit	180,000
Other income	10,000
Total income	190,000

Expenses	(113,000)
Taxable income	$77,000

3.

Net income per books	365,000
Federal income tax	280,000
Depreciation (140,000 - 85,000)	55,000
Life insurance proceeds	(100,000)
Taxable income	600,000

Code Section Recognition

1. Section 243
2. Section 248
3. Section 351
4. Section 301
5. Section 302
6. Section 331
7. Section 1361
8. Section 721
9. Section 707